Lifetime Fitness and Wellness

Fifth Edition

DORIS POGUE SCREWS
Alabama State University

ANGELA D. SHORTER
Delaware State University

Cover images copyright © Shutterstock, Inc.

Kendall Hunt
publishing company

www.kendallhunt.com
Send all inquiries to:
4050 Westmark Drive
Dubuque, IA 52004-1840

Copyright © 2002, 2006, 2009 by Kendall Hunt Publishing Company
Copyright © 2013, 2017 by Angela D. Shorter and Doris Pogue Screws

PAK ISBN: 978-1-5249-7243-1
TEXT ALONE ISBN: 978-1-5249-7244-8

All rights reserved. No part of this publication may be reproduced,
stored in a retrieval system, or transmitted, in any form or by any means,
electronic, mechanical, photocopying, recording, or otherwise,
without the prior written permission of the copyright owner.

Published in the United States of America

Contents

Preface	ix

Chapter 1 Getting on the Wellness Track — 1

Objectives	1
Understanding Health and Wellness	2
Dimensions of and Wellness	3
Barriers to Sound Fitness and Wellness	5
Benefits of Health-Related Fitness and Wellness	6
Making Behavior Modifications: Stages of Behavior Change	6
Summary	7
References	7
Internet Sources	8
Lab 1.1: Behavior Modification—Planning for a Healthy Lifestyle Change	9

Chapter 2 Nutrition for Wellness — 11

Objectives	11
Introduction	12
Nutrients for Wellness	12
The Wellness Diet	24
The Quest for an Ideal Diet	26
Nutrition and Physical Activity	29
Summary	31
References	32
Internet Sources	33

Lab 2.1:	Determining Basal Metabolic Rate	35
Lab 2.2:	Determining Estimated Daily Caloric Needs	37
Lab 2.3:	Three-Day Food Plan	39

Chapter 3 Health-Related Components of Physical Fitness — 43

Objectives	43
Introduction	44
Health-Related Components of Physical Fitness	44
Physical Fitness Training Principles	46
Designing a Physical Fitness Program	48
Exercise Precautions	52
Summary	52
References	53
Internet Sources	53
Lab 3.1: PAR-Q: The Physical Activity Readiness Questionnaire	55
Lab 3.2: Screening Questionnaire	57
Lab 3.3: Health-Related Fitness Goals	59

Chapter 4 Cardiorespiratory Endurance — 61

Objectives	61
Introduction	62
Understanding the Cardiorespiratory System	62
The Energy Systems	64
The Physiological Benefits of Improved Cardiorespiratory Endurance	66
Cardiorespiratory Endurance Program Design	68
Training Principles	69
Summary	70
References	70
Internet Sources	70
Lab 4.1: Your Resting Heart Rate	71
Lab 4.2: Target Heart Rate Zone	73
Lab 4.3: Cardiorespiratory Endurance Program	75

Chapter 5 Muscular Strength and Endurance — 77

Objectives — 77
Introduction — 78
Skeletal Muscle Structure — 79
Benefits of Resistance Training — 81
Factors Influencing Strength Production — 82
Resistance Training Program Design — 83
Resistance Training Methods — 85
Resistance Training Guidelines and Safety Tips — 86
Upper Body Exercises — 88
Lower Body Exercises — 94
Summary — 97
References — 97
Internet Source — 98

Lab 5.1: Muscular Strength and Endurance Program — 99

Chapter 6 Developing Flexibility — 101

Objectives — 101
Introduction — 102
Benefits of Flexibility — 102
Joint Classifications — 102
Factors Influencing Flexibility — 103
Types of Flexibility Training — 104
Flexibility Guidelines — 106
Stretching Exercises — 107
Stretching Exercises to Avoid — 112
Designing a Flexibility Program — 113
Back Health — 113

Summary — 114
References — 115

Lab 6.1: Flexibility Program — 117

Chapter 7 Fitness-Related Injuries — 119

Objectives — 119
Introduction — 120
Fitness-Injury Prevention—Tips for Exercising Safely — 120
Fitness-Related Injuries — 123
Treating Fitness-Related Injuries — 126
Injuries Caused by Environmental Conditions — 129

Summary — 131
References — 131
Internet Sources — 131

Chapter 8 Body Composition and Weight Control — 133

Objectives — 133
Introduction — 134
Obesity and Overweight — 134
Body Fat Distribution — 135
Body Composition Assessment Techniques — 136
Eating Disorders — 141
Strategies for Successful Weight Control — 142

Summary — 143
References — 144
Internet Sources — 144

Lab 8.1: Calculating Body Mass Index — 145
Lab 8.2: Body Composition Program — 147

Chapter 9 Understanding Emotional Wellness — 149

Objectives — 149
The Mind-Body Connection — 150
Characteristics of Emotionally Well Individuals — 150
Internal Influences Affecting Emotional Wellness — 151

External Factors Affecting Emotional Wellness	152
Mental Health Continuum	152
Stress	154
Stress Management Techniques	156
Suicide as a Consequence	158
Coping Strategies	159
Summary	160
References	161
Internet Sources	161
Lab 9.1: Health and Fitness Activity	163

Chapter 10 Sexual Wellness — 167

Objectives	167
Introduction	168
Sexually Transmitted Infections	168
The Sexually Transmitted Infection Epidemic and Risk Factors	176
Sexually Transmitted Infection Risk Factors	176
Guidelines for Preventing Sexually Transmitted Infections	176
Summary	177
References	178
Internet Sources	178
Lab 10.1: What Is Your Risk of Contracting a Sexually Transmitted Infection?	179
Lab 10.2: STI Attitudes	181

Chapter 11 Drug Use and Abuse — 183

Objectives	183
Introduction	184
Drugs and Their Effects	184
Drugs Commonly Used, Misused, and Abused	185
Addictive Characteristics	197
Strategies Used to Overcome an Addiction	198

Summary	199
References	199
Internet Sources	200
Lab 11.1: A Letter to My Best Friend	201

Chapter 12 Chronic Diseases — 203

Objectives	203
Introduction	204
Cancer	204
Cardiovascular Diseases	210
Diabetes Mellitus	214
Osteoporosis	217
Summary	220
References	221
Internet Sources	221
Lab 12.1: Assessing Your Risk for Cancer	223
Lab 12.2: Assessing Your Risk for Osteoporosis	227
Lab 12.3: Coronary Heart Disease Risk Appraisal	229

Appendices

Appendix A	231
Appendix B	235

Preface

This book is designed to help individuals understand how their lives can be enhanced by making and implementing appropriate healthy fitness and wellness choices throughout one's lifetime. Choices made today will shape your future in all dimensions of wellness. In order to enjoy the highest quality of life, combat degenerative diseases, and cope effectively with day-to-day stressors, a commitment must be made to implement and consistently practice positive fitness and wellness behaviors.

The fifth edition of *Lifetime Fitness and Wellness* has been revised and updated to provide practical and relevant content for today's college student and the adult population in general. It is organized into twelve chapters written in a straightforward reader friendly style. Chapter 1 introduces the concepts of health, wellness, and fitness and how they impact longevity. Chapter 3 introduces the health-related components of fitness, while Chapters 4, 5, 6 and 8 examine the health-related components in much greater detail. Chapter 6 and 7 explores safety considerations with regard to participation in physical fitness activities. Chapter 2 focuses on nutritional concepts critical to achieving personal fitness and wellness goals. Chapter 9 examines the emotional aspects of wellness and the effects of stressors in our lives. Chapters 10 through 12 respectively, discusses disease prevention and the impact of drug use and abuse related to inappropriate fitness and wellness choices. This text contains a plethora of information to aid the reader in fully taking charge of his/her personal well-being.

Chapter 1

Getting on the Wellness Track

Objectives
Understanding Health and Wellness
Dimensions of Health and Wellness
Barriers to Sound Fitness and Wellness
Benefits of Health-Related Fitness and Wellness
Making Behavior Modifications: Stages of Behavior Change
Summary
References
Internet Sources
Lab 1.1: Behavior Modification—Planning for a Healthy Lifestyle Change

Objectives

Upon completion of this chapter, you will be able to:

1. Define *wellness*, and *fitness*.
2. Differentiate between health and wellness.
3. Discuss the role of lifestyle choices as they relate to health and wellness.
4. Identify the dimensions of health and wellness.
5. Discuss how culture plays a role in an individual's degree of health-related wellness.
6. Know some of the barriers to sound health and wellness.
7. List and explain the benefits to health-related fitness and wellness.
8. Describe the stages of behavior modification.
9. Identify strategies that will facilitate behavior change.
10. Understand roadblocks that interfere with behavior change.

Understanding Health and Wellness

Wellness is a process in which one functions at an optimal level in all dimensions of health such that sound lifestyle choices are implemented on an ongoing basis. It is a marriage between the health and the physical well-being. The health aspect concentrates primarily on "healthful living" by emphasizing behaviors such as proper nutrition, smoking cessation, managing stress effectively, and creating productive positive relationships. The physical aspect emphasizes participation in physical activity consistently to prevent or control chronic illnesses.

Health is not merely the absence of disease but a state of well-being that enables a person to function at his or her optimum level. A healthy individual functions socially, spiritually, physically, intellectually, and psychologically. He or she experiences less stress and increased physical and mental fitness and can perform everyday activities. What a person does (health practices) and why one does it (health attitudes) are paramount in the scope of a truly healthy person.

An optimum level of wellness for one individual is not necessarily the same for all. The single parent who works full-time and attends college must maintain an adequate level of wellness in order to meet the heavy demands of a work, family and school life. He or she will experience demanding family and academic challenges that must be met. Each individual must develop and maintain their own optimum level of wellness in order to be able to meet the demands of his or her lifestyle.

Just as health is an individual matter (and choice), so is **lifestyle**. In general, we all have our own lifestyle—we complete certain activities each day with individual unique flair or fashion. Lifestyles involve choice. Whatever the choice, the daily activities in which an individual engages constitutes his or her lifestyle.

A Fit Individual

Physical fitness is the ability to perform daily activities with vigor, without excessive fatigue, and with enough energy to enjoy leisure-time activities. Fitness encompasses cardiorespiratory endurance, flexibility, muscular strength, and muscular endurance (these terms are defined in Chapter 3). It enhances health by controlling many of the risks associated with chronic disease or conditions such as high blood pressure, heart disease, cancer, osteoporosis, and diabetes—which are related to, or significantly influenced by, a lack of regular physical activity. Physical fitness activities can improve your appearance, help maintain desirable body weight, reduce stress, protect you from lower back problems, increase the efficiency of your heart and lungs, improve psychological functioning (make you feel better), and delay the aging process.

As an individual's level of health is unique, so is his or her level of fitness. Genetic factors, such as an individual's body composition, gender, and rate of metabolism, may affect his or her level of fitness. Lifestyle factors, such as a one's daily exercise, nutritional practices, and amount of sleep, also have an accumulative effect on his or her maintenance quantity of an optimum level of fitness. Any one of these components may individually, or in conjunction with each other, adversely affect an individual's level of fitness.

Dimensions of and Wellness

Wellness is a process, not a product. It encompasses continually making choices. Additionally, wellness involves balancing the various dimensions of one's life, such as intellectual, physical, psychological, social, environmental, and spiritual dimensions of living. Wellness is often characterized on a continuum, with one end representing a sound and healthy lifestyle and the other end representing an unwholesome lifestyle (see **Figure 1.1**). Therefore, it is a way of living, not a one-time phenomenon. We should all strive to operate at the optimal end of the continuum.

The dimensions of wellness in a fit and well individual are all encompassing. The potential for change in an individual's health status is ever present, thus prevention is preferred over treatment in every instance. Maintenance of a lifestyle that protects the individual's physical well-being, psychological and social health, spiritual and intellectual, and environmental prowess comprises the dimensions of health and wellness.

Intellectual Wellness

Intellectual wellness is ability to receive and process stimuli, formulate ideas, understand concepts to expand knowledge and skills. It is important for success in everyday life. Intellectual wellness means that one can apply learned concepts to create additional opportunities to enhance one's knowledge base and think critically about the world around you. Intellectual well persons are open-minded, accepting of others, embrace new and unfamiliar information or tasks and approach learning enthusiastically. The absence of these charcteristics makes it difficult to maintain normalcy in today's society. This includes but is not limited to becoming an informed consumer. This can be accomplished by taking a more active role in your medical care by writing down questions or concerns for your medical care professional to address during visits, obtaining and maintaining first aid credentials, employing effective time management skills, becoming more knowledgeable about financial matters and practicing sound financial strategies, and developing a plan to achieve your life goals.

Physical Wellness

Physical wellness involves recognizing the importance of regular physical activity, consuming healthy foods and other healthy lifestyle behaviors. A physically well individual who practices healthy lifestyle choices, such as getting adequate sleep, abstinence from unsafe sexual encounters, smoking, substance abuse, and exposure to violence will develop a high quality health status. Regular checkups, good nutritional habits, and moderate exercise on a consistent basis sets the foundation for good physical wellness.

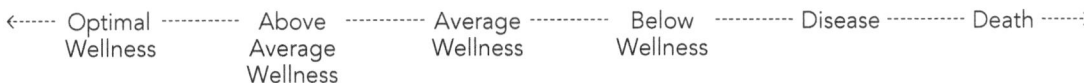

Figure 1.1 Wellness Continnuum.

Emotional Wellness

Emotional wellness is achieved when an individual is able to handle normal daily activities and tasks with the accompanying stressors. Good emotional health is characterized by moderate to high degrees of positive self-esteem, mental stability, and the ability to work closely with peers, and accept criticism while performing daily tasks in a proficient manner. Emotional wellness also includes the ability to accept one's own limitations, adjust to change, and view successes and failures in the proper perspective and continue to move forward in a positive manner. Emotionally well people are happy and possess the ability to rebound from minor setbacks while continuing to enjoy life. Emotional health status changes with maturity and, in some instances, with chemical or hormonal changes within the body. It is important to recognize these changes in order to maintain an acceptable level of mental functioning.

Social Wellness

Social wellness refers to developing and nurturing healthy, supportive relationships with individuals in your surroundings. Everyone needs to a sense of connection and belonging with others such as family, friends and peers. Thus, the ability to interact with others, the art of compromise, and to establish satisfying positive relationships are important to building self-confidence and good communication skills. A lack of adequate social wellness can lead to loneliness, distress and greater susceptibility to illness. Socially well individuals are willing to help others and seek help when needed. They are accepting of others from various cultures, backgrounds, and beliefs. People in healthy interpersonal relationships are free to openly express their needs, feelings and thoughts to their partner. They also feel valued and respected by their partner.

Spiritual Wellness

Spiritual wellness encompasses the ability to develop a sense of purpose and value system in one's life. Spiritually well individuals have a sense of meaning and direction in life as well as a relationship to a higher being or power. Research has clearly demonstrated a positive relationship between spiritual and emotional well-being and life satisfaction. Spiritual wellness is also linked to physical wellness. Individuals who are active in faith based organizations tend to have reduced age-related memory loss, lower incidence of disease and depression, and have stronger immune systems.

However, spirituality in a broader context assumes that the individual has a set of guiding principles and/or a belief system that transcends the basic purpose of serving as a beacon during dark times. An individual can exhibit a sense of spirituality through a belief system, guiding principles, and a value system, and be truly a spiritual being, but be void of love, compassion, and many of the traits that we attach to a spiritual being. It is important to distinguish spirituality from religion.

Environmental Wellness

Environmental wellness involves understanding how world conditions impacts one's well-being and taking action to cultivate positive, stimulating surroundings. Our world is filled with environmental concerns, such as global warming, terrorist attacks, pollution control, ozone deterioration, human genome cloning, new and rare diseases, and many new and unknown conditions yet to present themselves. It is important to know and understand the parameters of the various environmental concerns. We must be aware of how local, state, and federal laws affect the environment. As a society we must understand how special interest groups have vested interests in maintaining the status quo for environmental conditions associated with second-hand smoke, water and sewage disposal, atomic energy use and disposal, acid rain, rain forest deterioration, and other systemic conditions that threaten the environment and, ultimately, individual health.

Occupational Wellness

Occupational wellness encompasses one's ability to carry out work related tasks effectively and efficiently under conditions conducive to personal and group fulfillment. It allows an employee to operate in an environment with new and challenging demands and not merely routine demands. Occupational wellness is not related to a high salary or prestigious job title. Occupationally well individuals have opportunities to expand their current skill base and/or acquire new skills. They are encourages to collaborate and interact with coworkers creating an atmosphere of cooperation, teamwork and support.

Barriers to Sound Fitness and Wellness

There are many barriers to achieving a desirable quality of fitness and wellness. All individuals, need to be aware of potential barriers in order to prevent them from adversely affecting their lives. Examples of barriers to quality levels of fitness and wellness include the following:

- succumbing to negative peer pressure;
- failing to set and maintain positive health habits;
- failing to access the necessary knowledge bases related to healthy lifestyles;
- establishing negative attitudes toward sound fitness and wellness due to folkway and mores;
- lacking the motivation to achieve desirable levels of fitness and wellness;
- having low levels of self-esteem;
- unwilling to ask questions and maintain an assertive posture while pursuing knowledge;
- failing to take advantage of environmental resources; and
- exhibiting poor time management.

Benefits of Health-Related Fitness and Wellness

Optimal wellness assumes that a wholesome level of cardiorespiratory endurance, muscular strength and endurance, flexibility, weight control, nutrition, and psychological and sexual wellness are apparent in a person's life. It assumes that one is free from the use and abuse of alcohol, drugs, and tobacco, as well as free from chronic diseases. It is also desirable for a person to participate in lifetime activities and design a physical fitness program.

The following is a general list of benefits that a person may gain by implementing a effective wellness program:

- increased energy to carry out daily activities;
- a high level of self-esteem;
- improved physical fitness;
- a positive outlook on life;
- satisfying social relationships;
- a lower percentage of body fat;
- improved critical thinking;
- a sense of accomplishment;
- emotional stability;
- sound ethical values;
- increased understanding of how culture impacts health and wellness; and lower risk of chronic illness.

Making Behavior Modifications: Stages of Behavior Change

When seeking to achieve optimal health and wellness, setting personal lifelong goals is essential. We must recognize barriers that distract us from implementing strategies that help us reach our goals, and be willing to make necessary changes that lead to enhanced health and wellness. The following are various stages of change an individual progresses through on a journey to optimal health and wellness.

- *Precontemplation stage:* Trying to determine whether or not you have a problem that needs changing, and benefits of making the change.
- *Contemplation stage:* Acknowledging the problem and considering change.
- *Preparation stage:* Planning a strategy(ies) to make a behavior change.
- *Action stage:* Putting your plan into action to make a behavior change.
- *Maintenance stage:* Actively working to keep the change.

Behaviors that impede progress toward optimal health and wellness may be altered by understanding the stages of behavioral change **(Lab 1.1)**.

Summary

Important concepts that you have learned in this chapter include:

- **Wellness** is a process in which one functions at an optimal level in all dimensions of health such that sound lifestyle choices are implemented on an ongoing basis.
- A healthy individual experiences an optimum level of functioning in his or her daily activities.
- A lifestyle is the accumulation of all the daily activities in which an individual normally engages.
- A fit person is able to engage in physically active tasks throughout the day without experiencing undue fatigue.
- Each individual has his or her unique level of optimum health and wellness.
- Wellness is a process in which an individual demonstrates healthy choices in his or her intellectual, physical, psychological, social, spiritual, and environmental living.
- Psychological wellness is essential to daily functioning.
- Sound social wellness enhance an individual's total health and well-being.
- Knowledge of one's family background can impact lifestyle choices.
- Environmental conditions affect an individual's health and wellness.
- If given knowledge, resources and opportunities, all individuals can meet health and wellness objectives.
- Everyone must analyze and set their own health-related fitness and wellness goals.
- As health-related fitness and wellness goals are attained, adjustments may need to be made to reach future goals.
- Behavior modification enables individuals to establish personal short-term objectives that will lead to lifelong improvement in health and wellness.

References

Anspaugh, D.J., Hamrick, M.H., & Rosato, F.D. (2010). *Wellness: Concepts and Application,* 6th ed. Boston, MA: McGraw-Hill.

Corbin, C.B., Welk, G.J., Corbin, W.R., & Welk, K.A. (2010). *Concepts of Fitness and Wellness,* 7th ed. New York, NY: McGraw-Hill Publishing.

Dennis, K., Henson, B., & Adams, T.M. (2005). *Destination: Fit, Well and Healthy.* Dubuque, IA: Kendall/Hunt Publishing Company.

Donatelle, R., Snow, C., & Wilcox, G. (1999). *Wellness: Choices for Health and Fitness,* 2nd ed. Belmont, CA: Wadsworth Publishing Company.

Fahey, T.D., Insel, P.M., & Roth, W.T. (2014). *Fit and Well: Core Concepts and Labs in Physical Fitness and Wellness*, 9th ed. Mountain View, CA: Mayfield Publishing Company.

Hales, D. (2008). *An Invitation to Health,* 12th ed. Pacific Grove, CA: Brooks/Cole Publishing Company.

Powers, S, Dodd, S, & Jackson. E. (2014). *Total Fitness and Wellness*, 6th ed. Pearson Publishing Company.

Internet Sources

http://www.cdc.gov/nchs/products/pubs/pubd/hp2k/review/highl

Lab 1.1
Behavior Modification—Planning for a Healthy Lifestyle Change

Name: _____   Date: _____

Lab Equipment: None required

Purpose: To help you identify the stage of change for a target behavior and to guide you through the step-by-step process of behavior change.

Instructions: Lab 1.2 assesses your current lifestyle habits. Use the information from this lab to assess your current stage of behavior change relative to the various healthy behaviors listed in Part I, Stages of Change Questionnaire.

Part I. Stages of Change Questionnaire
Place an X in the box that most closely resembles the stage of change for each behavior.

Lifestyle	Pre-contemplation	Contemplation	Preparation	Action	Maintenance
Eating properly	❑	❑	❑	❑	❑
Managing stress	❑	❑	❑	❑	❑
Adopting safety habits	❑	❑	❑	❑	❑
Learning first aid	❑	❑	❑	❑	❑
Adopting personal exercise/fitness behaviors	❑	❑	❑	❑	❑
Protecting the environment	❑	❑	❑	❑	❑
Managing time	❑	❑	❑	❑	❑
Seeking and complying with medical advice	❑	❑	❑	❑	❑
Becoming an informed consumer	❑	❑	❑	❑	❑

Lab 1.1—Cont'd

Behavior Modification—Planning for a Healthy Lifestyle Change

Name: _____ Date: _____

Part II. Stage of Change

In step 1 select a behavior that you are ready to change and select one statement from 1-6 that most accurately describes the behavior you want to change. Then identify the Stage of Behavior change that most applies to you from page 6 (Do not select a behavior at a pre-contemplation stage.) Use the behavior that you are ready to change and complete step 2.

Example: I currently ____*exercise*____, but I have only done so within the last six months.

   Stage of Change: ____*Action*____.

Step 1-Behavior #1. Fill in only one blank.

1. I currently _____, and I do not intend to change in the foreseeable future.

2. I currently _____, but I am contemplating changing in the next six months.

3. I currently _____ regularly, but I intend to change in the next month.

4. I currently _____, but I have only done so within the last six months.

5. I currently _____, and I have done so for over six months.

6. I currently _____, and I have done so for over five years.

   Stage of Change: _____

Step 2-Goal Setting: Techniques for Change

List three techniques you will use to modify the behavior you selected in Step 1.

1.

2.

3.

Modified
Sources: Corbin C. et al. 2000, *Concepts of Fitness and Wellness*. 3rd ed. Boston: The McGraw-Hill Companies, Inc. Hoeger and Hoeger. 2002 Fitness and Wellness. 5th ed Belmont, CA: Wadsworth/Thomson Learning.

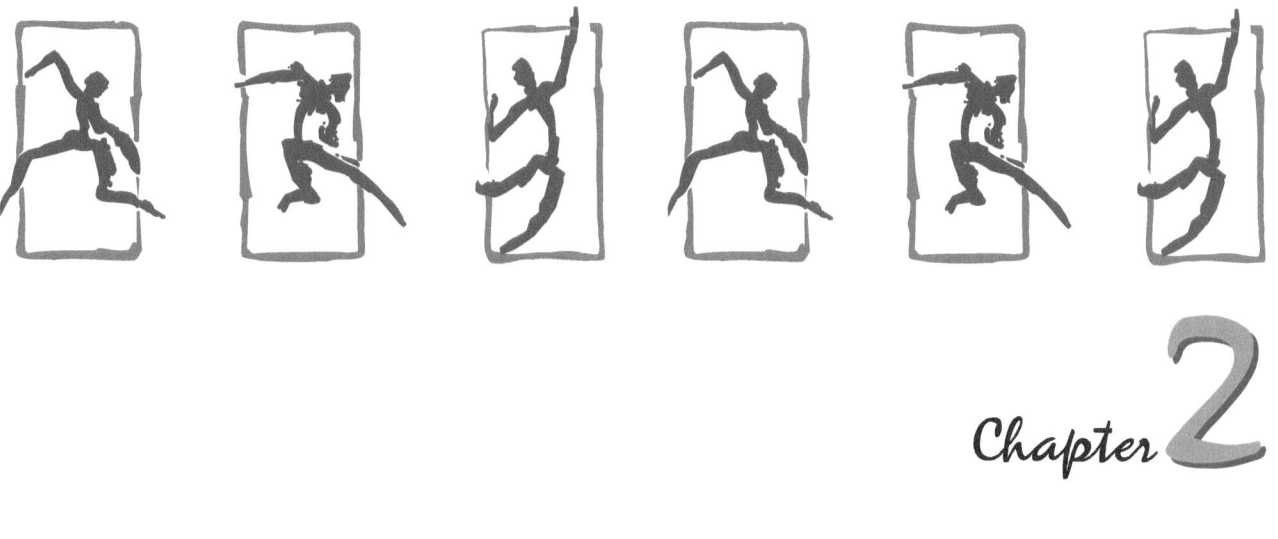

Chapter 2

Nutrition for Wellness

Objectives
Introduction
Nutrients for Wellness
The Wellness Diet
The Quest for an Ideal Diet
Nutrition and Physical Activity
Summary

References
Internet Sources
Lab 2.1: Determining Basal Metabolic Rate
Lab 2.2: Estimating Daily Caloric Needs
Lab 2.3: Three-Day Food Plan

Objectives

Upon completion of this chapter, you will be able to:

1. Describe the functions and purposes of the essential nutrients.
2. Explain dietary guidelines for Americans and healthy goals used to develop a healthy diet.
3. Describe the MyPlate healthy eating guide and explain its importance.
4. Identify nutritional information necessary for the development of an ideal diet.
5. Develop a personal plan for improving and maintaining your overall nutrition.

Lifetime Fitness & Wellness

Introduction

You've heard over and over that "we are what we eat." As you look at yourself and others around you this statement actually hits home, because our daily diet plays a major role in how we look and feel. For example, a diet high in unhealthy foods excess fat weight gain to weight gain and cardiovascular problems, and a diet low in nutrient content may not provide enough energy to permit you to function optimally. Making wise food selections and eating a healthy diet can be difficult for many people. The hectic and hurried lifestyle led by many people often results in the over consumption of fast foods and foods with a high sugar content. This chapter explores current information on nutrition that can be used to make wise food choices that contribute to wellness.

Nutrients for Wellness

The human body must have **nutrients** to function properly. Nutrients are chemical substances found in food that serve three functions in the body: (1) regulatory—regulate body processes, (2) structural—support growth and repair of body tissue, and (3) provide energy. There are six classes of nutrients found in dietary foods: water, carbohydrates, fats, proteins, vitamins, and minerals. Water, proteins, fats, and mineral are nutrients that contribute to the structural roles in the body; vitamins, minerals, and proteins have regulatory roles; and carbohydrates, fats, and, to a lesser degree, protein serve as dietary sources of energy. There are more than 40 **essential nutrients** found in food. These nutrients are considered necessary for the body's growth, maintenance, and repair.

The foods we eat provides the fuel needed to produce energy for all bodily activities. **Calorie** is the term used to measure the amount of energy found in food. You must consume the proper nutrients and the right amounts of foods to produce enough energy to carry out your daily functions.

You should select foods that have a **low energy density. Energy density** refers to the amount energy provided relative to the number of calories per serving. For example one cup of raisins contains approximately 420 calories (high energy density) while one cup of grapes contains approximately 104 calories (low energy density). Beware of foods that are considered to have **empty calories.** They lack a significant amount of vitamins and minerals, but are high in sugar and fat (soft drinks, candy bars, cakes, fruit drinks, and fruit punch).

Water

Water is a nutrient that is often undervalued, yet is the most important. Water is involved in almost all biological processes, including the elimination of waste through urine, controlling body temperature through the production of sweat, lubricating joints, protecting a fetus, and aids the respiratory system by moistening the lungs to facilitate intake of oxygen and excretion of carbon dioxide. Water also aids in the digestion of food, energy production, nutrient transportation, and body metabolism. It helps regulate fluid balance in the body, as well as the balance of electrolytes. Water makes up 85 percent of blood, 70 percent of muscle, 60 percent of an adult's body weight, about 75 percent of the brain and 20 percent of bone tissue. After oxygen, water is the most important element for sustaining life. When compared to food, the average person can go weeks without food but can survive only a few days (3) without water. Research has reported a reduction in the development of kidney stones, colon cancer, and bladder cancer as a result of high water intake.

On the average a person loses about 64 to 80 ounces of water a day, which is equivalent to about 8 to 10 eight-ounce glasses of fluid. You lose water each day in feces, urine, sweat, and through evaporation in your lungs. Water is lost at a higher rate if you live in a dry climate or high altitude, exercise, consume large amounts of alcohol and caffeine, or become ill.

Water lost each day must be replenished. Dehydration, an abnormal depletion of body fluids may occur if the body loses 5% of body water. A loss of 15%–20% can be harmful or even fatal. It is recommended that 8 to 10 glasses of water be consumed on a daily basis to re-hydrate the body from fluid loss. A **hydrated** state is maintained when daily water intake is equal to daily water lost. Although, beverages provide most of the water intake (60 percent), solid foods (30 percent) also play a significant role in water replacement, and the remainder is generated through metabolism (10 percent). Most fruits and vegetables are composed of approximately 80–90 percent water, meats 50 percent, bread 33 percent, and butter 15 percent. The actual amount of water needed by an individual can be influenced by such factors as age, sex, dietary intake, environmental conditions, fitness level, activities in which you may participate, and body weight.

Carbohydrates

Carbohydrates are vital in supplying the body's energy requirements, fueling the brain and nervous system and to keep the digestive system functioning optimally. Carbohydrates have been falsely been accused of being fattening resulting in the avoidance of carbohydrates by many weight conscious people. Individuals who wish to reduce fat weight, maintain lean mass and remain healthy should do so by closely attending to portion sizes, caloric intake and dietary consumption of carbohydrate-rich whole foods that possess high nutrient density and low in energy density.

Carbohydrates (glucose) are the primary energy source that fuels your muscles and brain. The body receives approximately 90% of its energy from the metabolism of carbohydrates. The majority of daily food intake should come from foods that provide carbohydrates. Healthy carbohydrates are mostly of plant origin, primarily found in grains (rice, corn, wheat), fruits, beans, and vegetables; they can also be found in milk and other dairy products (animal sources). Each gram of carbohydrates provides the body with four calories, which provide energy more quickly and efficiently than fat and proteins. Carbohydrates should comprise approximately 45–65 percent of our total daily caloric intake and 45–55 percent should come from complex carbohydrates with 10 percent or less from simple carbohydrates. Endurance athletes should increase their intake to approximately 70 percent.

Simple sugars serve as the basic structural unit of all carbohydrates. During metabolism and the digestive process, carbohydrates break down and are changed to glucose—the body's primary source of energy. Any excess glucose not used immediately is stored as glycogen in muscle and liver cells to be released as needed. Only a limited amount of glucose can be stored as glycogen; any leftover is converted to fat and stored in fatty cells.

There are two major types of carbohydrates: simple carbohydrates and complex carbohydrates (starches and fiber). **Simple carbohydrates**, or sugars, are also referred to as **monosaccharides** and **disaccharides.**

Monosaccharides are single sugars consisting three types: glucose, fructose, and galactose. Glucose and lactose are very common monosaccharides found in nature. Glucose is the most important monosaccharide in the body. It is used by plant and animal tissues for energy, formed through the process of photosynthesis. Photosynthesis is the process used by green plants to make carbohydrates using carbon and water. Fructose or fruit sugar is found mostly in fruits and is a constituent of table sugar is formed by rearranged glucose molecules. Fructose provides the intense sweetness of fruit. Other sources include ready-to-eat cereal, soda, and products sweetened with high fructose corn syrup. Galactose is a single sugar that does not occur alone in foods but is bound to lactose and released during digestion. Foods containing monosacchaarides are directly absorbed into the bloodstream.

Disaccharides are double sugars (pairs of sugars) formed by joining two monosaccharides. The three disaccharides are sucrose, maltose and lactose. Sucrose consists of fructose and glucose and is commonly known as table sugar. Sucrose also occurs naturally in many fruits. Maltose consists of two glucose units and appears when starch is being digested in the body. Lactose is made up of glucose and galactose. Foods containing disaccharides must be digested using enzymes before being utilized by the body.

Simple carbohydrates provide a quick burst of energy. They constitute 16 percent of the American caloric daily intake, and 20 percent of a teenagers daily caloric intake. Monosaccharides are naturally occurring sugars including fructose (fruit sugar, honey). Disaccharides are concentrated or double sugars, meaning that they are pairs of monosaccharides chemically linked and include such sources as sucrose (table sugar), lactose (milk sugar), and maltose (malt sugar).

Complex carbohydrates are the foundation of a healthy diet. Starches and fiber, also known as **polysaccharides**, are considered complex carbohydrates. They are obtained by eating yellow fruits and vegetables (carrots, yams), cruciferous vegetables (kale, brassels sprouts, greens, water cress, Wasabi, broccoli), root vegetables (potatoes) and dark green leafy vegetables, legumes, whole grain (rice, wheat, corn, millet, rye, barley, and oats). All starchy foods are plant foods and are the preferred source of carbohydrates because they also contain fiber, vitamins, and minerals. Diets high in starch rather than simple sugars help the body maintain a normal blood sugar level through slower digestion and absorption of glucose.

Dietary fiber is considered a complex carbohydrate that resists human digestive enzymes, and is often referred to as bulk or roughage. Although it resists digestion, it helps maintain the health of the digestive track by providing bulk in the intestines. The bulk from the fiber reduces the amount of time required for waste to move through the digestive track. The American Dietetic Association recommends that you consume 25 to 35 grams of fiber per day, the equivalent of five or six servings of high-fiber foods such as whole-grain cereals and fruits. High fiber foods are generally high in B vitamins and iron.

Dietary fiber is referred to as insoluble or soluble. **Insoluble fiber** does not dissolve in water. It does play an important role in the elimination of waste by speeding up the transit time of food through the small and large intestines. By reducing the amount of time waste material remains in the digestive tract several healthful benefits are accomplished: the body's exposure to cancer-causing agents is decreased, constipation is prevented because of softer stools, diverticulitis (a painful inflammation of the bowel) is prevented, and the risk of colon cancer may be reduced. The best source of insoluble fiber is wheat bran. Wheat bran is the outer shell of the whole wheat kernel. Many high-fiber cereals such as bran flakes, shredded wheat or oatmeal are good sources of wheat bran. Any whole grain products such as barley, brown rice and whole-wheat bread, pasta or crackers also contain bran. Whole grains haven't had their bran and germ removed by milling, making them better sources of fiber.

Soluble fiber absorbs water and cleanses the intestinal tract, provides some energy to the body by producing fatty acids through fermentation in the large intestine, assist in decreasing cholesterol and increasing cholesterol excretion, and slows stomach emptying, which helps control blood sugar levels. Good sources of soluble fiber are the pulp of many citrus fruits, vegetables, apples, oats, dried beans, and barley. Whole-grain breads are excellent sources of soluble fiber when compared to refined grains, such as white rice or white flour.

Glycemic Index

Not all carbohydrate foods are created equal. In fact, they behave quite differently in our bodies. The **glycemic index** or GI describes this difference by ranking carbohydrates according to their effect on our blood glucose levels. Carbohydrates are ranked on a scale ranging from zero to 100. Glucose serves as the reference tem and is arbitrarily given a score of 100 because it is considered to be one of the fastest carbohydrates to raise blood sugar levels. A food's GI rating is determined by measuring the blood samples taken from ten healthy individuals who have consumed a food containing 10-50 grams of carbohydrate after an overnight fast. Carbohydrates with a GI ranking of 55 and less are considered low, while those with a ranking of 70 or greater are deemed high.

Foods with a low GI diet rating gradually raise blood sugar levels and are slowly digested and absorbed. A low GI has several healthful benefits such as: assists with weight loss and control, lower risk of heart disease, replenish carbohydrate stores after exercise, allows you to feel full longer thereby reducing hunger, increases the body's sensitivity to insulin, improves control of diabetes, and reduces blood cholesterol levels. Choosing low GI carbohydrates, the ones that produce only small fluctuations in our blood glucose and insulin levels, is the secret to long-term health and is the key to sustainable weight loss. Examples of low GI foods include specific whole grains, beans, pasta, and nuts. You should consume at least one low GI food with each meal. This can be accomplished by gradually replacing high GI foods.

Foods with a GI of 70 or above are considered high and are rapidly digested and absorbed, and produced significant fluctuations in blood sugar levels. The specific influence of a food on blood sugar level depends on a number of factors such as cooking method, ripeness, fat and fiber content, time of day, individual differences, and blood sugar levels. Examples of foods with a high GI include white bread, potatoes, Corn Chex cereal, corn chips, and french fries. **Table 2.1** contains various foods and their corresponding GI ranking.

Fats

Fats (or lipids) found in meat, dairy products, and oils are the most abundant sources of fuel in the diet. When energy is not burned, it is converted to fat and stored for usage at a later time. Fats in the diet are necessary for good health. They are important in the transport and absorption of fat-soluble vitamins A, D, E and K; are used as stored energy; cushion vital organs; make up part of all body cells; and help to maintain body temperature. Fat also delays pains of hunger by providing a feeling of fullness. Fats are the most concentrated source of energy in the body. They provide more than twice the food energy of either carbohydrates or protein: one gram of fat provides 9 calories versus 4 calories for carbohydrates and protein. It is recommended that fat intake should be 20 to 35 percent of daily caloric intake with saturated fat no more than 10 percent.

Almost 95 percent of the fat stored in the body is in the form of **triglyceride.** These are a collection of three fatty acids joined to glycerol, with the remaining 5 percent consisting of other glycerides and cholesterol. **Fatty acids** are long chains of carbon atoms with hydrogen atoms attached and are characterized as saturated or unsaturated.

Saturated fats usually are solid at room temperature and of animal origin, such as cheese, butter, lard, and meats. But some plants, such as the avocado, are high in saturated

Table 2.1 Glycemic Index Food Chart

Low Glycemic Index Food (less than 55)
Medium Glycemic Index Food (between 55 and 70)
High Glycemic Index Food (more than 70)

Food List	Rating	Food Glycemic Index
Waffles	High	76
Doughnut	High	76
Apple juice	Low	41
Pineapple juice	Low	46
Grapefruit juice	Low	48
Orange juice	Low	52
Rice cakes	High	77
Multi grain bread	Low	48
Rice Krispies	High	82
Corn flakes	High	83
Rye	Low	25
Rice, instant	Low	46
Croissant	Medium	67
Danish pastry	Medium	59
Cheese pizza	Medium	60
Whole grain	Low	50
White bread	High	71
White rolls	High	73
Hamburger bun	Medium	61
All bran	Low	42
Oat bran	Medium	55
Rice, brown	Medium	55
Taco Shell	Medium	68
Yogurt low-fat (sweetened)	Low	14
Milk, chocolate	Low	14
Milk, whole	Low	27
Milk, fat-free	Low	32
Milk, skimmed	Low	32
Popcorn	Medium	55
Pretzels	High	81
Tomatoes	Low	15

fat, as well as coconut and palm oil. Saturated fats are known to raise the level of cholesterol in the blood and contribute to heart disease. Manufacturers, in a response to consumer demands to lower saturated fat in food, placed partially hydrogenated oil in their products. The **hydrogenation** process produces unsaturated fatty acids known as **trans fats.** This process also increases shelf life, improves the texture of the product, and makes it more spreadable. Trans fats are found in foods that contain partially hydrogenated oils, such as margarine products, fried foods, and baked goods. Studies have linked trans fats to cardiovascular disease and concluded that they are just as dangerous as saturated fat.

Unsaturated fats remain in liquid form at room temperature. Unsaturated fats can be monounsaturated or polyunsaturated. These fats are considered "good" fats because they have been associated with a lower incidence of heart disease, including stroke and heart attack, and a lower blood cholesterol level. **Monounsaturated fats** are oils derived from plant sources such as corn, sunflowers, soybean, canola, cottonseed, and olives. **Polyunsaturated** fats are of two types: omega-3 and omega-6. Omega-3 polyunsaturated fatty acids are acquired by eating deep water fish like salmon, mackerel, sardines, herring, whitefish, bluefish, swordfish, rainbow trout, striped bass, and Pacific oysters. The consumption of omega-3 is linked with cardiovascular benefits, including lower cholesterol levels, reduced blood clotting, and prevention of abnormal heart rhythms. Omega-6 polyunsaturated fatty acids can be found in vegetable oils, such as soybean, corn, sunflower, and safflower. Its dietary intake is linked with the reduction of cardiovascular diseases.

Cholesterol is a waxy form of fat made by the liver and consumed in the diet. The liver produces approximately 80% of the cholesterol in the blood and tissues, and 20% is obtained from dietary sources. Dietary cholesterol is of animal origin found in egg yolks, liver, red meat, whole milk, and shellfish. Cholesterol in the body is necessary to form digestive juices, serves as a structural component of cell membranes and steroid hormones (such as estrogen and testosterone), and aids in vitamin D synthesis. Cholesterol of animal origin is linked to the development of heart disease. When the body cells cannot absorb any more cholesterol, excess begins to accumulate in the walls of the blood vessels and gradually narrow them. This condition may lead to a heart attack or stroke. The American Heart Association recommends that the daily intake of dietary cholesterol not exceed 300 milligrams (mg) per day. The National Cholesterol Education Program (NCEP) recommends 200 mg per day.

In order for fats to travel throughout the body they must combine with protein. When this happens they form lipoproteins, whose major responsibility is to transport cholesterol in the blood. There are two types of cholesterol: low-density lipoproteins and high-density lipoproteins. **Low-density lipoproteins** (LDL), also known as "bad" cholesterol, transport large amounts of cholesterol to the body's cells. **High-density lipoproteins** (HDL), or "good" cholesterol, contain a high percentage of protein which aid the removal of cholesterol from the arterial walls and carries it to the liver for elimination from the body.

HDL and LDL cholesterol levels are considered predictors of one's risk for developing coronary heart disease. Having a low level of HDL is linked to a greater risk of developing coronary heart disease compared to individuals who have elevated HDL levels. Many studies have shown that high levels of LDLs are associated with increased risk of heart attack because these lipoproteins harm arteries. The NCEP classifies cholesterol levels as follows (all measurements are in milligrams per deciliter):

Total cholesterol levels less than 200 are desirable

Total cholesterol levels between 200 and 239 are borderline-high

Total cholesterol levels 240 or higher are high

Regular cholesterol screenings are important. The NCEP recommends that males and females 20 years or older have a cholesterol tests every five years. Individuals who have risk factors such as obesity, diabetes, or a family history of cardiovascular disease should have regular cholesterol screenings. To reduce elevated cholesterol levels select foods that are low in saturated fats and trans-fats, increase your intake of fruits and vegetables, and exercise regularly.

Proteins

Proteins contain nitrogen as well as hydrogen, carbon, and oxygen which makes its chemical structure different from that of carbohydrates and fats. Proteins are the major source of nutrients used to build and repair tissues such as bones, muscles, cartilage, skin, hair,

Lifetime Fitness & Wellness

blood, internal organs, and nails. In addition, proteins are the foundation of antibodies that protect us from disease, of enzymes that control chemical activities in the body, and of hormones that regulate bodily functions. Protein produces four calories of energy per gram, similar to that of carbohydrates. They are used by the body as a source of energy only if there are not enough carbohydrates and fats available.

The building blocks of protein are chemical structures called **amino acids.** These small chemical structures are necessary for growth and repair of the body. There are 20 amino acids that are required to carry out several physiological functions. There are nine amino acids that the body cannot produce and are considered **essential amino acids.** These amino acids must be supplied by the diet. Eleven amino acids are considered **nonessential amino acids** because they can be produced in the body by rearranging other amino acids, if the diet is adequate in protein.

Recommendations for protein intake should be based on both the **quality** and **quantity** of amino acids in the diet. Protein sources that contain all nine essential amino acids are of **good quality** or **complete protein**, and include almost all animal sources. Animal sources of protein (egg whites, dairy products, milk, meat, fish, poultry) are generally superior to plant sources. On a scale of 1 to 100, an egg white is rated 100, which is used as the standard with which other proteins are compared to determine protein quality. Protein sources that are lacking in one or more essential amino acids are considered **incomplete proteins** and include most plant sources of protein (legumes—dried beans, peas, peanuts, soy products; grains—whole grain, corn, pasta products; and nuts and seeds). Incomplete proteins may be complemented by each other through a practice called **protein complementing**. This practice involves eating two or more incomplete proteins to make a complete protein. For example, peanut butter and bread, red beans and rice, corn and pinto beans, corn and lima beans, soybeans and sesame seeds, or a bean burrito each provides a complete protein meal. Plant and animal sources of protein such as cereal and milk, macaroni and cheese, and a cheese sandwich can also be combined to make a complete protein.

The Recommended Dietary Allowances (RDA) for protein varies with both weight and age. The RDA for adults is 0.8 grams of protein per kilogram of body weight with additional protein needed during pregnancy and lactation. Athlete's may need as much as 1.2 grams per kilogram of body weight per day. According to the dietary guidelines Americans should consume 12 to 15 percent of their daily caloric intake as protein. Americans consume double the RDA for protein each day. If protein intake exceeds the body's requirement, the excess will be used as energy or converted to fat. Problems with such a high protein intake may include: dehydration, calcium loss, high serum cholesterol levels, and obesity.

Vitamins

Vitamins are organic compounds (they contain carbon), have no caloric value, and provide no energy for the body. Even though they provide no energy, without them the body would be unable to digest, absorb, and metabolize energy nutrients. They are not only needed for energy production, but are essential for normal growth and the regulation of body activities. Together with the enzymes in the body, they help produce the right chemical reactions at the right time. They also aid in the production of blood cells, hormones, and other compounds. Some vitamins interact with minerals. For example, vitamin D improves calcium absorption, and vitamin C assists in iron absorption.

The body produces some vitamins, such as D, K, and B^{12}, but in general, the body cannot manufacture vitamins, and they must be obtained from food sources. There are two major classifications of vitamins: fat soluble and water soluble. Vitamins A, D, E, and K are fat-soluble. The **fat-soluble vitamins** are found in the fat and oily parts of food.

They are absorbed into the lymph system and then the blood, require protein (lipoproteins) carriers for transport, may become trapped in cells associated with fat when consumed in excess, are needed in periodic doses, and toxic levels can accumulate in the liver, resulting in cirrhosis-like symptoms. **Water-soluble vitamins** include vitamin B complex and vitamin C. They are absorbed directly into the blood, travel freely in the blood, freely circulate into the water-filled compartments of the body, leave the body in urine, must be ingested daily in small doses, and are unlikely to reach toxic levels when taken in megadoses. A well-balanced diet should provide adequate vitamins. **Table 2.2** summarizes the major dietary sources of each vitamin, functions, symptoms of deficiency and excess, and DRI of each vitamin.

Minerals

Minerals are neither animal nor plant—they are inorganic elements found in the body and food. They serve some of the same purposes in the body as vitamins. They are easily excreted and are usually not toxic. Almost all foods contribute to a varied intake of essential minerals. Most minerals are easy to obtain in quantities required by the body. Minerals are important in maintaining water balance, enzyme activity, and nerve function. They are also important in the formation of teeth, bones, hemoglobin, enzymes, myoglobin, and connective tissue.

Minerals are classified in two groups: **major minerals** or macrominerals, and **trace minerals** or microminerals **(Table 2.3)**. The major minerals are those the body needs in large amounts (more than 100 mg, or 0.02 teaspoon per day) including chloride, potassium, sodium, calcium, phosphorus, magnesium, and sulfur. 60 to 80 percent of all organic material in the human body would be from major minerals. Trace minerals are those the body needs in smaller dosages (less than 100 mg per day), including zinc, manganese, copper, cobalt, and iodine. Three important minerals that need further explanation are calcium, iron, and sodium.

Calcium. Everyone at any age needs calcium. Ninety-eight percent of the calcium found in the body is located in the skeleton. This mineral builds strong bones and teeth, is necessary for blood clotting, nerve impulse transmission, muscle contraction, regulating heartbeat, and fluid balance in cells. Recommended Adequate Intake (RAI) by the Institute of Medicine (IOM) for calcium is 1300 mg/day for males and females ages 14 to 18 years, 1000 mg/day for males and females ages 19 to 50 years, and 1200 mg/day for males and females 51 years and older. These recommended average intake levels are based on observed or experimentally determined levels.

There is a widespread concern that Americans are not meeting the recommended intake for calcium. Inadequate calcium can contribute to osteoporosis. This is an age related condition of insufficient bone mass found in both men and women, but it is more prevalent in women. The best sources of calcium are dairy foods such as milk and cheese. Other sources are leafy greens, nuts, and small fish (such as sardines) with bones that can be eaten.

Iron. Iron helps to build red blood cells and assists the blood in carrying oxygen from the lungs to each body cell. It also plays a vital role in the breakdown of carbohydrates, fat, and protein into energy and supports the immune system. Most minerals are easy to obtain in quantities required by the body. A major exception is iron for children under age four and adolescent girls and women in the childbearing years. Iron deficiency can lead to **anemia**, a problem resulting from the body's inability to produce hemoglobin caused by an insufficiency of iron intake. Women tend to need more iron than men because of iron lost during menstruation. The suggested RDA for iron is 18 mg per day for women and 10 mg per day for men.

Table 2.2 Vitamins and Functions

Vitamin/Dietary Reference Intake	Major Functions	Food Sources	Signs of Deficiency	Signs of Toxicity
Fat-Soluble Vitamins				
Vitamin A Males 19-50; 900 µg Females 19-50; 700 µg	Antioxidant, formation of visual pigments, maintenance of epithelial cells, immunity	Green or yellow fruits and vegetables, liver, eggs, milk products	Anemia, painful joints, night blindness, frequent infections, growth retardation	Dry skin, nausea, headache, hair loss, fatigue, birth defects
Vitamin D Males 19-50; 5 µg Females 19-50; 5 µg	Absorption of calcium and phosphorus, bone formation	Vitamin D fortified milk, eggs, liver, sardines, exposure to sunlight	Rickets (bone deformities), joint pain, soft bones, malformed teeth	Calcium deposits in soft tissues, growth failure, excessive thirst, headaches, kidney stones
Vitamin E Males 19-50; 15 mg Females 19-50; 15 mg	Antioxidant needed for stabilization of cell members	Polyunsaturated vegetable oils, green and leafy vegetables, nuts, seeds	Leg cramps, difficulty walking, muscle degeneration, anemia	Muscle weakness, blurred vision, interference with anticlotting medication and vitamin K metabolism
Vitamin K Males 19-50; 120 µg Females 19-50; 90 µg	Synthesis of blood clotting proteins	Green leafy vegetables	Hemorrhage	Anemia, interference with anticlotting medication
Water-Soluble Vitamins				
Thiamin (B_1) Males 19-50; 1.2 mg Female 19-50; 1.1 mg	Coenzyme used in energy metabolism	Pork, whole grains, seeds, nuts	Edema, mental confusion, nervous/muscular system degeneration	None reported
Riboflavin (B_2) Males 19-50; 1.3 mg Females 19-50; 1.1 mg	Coenzyme used in energy metabolism, supports normal vision and skin health	Leafy green vegetables, milk, dairy products, meat, whole grain or enriched breads and cereals	Dry skin, cracks at corner of mouth, skin rash, hypersensitivity to light	None reported
Niacin Males 19-50; 16 mg Females 19-50; 14 mg	Coenzyme used in energy metabolism	Enriched bread and cereals, nuts, all protein-containing foods, fish, poultry, wheat bran	Diarrhea, depression, dizziness, weakness, mental confusion	Nausea, vomiting, painful flushing and rash on the skin, liver damage
Pantothenic acid Males 19-50; 5 mg Females 19-50; 5 mg	Coenzyme used in energy metabolism	Widespread in foods	Insomnia, fatigue, vomiting	None from food, water retention
Vitamin B_6 Males 19-50; 1.3 mg Females 19-50; 1.3 mg	Coenzyme used in fatty acid and amino acid metabolism	Animal protein, legumes, whole grains, fruits, soy products	Convulsions, anemia, headaches, depression	Numbness, damage to nerves, headaches, loss of reflexes, impaired memory

Continued.

Table 2.2 Vitamins and Functions

Vitamin/Dietary Reference Intake	Major Functions	Food Sources	Signs of Deficiency	Signs of Toxicity
Vitamin B$_{12}$ Males 19-50; 2.4 µg Females 19-50; 2.4µg	Coenzyme used in metabolism of amino acids and producing red blood cells	Animal products (meat, cheese, milk, fish, poultry)	Anemia	None reported
Biotin Males 19-50; 30 µg Females 19-50; 30 µg	Coenzyme used in metabolism of energy from carbohydrate, fat, and amino acids	Liver, cheese, egg yolk, peanuts, widespread in foods	Rare	Rare
Folate Males 19-50; 400 µg Females 19-50; 400 µg	Coenzyme for nucleic acid and amino acid synthesis (new cell synthesis)	Leafy green vegetables, liver, fortified breads, cereal, pasta and grains	Anemia, embryonic neural tube defects, frequent infections	None from food, masks vitamin B$_{12}$ deficiency
Vitamin C Male 19-50; 90 mg Female 19-50; 75 mg	Antioxidant, collagen synthesis, strengthens resistance to infection, aids iron absorption, amino acid metabolism, aids iron absorption	Broccoli, citrus fruits, dark green vegetables, cantaloupe, tomatoes, potatoes, strawberries, peppers, lettuce	Scurvy, poor wound healing, bruises, bleeding gums, frequent infections	Kidney stones, diarrhea, urination, headache, insomnia,

There are two types of iron found in dietary food: animal sources (heme iron) and plant sources (nonheme iron). Animal sources of iron are more easily absorbed by the body than the plant sources. The absorption of plant sources can be enhanced when consumed with vitamin C. Good sources of heme iron include meat, poultry, and fish. Good sources of nonheme iron include whole grains, legumes, and enriched cereals. Cooking with cast iron pots provides additional iron to food. This is known as contamination iron. Do not drink tea with your meal, because the tannin in it may interfere with iron absorption.

Sodium. Sodium is the primary electrolyte that regulates the extracellular fluid levels in the body. In turn, potassium pumps the by-products of cellular processes out of the cell, eventually eliminating these "wastes" from the body. Working in conjunction with potassium and chloride these electrolytes regulate blood and body fluids, aid in the transmission of nerve impulses, aid in the regulation of heart activity and muscle contraction, and enhance certain metabolic functions. Americans consume too much sodium. The estimated average intake of sodium for Americans two years and older is approximately 3400 mg per day. Sodium intake should be reduced to 1500mg in persons 51 years and older, anyone who is hypertensive, diabetic or has chronic kidney disease, and African Americans.

Some individuals are sensitive to salt, which in some cause high blood pressure, or hypertension, as well as edema. Hypertension increases your risk of developing kidney disease, a stroke, and heart disease. High intakes of sodium can also lead to osteoporosis because sodium can increase urinary calcium losses. Common dietary sources of sodium are often processed food to which salt is added during preparation, such as cheeses, soups, pickles and pretzels. Salt is added to most canned and some frozen vegetables,

Table 2.3 Minerals and Functions

Minerals	Major Functions	Food Sources	Signs of Deficiency	Signs of Toxicity
Major Minerals				
Sodium	Needed to maintain fluid and acid base balance in body cells, nerve transmission, muscle contraction	Table salt, seafood, processed foods, pickled food	Mental apathy, nausea, vomiting, muscle cramps	Possible hpertention (high blood pressure)
Potassium	Needed to maintain fluid and acid base balance in body cells, nerve transmission, muscle contraction,	Fruits and vegetables, legumes, grains, all whole foods	Heart irregularities, muscle cramps, mental confusion, paralysis	Slowed heart rate, heart attack, muscular weakness
Chloride	Aids in digestion, needed to maintain fluid and acid-base balance in body cells, aids digestion in stomach	Table salt, processed food, soy sauce	Rare, muscle cramps, growth failure in children	Possible hypertension, vomiting
Calcium	Component of bone and teeth, blood clotting, muscle contraction, nerve transmission, blood clotting, blood pressure	Dairy products, canned fish with bones, greens, legumes, tofu	Osteoporosis, stunted growth in children, muscle cramps, weight gain	Rare, kidney stones, constipation
Phosphorus	Component of bone and teeth, energy transfer (ATP), component of cell membrane, metabolism of fats and starches, acid base balance	Milk products, fish, eggs, poultry, beef, fish, legumes, nuts, soft drinks	Unknown	Relative deficiency of calcium
Magnesium	Aid in bone mineralization, promote muscle and nerve activity, absorption of calcium, vitamin C, phosphorus, sodium and potassium	Beef, tuna, scallops, milk, yogurt, legumes, seafood, chocolate, dark green vegetables, mineral water	Weakness, confusion, hypertension, heart arrhythmia, muscle spasms, growth failure	Rare, diarrhea
Trace Minerals				
Sulfur	Important to cell respiration, component of some amino acids and insulin	All protein-containing foods, onions, garlic	None known: protein deficiency would occur first	Depresses growth in animals
Iron	Aids in oxygen transport, energy formation, hemoglobin synthesis, and myoglobin formation in muscle	Liver, meat, enriched breads and cereals, eggs, legumes, dried fruits, foods cooked in cast iron pots	Anemia, weakness, headaches, depressed immunity, fatigue	Constipation, decreased zinc absorption, "Iron poisoning"

Continued.

Table 2.3 Minerals and Functions—cont'd

Minerals	Major Functions	Food Sources	Signs of Deficiency	Signs of Toxicity
Zinc	Transport of vitamin A, sense of taste, wound healing, sexual development, immune health, component of many enzymes, hormones and proteins	Protein-containing foods, green vegetables, seafood, whole grain	Delayed sexual maturation, slow wound healing, hair loss, skin rash, growth failure in children, reduced immune function	Excessive intake may interfere with iron absorption, diarrhea, dizziness, vomiting, fever, metallic taste in mouth
Selenium	Part of antioxidant enzymes, act as a free radical scavenger and protects against oxidation	Seafood, meats, eggs, milk, whole grains, wheat germ, legumes, Brazil nuts, tomatoes, onions	Anemia (rare), possible increased risk of heart disease and cancer	Rare; digestive disorder, dermatologic lesions
Molybdenum	Component of enzymes, helps the body use iron and burn fats	Legumes, cereals, organ meats, leafy vegetables, meats	Rapid heartbeat and breathing	Joint pain, growth failure, anemia, gout
Iodine	Thyroid hormone production that helps regulate energy production and growth	Milk and milk products, sea-weed, seafood, iodized salt	Goiter, cretinism (mental retardation) in newborn	Interference with thyroid function, pimple
Copper	Absorption of iron, component of enzymes, necessary for formation of collagen, regulate oxygen levels, essential to utilization of vitamin C	Beef, fish, shellfish, shrimp, dried beans, liver, whole grains organ meat, green leafy, vegetables, cocoa and chocolate	Anemia, growth retardation,	Rare, vomiting, Wilson's disease, diarrhea, liver disease
Manganese	Component of enzymes, component of thyroid hormone, needed for digestion and utilization of food, helps build bone	Legumes, tea, oatmeal, apples, brewer's yeast, vegetables, coffee, nuts, fruit juice	Rare, weight loss, nausea and vomiting	Rare, nervous system disorders, schizophrenia
Fluoride	Decreases dental caries, bone and teeth formation	Fluoridated water, tea, seafood	Tooth decay, bone loss, dental disease	Discolored teeth, nerve abnormalities, brittle bones
Chromium	Energy release, sugar and fat metabolism, protein transport	Chicken, ham, vegetable oils, whole grains, seeds, black pepper, potatoes, brown rice, lettuce, peaches, beer, brewer's yeast	Impaired glucose tolerance, elevated circulating insulin, weight loss	Kidney and skin damage

and to smoked and cured meats. One of the Dietary Guidelines for American is to avoid too much sodium. Use the following suggestions to reduce sodium in your diet:

- Season foods with herbs and spices rather than salt.
- Choose fresh, frozen or canned food items without added salts.
- Limit the amount of salty snacks you eat, like chips and pretzels.
- Select fat-free or low-fat milk, low sodium, low fat cheese, as well as low-fat yogurt.
- Specify what you want and how you want it prepared when dining out. Ask for your dish to be prepared without salt, or order foods lower in sodium.
- Select unsalted, fat-free broths, bouillons, or soups.
- Select unsalted nuts or seeds, dried beans, peas, and lentils.
- Taste your food before you salt it.
- Try products with low or reduced sodium to curb sodium intake.
- Consume more fresh foods and fewer processed foods.

The Wellness Diet

Foods that are eaten on a regular basis make up one's diet. The foods that you select should constitute a balanced diet and consist of dietary sources from the six essential nutrients, and in adequate amounts. When planning your dietary intake, take into consideration the *Dietary Guidelines for Americans* from *2015 to 2020 and key recommendations*.

Dietary Guidelines for Americans 2015–2020

The *Dietary Guidelines* are jointly disseminated and updated every five years by the Department of Agriculture (USDA) and Health and Human Services (HHS). The *Guidelines* provide science-based information on effective food and physical activity choices for good health. The 2015–2020 *Dietary Guidelines* encourages healthy eating patterns two years and older. The goal of the 2015–20120 *Dietary Guidelines* is to help individuals improve and maintain overall health and reduce the risk of chronic disease. *The Key Recommendations* for healthy eating patterns provide additional strategies relative to the implementation of the Dietary Guidelines.

- **Follow a healthy eating pattern across the lifespan.** Choose a healthy eating pattern at an appropriate calorie level to help achieve and maintain a healthy body weight, support nutrient adequacy, and reduce the risk of chronic disease. A healthy eating pattern includes fruits, vegetables, protein, dairy, grains and oils.

- ≈ **Focus on variety, nutrient density, and amount.** Select a variety of nutrient dense foods across and within all food groups in recommended amounts to meet nutrient needs within calorie limits.

- ≈ **Limit calories from added sugars and saturated fats and reduce sodium intake.** Adopt and implement an eating pattern low in added sugars, saturated fats, and sodium. Reduce foods and beverages higher in these components to amounts that fit within healthy eating patterns.

- ≈ **Shift to healthier food and beverage choices.** Select nutrient dense foods and beverages across and within all food groups in place of less healthy choices. Consider cultural and personal preferences to make these shifts easier to accomplish and maintain.

- ≈ **Support healthy eating patterns for all.** Everyone has a role in helping to create and support healthy eating patterns in multiple setting nationwide, form home to school to work to communities.

Key Recommendations

Consume a healthy eating pattern that accounts for all foods and beverages within an appropriate calorie level. A healthy eating plan includes:

A variety of vegetables from all of the subgroups-dark green, red and orange, legumes (beans and peas), starchy

Fruits, especially whole fruits

Grains, at least half of which are whole grains

Fat-free or low-fat dairy, including milk, yogurt, cheese, and/or other fortified soy beverages

A variety of protein foods, including seafood, lean meats and poultry eggs, legumes, and nuts, seeds, and soy products

Oils

Criteria for Healthy Living Pattern:

Limit saturated fats, trans fats, added sugars and sodium

Consume less than 10 percent of calories per day from added sugars

Consume less than 10 percent of calories per day from saturated fats

Consume less than 2,300 milligrams per day of sodium

If alcohol is consumed, it should be consumed in moderation- up to one drink per day for women and up to two drinks per day for men – and only by adults of legal drinking age

Meet the Physical Activity Guidelines for Americans

The Quest for an Ideal Diet

Understanding Food Labels

An excellent way to determine whether your daily food intake meets the requirements of a healthy diet is to read the nutritional information located on the food labels. If you are eating foods without labels, use a food composition table. Most experts agree that a healthy diet includes foods that are low in sodium, sugar, and fat; high in carbohydrates; and consist of sufficient amounts of calcium, protein and essential vitamins and minerals.

The Food and Drug Administration (FDA) is responsible for labeling all food products except meat and poultry. There are certain regulations that the FDA put into practice to make food labels user-friendly. **Food labels** (see **Figure 2.2**) must indicate the manufacturer and the packer or distributor, the quantity of contents by net weight or by volume, and list the common name of each ingredient in descending order of prominence. The food labels must include the following information.

1. **Serving size** and the number of servings per container. A serving is a specific amount of food that contains the amount of nutrients described on the label, while a **portion** is the amount you choose to eat at one time and may be more or less than a serving on food labels.

2. Information about nutrients that are associated with chronic disease risk factors—that is, the amount of total fat, saturated fat, cholesterol, sodium, sugar, dietary fiber, total carbohydrate, and protein per serving.

3. The number of calories per serving and calories from fat, and the number of grams of fat, carbohydrates, and protein.

4. Percent Daily Values describes what percentage of a day's worth of a nutrient the item contains, based on a recommended diet. **Percent Daily Values (DVs)** are based on a 2,000 calorie diet. Your DV may be higher or lower.

5. All sweeteners are listed together under the term sweeteners in the ingredients.

6. The use of descriptive terms to describe food products has been limited and their meanings standardized. For example:

   - **High-fiber.** Contains 5 grams of fiber (or more per serving).
   - **Calorie-free.** Fewer than 5 calorie per serving
   - **Sodium-free.** Less than 5 milligrams per serving and no sodium chloride.
   - **Very low sodium.** Contains 35 milligrams of sodium or less per serving
   - **Low sodium.** Contains 140 milligrams or less per serving.
   - **Fat-free.** Contains less than 0.5 gram of fat per serving.
   - **Low fat.** Contains 3 grams of fat or less per serving.
   - **Reduced fat.** At least 25% less fat per serving than the highest fat version.
   - **Lean.** Less than 10 grams of fat, 4 grams of saturated fat, and 95 milligrams of cholesterol per serving.

Chapter 2   Nutrition for Wellness   27

Serving Size
Is your serving the same size as the one on the label? If you eat double the serving size listed, you need to double the nutrient and calorie values. If you eat one-half the serving size shown here, cut the nutrient and calorie values in half.

Calories
Are you overweight? Cut back a little on calories! Look here to see how a serving of the food adds to your daily total. A 5'4", 138-lb, active woman needs about 2,200 calories each day. A 5'10", 174-lb, active man needs about 2,900. How about you?

Total Carbohydrate
When you cut down on fat, you can eat more carbohydrates. Carbohydrates are in foods like bread, potatoes, fruits and vegetables. Choose these often! They give you more nutrients than **sugars** like soda pop and candy.

Dietary Fiber
Grandmother called it "roughage," but her advice to eat more is still up-to-date! That goes for both soluble and insoluble kinds of dietary fiber. Fruits, vegetables, whole-grain foods, beans and peas are all good sources and can help reduce the risk of heart disease and cancer.

Protein
Most Americans get more protein than they need. Where there is animal protein, there is also fat and cholesterol. Eat small servings of lean meat, fish and poultry. Use skim or low-fat milk, yogurt and cheese. Try vegetable proteins like beans, grains and cereals.

Vitamins & Minerals
Your goal here is 100% of each for the day. Don't count on one food to do it all. Let a combination of foods add up to a winning score.

Nutrition Facts
Serving Size ½ cup (114g)
Servings Per Container 4

Amount Per Serving

Calories 90   Calories from Fat 30

                                    % Daily Value*
Total Fat 3g	5%
Saturated Fat 0g	0%
Cholesterol 0mg	0%
Sodium 300mg	13%
Total Carbohydrate 13g	4%
Dietary Fiber 3g	12%
Sugars 3g	
Protein 3g	

Vitamin A	80%	Vitamin C	60%
Calcium	4%	Iron	4%

*Percent Daily Values are based on a 2000 calorie diet. Your daily values may be higher or lower depending on your calorie needs:

	Calories	2000	2500
Total Fat	Less than	65g	80g
Sat Fat	Less than	20g	25g
Cholesterol	Less than	300mg	300mg
Sodium	Less than	2400mg	2400mg
Total Carbohydrate		300g	375g
Fiber		25g	30g

Calories per gram:
Fat 9 • Carbohydrates 4 • Protein 4

More nutrients may be listed on some labels.

g = grams (About 28 g = 1 ounce)
mg = milligrams (1,000 mg = 1 g)

Total Fat
Aim low: Most people need to cut back on fat! Too much fat may contribute to heart disease and cancer. Try to limit your **calories from fat.** For a healthy heart, choose foods with a big difference between the total number of calories and the number of calories from fat.

Saturated Fat
A new kind of fat? No—saturated fat is part of the total fat in food. It is listed separately because it's the key player in raising blood cholesterol and your risk of heart disease. Eat less!

Cholesterol
Too much cholesterol—a second cousin to fat—can lead to heart disease. Challenge yourself to eat less than 300 mg each day.

Sodium
You call it "salt," the label calls it "sodium." Either way, it may add up to high blood pressure in some people. So, keep your sodium intake low —2,400 to 3,000 mg or less each day.*

*The AHA recommends no more than 3,000 mg sodium per day for healthy adults.

Daily Value
Feel like you're drowning in numbers? Let the Daily Value be your guide. Daily Values are listed for people who eat 2,000 or 2,500 calories each day. If you eat more, your personal daily value may be higher than what's listed on the label. If you eat less, your personal daily value may be lower.

For fat, saturated fat, cholesterol and sodium, choose foods with a low **% Daily Value.** For total carbohydrate, dietary fiber, vitamins and minerals, your daily value goal is to reach 100% of each.

Figure 2.2 How to read food labels.

≈ **Extra lean.** Less than 5 grams of fat, 2 grams of saturated fat, and 95 milligrams of cholesterol per serving.

≈ **Good source of fiber.** Contains 2.5 to 4.9 grams of fiber per serving.

≈ **Sugar-free.** Less than 0.5 gram of sugar per serving.

≈ **Cholesterol-free.** Contain less than 2 milligrams of cholesterol and 2 grams of saturated fat per serving.

- **Low cholesterol.** Contains 20 milligrams of cholesterol or less and 2 grams of saturated fat or less per serving.
- **Reduced cholesterol.** At least 25% less cholesterol than the highest-cholesterol version and 2 grams or less of saturated fat per serving.

The Vegetarian Diet

Individuals have chosen vegetarian diets for many reasons, including religious beliefs, animal rights, inability to afford animal products, and proven health benefits. Vegetarianism is linked with low cholesterol levels, lower incidences of colon, breast, and prostate cancer; and lower incidences of high blood pressure, osteoporosis and heart disease. Vegetarians seldom are overweight or have diabetes.

There are several types of vegetarian diets, ranging from no red meat, to just fish and vegetables. The common types of vegetarian diets include **lacto-vegetarians**—which includes diary products as well as grains, fruit, and vegetables; **ovo-lacto-vegetarians**—which includes eggs, dairy products, and fruits and vegetables but not meat, poultry, or fish; **pesco-vegetarians**—which includes fish as well as vegetables and grains; and **vegans**—which includes only food of plant origin. Vegans often take vitamin B^{12} supplements, because that vitamin is usually found only in animal products. Vegetarians must learn how to plan and select dietary foods carefully by modifying the MyPlate so that they can consume adequate amounts of protein, vitamin B^{12}, iron, calcium, and other essential vitamin and mineral requirements without taking supplements.

Fast Food Selection

Many Americans—especially college students—eat on the run, which probably means that they are eating lots of fast foods. Fast-food restaurants are generally associated with lots of salt, sugar, fat, and calories, and low in nutrients. The good news is that fast-food restaurants have responded to people's desire to eat more nutritious meals. Today you see more light menu items, such as salad bars, grilled chicken, nonfat yogurt, and fresh fruits/vegetables. In addition, fast-food venues have changed from frying in lard to vegetable oils, reduced sodium in their products, and removed additives from products.

You can also get a good nutritious meal that is low in calories, fat, and salt when eating out in a regular restaurant. For example, request a baked potato instead of french fries, baked or broiled items, steamed vegetables without butter or salt, lunch instead of dinner portions, and appetizers or side dishes in place of an entree. Always remember, whether eating at a fast-food or regular restaurant, that you are responsible for selecting a balanced and nutritious diet that includes foods from the MyPyramid Plan.

Supplements

Over half of Americans take **dietary supplements** in the form of vitamins, minerals, and botanical and biological substances. The Dietary Supplement Health and Education Act (DSHEA) defines dietary supplements as any product which contain one or more dietary ingredients such as vitamins, minerals, herbs, or other botanicals, amino acids or other ingredients used to supplement the diet. These supplements are marketed in most advertising venues and capture the attention of children and adults. This industry makes millions of dollars each year as a result of poor eating habits in America. Vitamins and minerals needed for normal physiological functioning of the body can be provided by eating a variety of foods. There are many Americans who depend on supplements and fortified foods to make up for poor dietary choices. Large doses of some vitamins and minerals may prove to be more dangerous than healthful. Research the benefits and dangerous effects of dietary supplements before consuming them.

Doctors recommend supplements for some individuals. If you belong to one of the following groups, ask your doctor about adding supplements to your diet: the elderly; strict vegetarians; women who are pregnant, breast-feeding or menopausal; people with chronic illnesses; at risk for heart disease; and people on medications that affect appetite or those whose lacks foods from one or more food groups.

Ergogenic supplements or aids are often used by adults under the assumptions that they enhance performance and appearance; they are safe and have been approved by the Food and Drug Administration (FDA). **Ergogenic** dietary supplements are considered to be performance-enhancing drugs or aids and most are available over the counter, without a prescription. The FDA does not agree with the assumptions about supplements and have great concerns that they may have dangerous side effects. Examples of these supplements include growth hormones, ephedrine, anabolic steroids, amino acids, chromium picolinate, creatine monohydrate, amino acids, and adrenal androgens: DHEA and androstenedione.

Nutrition and Physical Activity

Water Intake

Your muscles generate heat while participating in physical activity. In order for your body to cool down, you sweat. When sweating, water is lost from the body's water supply. Water lost during exercise must be replaced to prevent dehydration. Always **rehydrate** or replenish the water lost during physical activity in order to maintain all physiological functions of the body. It has been recommended by some experts that if you are a moderate exerciser, drink 16 ounces of fluid before you exercise, 4 to 8 ounces every 15 to 20 minutes, and at least twenty-four ounces after exercise.

It has been suggested that rehydration after dehydration will occur more rapidly and completely if the beverage contains sodium. When you drink plain water, the blood becomes more diluted, which alleviates the thirst and stimulates urine production. By placing 50 to 100 milligrams of sodium per cup in your water, the thirst is maintained, and you continue to drink enough fluid to restore body water more effectively. Sport drinks are often recommended to replace sodium and potassium lost in sweat during exercise, but water will do the job unless you are an elite athlete.

Pre-Competition Meal

The pre-competition meal provides the participant with enough nutrient energy and fluids for competition. It is very important to time the meal to allow for digestion to take place so that you can avoid the discomfort of exercising on a full stomach. Allow three to four hours between the time you eat and the time you participate in vigorous exercise. If participating in light to moderate activity, the time may be shortened between the meal and exercise. Stay away from spicy and high-fiber foods, as they may cause stomach discomfort.

During competition an ample supply of glycogen must be stored in the muscles and liver. Foods high in carbohydrates such as bagels, toast, and fruits are good sources because they are easy to digest, which makes glucose readily available for the muscles.

Proteins

High protein diets for physically active individuals and athletes have been questioned by many in the areas of health, physical activity, and nutrition. The American Dietetics Association (ADA) recommends 1.0 grams of protein per kg of body weight for active people such as athletes. This is higher than the 0.8 per kg recommended for normal adults. Most athletes do not need more protein, unless they are involved in an intense training program. On the average, athletes and non-athletes get more than the RDA of protein in their diet.

Carbohydrates

Carbohydrates are a major source of energy during exercise, but most are used on a daily basis, and little stored as muscle and liver glycogen. Physically active individuals and athletes often use more calories than sedentary individuals, so extra calories are needed in the diet. Since carbohydrates are the best source of energy, it is recommended that 70 percent of total daily caloric intake come from carbohydrates (complex) instead of 45 percent to 65 percent. This increase is necessary to replenish muscle glycogen stores between workouts.

Healthy Eating Suggestions

1. Increase your daily intake of fruits and vegetables. Add a fruit or vegetables serving daily. Allow yourself to adjust, and then add another serving until you reach eight to ten servings per day. Eat fruit for dessert instead of cake, pie or other high calorie, and low nutrient foods.

2. Your plate should contain one-half vegetables and other grains daily.

3. Eat whole-grain bread, pasta, rice and other grains daily.

4. Eat 5-6 small meals evenly spaced throughout the day (eat approximately every three hours). Eat healthy snacks between major meals.

5. Eat a breakfast everyday. Individuals who eat a healthy breakfast are less likely to overeat later in the day.

6. Approximately fifty percent of your daily calories should consist of complex carbohydrates, thirty-five percent from protein, and 15 percent fats.

7. Choose fresh or canned fruit more than fruit juice. Fruit juice has little or no fiber and added sugars.

8. Drink at least 72 ounces of water per day.

9. Reduce or eliminate your soda and alcohol consumption.

10. Snack on nuts, seeds, or fruit instead of processed foods.

11. Eat at least two vegetarian meals twice a week.
12. Have a large leafy green salad with your dinner.
13. Eat baked, broiled or steamed (not fried) fish at least twice a week.
14. When cravings arise, try to divert your attention to something unrelated to food for 15 minutes. These cravings usually stop in a short time period.
15. Eat slowly to savor every bite of food. Eat at a pace such that you take time to completely enjoy the food as you eat it. Eating fast or when your attention is focused elsewhere (such as when watching television) can cause consumption of excess calories.
16. Avoid eating oversized portions. Select portion sizes before eating. Use smaller plates, bowls and glasses when eating. When eating out, select a smaller size option, share a dish, or take part of your meal home.

Summary

Important concepts that you have learned in this chapter include the following:

- Dietary food contains the nutrients your body needs to produce energy, to regulate physiological functions of the body, and build and repair body tissue.
- The six classes of nutrients your body needs are water, carbohydrates, fat, proteins, vitamins, and minerals.
- The main dietary source of energy is carbohydrates.
- The most concentrated source of energy comes from fats, which may be saturated or unsaturated.
- Protein's major role in the body is for structural purposes that regulate cellular reactions.
- Vitamins regulate the energy-yielding reaction of cells.
- Minerals are important in the structure of bones, teeth, connective tissue, enzymes, hemoglobin, and myoglobin.
- Sodium, iron, and calcium are important minerals because they are linked to hypertension, anemia, and osteoporosis, respectively.
- Focus on your own particular needs and develop dietary goals to meet them, because no single diet provides wellness for everyone.
- The Dietary Guidelines and key recommendations to
- Learning to read and interpret food labels is necessary to achieve a healthy eating pattern.
- A vegetarian diet requires special planning but can meet all human nutritional needs.

References

American Dietetic Association and Canadian Dietetic Association. Nutrition for physical fitness and athletic performance in adults. www.eatright.org.

Anspaugh, D.J., Hamrick, M.H. & Rosata, F.D. (2008). *Wellness fundamental concepts and applications,* Boston, MA: McGraw-Hill.

Corbin, C.B., Welk, G.J., Corbin, W.R. & Welk, K.A. (2008). *Concepts of fitness and wellness.* New York, NY: McGraw-Hill Publishing Company.

Cowart, V.S. (1992). Dietary Supplements. *Physician and sports medicine,* 17, 169.

DeMarco, H.M. (1999). Pre-exercise carbohydrate meals: Application of the glycemic index. *Medicine and science in sports and exercise,* 31(1):164.

Floyd, P.A., Mimms, S.E. & Yielding, C. (2008). Personal Health: Perspective and Lifestyles, 4th ed. Belmont, CA: Thompson & Wadworth.

Food and Drug Administration (n.d.). *Dietary supplements.* Retrieved on May 12, 2006 from http://vm.cfsan.fda.gov/,dms/supplmnt.html.

Hale, Dianne (2008). *An invitation to fitness and wellness.* Belmont, CA: Wadsworth.

Jenkins, F.C. (2001). *Dynamics of fitness and health,* 8th ed. Dubuque, IA: Kendall/Hunt.

Liebman, B. (1998). Vitamins and minerals: what to take. *Nutrition action health letter,* 25(4), 3–7.

Schumann, S. (2005). *Essential knowledge for exercise and training,* 2nd ed. Dubuque, IA: Kendall/Hunt Publishing Company.

United States Department of Agriculture. National center for nutrition policy and promotion (2010, April. *MyPlate Results.* Retrieved on July 28, 2011 from http://www,myplate.gov/professionals/food_download.html.

United States Department of Agriculture (2005, January). U.S. Department of Health and Human Services. *Dietary guidelines for americans,* 2005. Retrieved on Feb. 18, 2008 from http://www.health.gov/dietguidelines/dga2005.

United States Department of Agriculture. (April, 2010). *What are discretionary calories?* Retrieved on July 28, 2011 from http://www.myplate.gov/pyramid/discretionary_calories.html.

Welland, D. (2000). Drink to good, especially water: Here is why and how much. *Environmental nutrition,* 33(10), 123.

Internet Sources

http://www.mayoclinic.com/health/whole-grains/NU00204

http://www.glycomicindex.com/main.htm

http://ods.od.nih.gov/factsheets/calcium.asp

www.healthierus.gov/dietaryguidelines

http://www.usda.gov

http://www.crnusa.org/about_bots.html

http://www.anglefire.com/:12/figskating/competitive/minerds.html

http://www.crnusa.org/about_pyramid.htm/

http://www.anyvitamins.com/rda.htm

www.nap.edu

http://www.ext.colostate.edu/pubs/foodnut/09354.html

http://www.feinberg.northwestern.edu/nutrition/factsheets/sodium.html

http://www.ohioline.osu.edu/hy-fact/5000/5559.html

www.chooseMyPlate.gov

Lab 2.1
Determining Basal Metabolic Rate

Name: _____ Date: _____

Purpose: To estimate your basal metabolic rate.

Instructions: Determine your estimated metabolic rate by completing the following steps.

Step 1: Determine standing height in inches and convert it into centimeters.

Height (inches): _____

Calculation: _____ × 2.54 = _____
     Height (in)   Height (cm)

Converted height (cm): _____

Step 2: Convert body weight in pounds to weight in kilograms.

Body Weight (lbs): _____

Calculation: _____ × .454 = _____
     Weight (lbs)   Weight (kg)

Converted Body Weight (kg): _____

Step 3: Estimate your basal metabolic rate by placing height (cm), weight (kg) and age (years) into the following equations.

Women:

Formula: BMR = 447.59 + (3.098 × height in cm) + (9.247 × weight in kg) − (4.33 × age in years)

_____ = 447.59 + (3.098 × _____) + (9.247 × _____) − (4.33 × _____)

_____ = 447.59 + _____) + _____) − _____)

BMR (kcal per day) = _____

Lab 2.1—Cont'd
Determining Basal Metabolic Rate

Name: _____   Date: _____

Men:

Formula: BMR = 88.362 + (4.799 × height in cm) + (13.397 × weight in kg) − (5.677 × age in years)

_____ = 88.362 + (4.799 × _____) + (13.397 × _____) − (5.677 × _____)

_____ = 88.362 + _____) + _____) − _____)

BMR (kcal per day) = _____

Lab 2.2
Determining Estimated Daily Caloric Needs

Name: _____   Date: _____

Purpose: This laboratory will estimate daily caloric needs based on basal metabolism and current physical activity levels.

Precautions: None

Equipment: Calculator, stadiometer, body weight scales.

Procedure: Determine estimated daily caloric needs (Food and Nutrition Board, National Research Council, 1989).

Step 1: Determine basal metabolic rate by completing **Lab 2.1.**

Estimated BMR (kcal per day): _____

Step 2: Determine current activity status correction factor.

Activity Correction Factor	Description
1.4	Limited weekly physical exertion—No regular exercise program
1.6	Moderate activity—Regular submaximal exercise at least 3 days per week
1.8	Vigorous activity—Regular vigorous work-related or exercise-related activity 4 or more days per week

Step 3: Determine estimated daily caloric need.

Daily Caloric Need (kcal per day) = BMR (kcal per day) × Activity Correction Factor

Daily Caloric Need (kcal per day) = _____ × _____

Scoring: Daily caloric need can be estimated using the procedures of the Food and Nutrition Board of the National Research Council (1989).

Data/Calculations:

Subject: _____ Date: _____

Gender: _____ Age: _____ Height: _____ Weight: _____

Estimated Daily Caloric Need (kcal per day): _____

Source: *Concepts of Health-Related Fitness*. Author: Thomas M. Adams II. Reprinted with permission.

Lab 2.3
Three-Day Food Plan

Name: _____   Date: _____

Use the chart below to devise a three day food plan for yourself based on the recommendations of the Dietary Guidelines. Each day will consist of three meals and three snacks. Maintain the proportions suggested in the Dietary Guidelines.

DAY 1

Meal	Food Selections	Portion
Breakfast		
Snack		
Lunch		
Snack		
Supper		
Snack		

Lab 2.3—Cont'd
Three-Day Food Plan

Name: _____ Date: _____

DAY 2

Meal	Food Selections	Portion
Breakfast		
Snack		
Lunch		
Snack		
Supper		
Snack		

Lab 2.3—Cont'd
Three-Day Food Plan

Name: _____ Date: _____

DAY 3

Meal	Food Selections	Portion
Breakfast		
Snack		
Lunch		
Snack		
Supper		
Snack		

Chapter 3

Health-Related Components of Physical Fitness

Objectives
Introduction
Health-Related Components of Physical Fitness
Physical Fitness Training Principles
Designing a Physical Fitness Program
Exercise Precautions

Summary
References
Lab 3.1: PAR-Q: The Physical Activity Readiness Questionnaire
Lab 3.2: Screening Questionnaire
Lab 3.3: Health-Related Fitness Goals

Objectives

Upon completion of this chapter, you will be able to:

1. Define the health-related components of physical fitness.
2. Discuss how each health-related component of physical fitness influences your total fitness level.
3. Define the skill-related components of physical fitness.
4. Identify and explain the basic principles of training applied when designing a physical fitness program.
5. Identify the steps involved in designing a safe and effective fitness program.
6. Identify the three basic elements of a daily exercise session.
7. Identify health factors that may warrant consulting a physician before starting an exercise program.

Introduction

People engage in physical activities for several reasons. Many participate to enhance the dimensions of health-related physical fitness. Most authorities agree that health-related physical fitness consists of cardiorespiratory endurance, muscular strength, muscular endurance, flexibility and body composition. Research data supports the notion that the dimensions of health-related physical fitness impact total well-being including social, spiritual, psychological, physical, intellectual, and environmental health. People participate in physical activities to help control weight, manage stress, to protect against osteoporosis, high blood pressure, some types of cancer, diabetes, heart disease, and to release anxiety and tension. Many individuals in the United States are exercising regularly, eating well-balanced diets, and participating in various types of physical activities today than in the past. As a society we are increasingly becoming aware of the benefits of regular physical activity.

This chapter explores the health-related components of physical fitness, and how the development of each component, through physical activity, impacts your overall fitness and wellness. You will learn the training principles that describe how the body responds to physical demands placed on it—important components necessary for designing a physical fitness program, training guidelines, and exercising precautions. Chapters 4, 5, 6, and 8 will address the components of health-related physical fitness and how to develop the components into an integrated fitness program utilizing the training principles.

Health-Related Components of Physical Fitness

Physical fitness is important both for skill performance and health. The health-related components of physical fitness include cardiorespiratory endurance or aerobic fitness, muscular strength and endurance, flexibility, and body composition. Athletic performance depends on the skill-related components of physical fitness, such as balance, speed, power, coordination, agility and reaction time (see **Table 3.1**). Many individuals other then athletes use the skill-related components of fitness to enhance their health-related components by

Table 3.1 Skill-Related Fitness Components

Component	Definition	Activities
Balance	The ability to maintain equilibrium while moving or stationary	walking on balance beam, gymnastics, water skiing
Speed	The ability to perform a movement in a short time frame	runner on a track team
Power	The ability to rapidly produce force	discus thrower, shot-putter
Coordination	The ability to integrate body parts (i.e., eye, hand, foot) to move smoothly	juggling, sports (i.e., baseball, tennis, softball)
Agility	The ability to rapidly change bodily positions and maintain the movement of the entire body	skiing, wrestling
Reaction Time	The amount of time that elapsed between a stimulus and the start of a movement	swimming, track, karate, ping pong

participating in activities that use these skills. Always keep in mind that skill is not necessary to maintain the health-related components of physical fitness.

Cardiorespiratory Endurance

Cardiorespiratory endurance is the ability of the heart, lungs, and blood vessels to deliver adequate amounts of oxygen to the body during extended periods of physical activity. Cardiorespiratory endurance has also been called aerobic fitness or cardiovascular fitness. Aerobic dance, swimming, running, walking, and cycling are examples of activities used to enhance cardiorespiratory endurance.

Cardiorespiratory endurance is an important part of health-related physical fitness and may be the most important. As cardiorespiratory fitness improves, the following health benefits are experienced: (1) resting heart rate slows, blood volume increases, and resting blood pressure decreases as a result of the heart functioning more efficiently; (2) a reduction in body fat and an increase in high-density lipoproteins as a result of energy use during exercise; and (3) other benefits include a lower risk for developing heart disease, high blood pressure, and diabetes, as well as aiding in managing stress. (Cardiorespiratory endurance is discussed in Chapter 4.)

Muscular Strength

Muscular strength refers to the amount of force a muscle can generate with a single maximum effort (for example: lifting, pressing, pulling, or pushing). Strong muscles improve posture, enhance athletic performance, and help in everyday activities, such as lifting and carrying boxes. They help prevent back and leg aches, as well as help keep the skeleton in proper alignment. As muscle mass increases, along with strength, both contribute to a higher metabolic rate and healthier body composition. Muscular strength is tested by determining the maximal amount of weight you can lift one time, such as leg lifts or biceps curls.

Resistance training can be used to maintain or develop muscular strength. This type of training is performed by lifting weights, which stress the muscles and make them contract. The type of resistance equipment selected depends largely upon availability and personal preference. Some individuals apply resistance by using free weights (barbell and dumbbells) or a weight-training machine. Others use their own body weight to apply resistance to perform pull-ups or push-ups. You can also use equipment found at home to add resistance, such as plastic gallon milk jugs or two-liter soda containers filled with water or sand. No matter what method chosen, resistance training helps maintain and develop muscular strength, which declines with age. (Muscular strength is discussed in Chapter 5.)

Muscular Endurance

Muscular endurance is the ability of a muscle group to develop force or contract repeatedly for a long period. Muscular endurance is essential for good posture and injury prevention. It is also essential for leisure, recreational, and fitness activities. Muscular endurance is measured by counting the number of times you can repeat lifts with a fixed weight, such as lifting 30 pounds in a biceps curl, or by the number of sit-ups, pull-ups, or pushups executed in a certain period of time. Resistance training should be included in your exercise program to maintain or develop muscular endurance and muscular strength. (Muscular endurance is discussed in Chapter 5.)

Flexibility

Flexibility is the range of possible movement in a joint, such as the knee, hip, ankle, or elbow. Flexibility can depend upon such factors as age, gender, body composition, body physique, and posture. People who are flexible are less likely to be injured while playing a sport, usually have good posture, have less lower back pain, have less stiffness and soreness of muscles, and have less tearing of ligaments and muscles during physical activity. Everyone can increase their flexibility. The key is starting a stretching program slowly and maintaining it. Stretching exercises increase the range of motion of the joints and will soothe and relax you. (Flexibility is discussed in Chapter 6.)

Body Composition

Body Composition refers to the relative amounts of fat and lean tissue (bone, muscle, organs, and water) in the body. People with excessive amounts of body fat are more susceptible to high blood pressure, heart disease, joint problems, gallbladder disease, back pain, stroke, diabetes, gout, and some types of cancer. College-aged males and females average 15 percent and 23 percent body fat, respectively. The level at which males and females are considered obese is 25 percent and 32 percent respectively. Body composition, especially body fat, is best controlled by a combination of regular exercise and a balanced diet. In order to increase muscle mass, resistance weight training must be included in a regular exercise program. (Body composition and weight control are discussed in Chapter 8.)

Physical Fitness Training Principles

Your body is what you make it. It is designed for numerous purposes and can easily adjust to meet physical demands. When rushing to your car, the heart will speed up to pump a greater amount of blood to the legs and your breathing rate will increase. These short-term, immediate adaptations can easily be transformed into long-term changes in heart rate and oxygen consumption with **physical training.** Physical training over a period of time allows the body to make these long-term changes and enhances body functioning. Although individuals exhibit different limits on the maximum levels of physical fitness and performance they can achieve, regular participation in different types of activities can improve everyone's wellness and fitness level.

Developing the components of fitness and working toward wellness involves being aware of various types and amounts of exercises you should perform. As you begin the process, it's important to comprehend the principles of physical training. Principles of importance include overload, specificity-of-training, reversibility-of-training, and individual differences.

Overload

The principle of **overload** (also called stress) means subjecting the body to a greater demand than it is accustomed to. In order for muscles to get stronger, they must work against an amount of resistance greater than normal. For body to continue to get stronger, greater workload must continuously be applied in increments over a period of time. **Progressive overloading** involves gradually increasing the amount of exercise as the body adapts to the stress placed upon it. Progressive overloading provides the opportunity for improvement in fitness without the risk of injuries.

The overload principle applies equally to all aspects of fitness: flexibility, muscle strength, muscle endurance, and cardiorespiratory endurance. It also applies to the skeleton. To develop a strong, dense skeletal system, you must start by demanding that the bones bear slightly more stress (through weight-bearing exercises such as walking, running, weightlifting, or aerobic dance) than they are accustomed to. The amount of overload is very important. To improve fitness one must work harder, that is, at a greater intensity, although basic health can be enhanced through slow and moderate activity. Whatever exercise you do, there is a level, or training threshold at which fitness benefits begin to improve—a target zone. There is also an upper level of safe training at which potential risks outweigh any further benefits.

The acronym **FIT** describes the three dimensions of progressive overload that are put into practice by those who are trying to maintain or improve a specific level of fitness: frequency (how often use exercise), intensity (how hard), and time (how long). Sometimes a second *T* is added to create the **FITT** formula, which indicates the **T**ype of physical activity to be performed. The specificity principle stresses the point at which various types of activities enhance different components of fitness and improve different areas of health and wellness.

Frequency (how often). Physical activity must be performed regularly to be effective. The recommended frequency varies with different types of exercises and with an individual's fitness goals. The minimum frequency for most people is three to five days of cardiorespiratory endurance or aerobic exercise a week and two to three days of resistance and flexibility training a week, but frequency ultimately depends on the specific benefits desired.

Intensity (how hard). Exercise intensity varies both with personal goals and types of exercise. Physical activity must be performed harder than your normal level of activity (overload) to produce benefits. To improve cardiorespiratory endurance, you need to increase your heart rate to a target zone. To develop muscular strength, increase the amount of weight lifted. To develop muscular endurance, increase the number of repetitions; and to enhance flexibility, a person needs to stretch muscles beyond their normal length.

Time (how long). Physical activity must be performed for an adequate length of time, or duration in order to gain fitness benefits, particularly for cardiorespiratory endurance. Experts suggest that cardiorespiratory endurance exercise bouts last 20–60 minutes. Similar health benefits have been found in individuals that performed a single 30 minute session of moderate exercise and three 10 minute sessions of exercise throughout the day. The higher the intensity of exercise, the shorter time you have to exercise—for instance, running at a brisk pace. The lower the intensity of exercise, the longer you have to exercise—for instance, walking at a moderate pace. As the length of time increases, intensities of exercises may be decreased.

For muscular strength, muscular endurance, and flexibility, time (duration) is defined by the number of sets or repetitions of particular exercises rather than the number of minutes.

Specificity-of-Training

The **specificity** principle refers to the body's adaptation to a particular type and amount of stress placed upon it relative to parameters such as physical fitness goals, types of movement, and energy systems targets during physical activity. In order to develop a particular body part and component of fitness, perform exercises specifically designed for those areas. Running, for example, trains the lungs and heart to work more effectively and efficiently, and makes certain muscles in the legs stronger. However, it does not improve flexibility or arm strength.

Overloading is specific to each body part and to each component of fitness. In order to improve all components of fitness, develop a comprehensive exercise program that overloads each component, as well as different body parts. To compete in a particular sport, training to develop sport-specific skills is required, such as a strong power serve in volleyball, or a strong, efficient backhand in tennis.

Reversibility-of-Training

The principle of **reversibility** or disuse is the opposite of the overload principle. To put it simply, if you don't use it, you lose it. The body adapts to higher physical demands, just as it also adjusts to lower levels. If you stop exercising, within two months you can lose as much as 50% of fitness improvements. If you must modify your exercise program temporarily, you can maintain your fitness by reducing time (duration) and frequency, and keeping the intensity constant.

Individual Differences

Take a look around; we are all different. There are no two bodies alike, no two fitness levels the same; and there are great differences in athletic performance and sport skills. Some people perform sports or various activities more skillfully than others, no matter how much those others train. There are individual limits on each person's adaptability and potential for improvements. For example, the body's ability to transport and use oxygen can be improved only by about 15 to 30 percent through training. This improvement may not be enough to encourage you to engage in activities at the competitive level, but it can enhance health benefits. Scientists have identified certain genes that control strength, endurance, and body fat. So an endurance athlete must be born with certain genes to reach competitive performance levels.

Designing a Physical Fitness Program

One of the best ways to improve your fitness level is to start an exercise program that helps you realize your goals. By developing a written plan you make a promise to be physically active. Research shows that you are more inclined to be physically active when you put your physical fitness program in writing. An established plan allows you opportunities to monitor your progress toward your goals. Designing a physical fitness program involves assessing your present fitness level, determining long range goals, and selecting activities to help reach fitness goals.

Assessment

In order to develop a successful fitness program you must first assess your current level of physical fitness and activity for each of the five health-related fitness components. The assessment data will allow you to establish specific fitness goals and design your physical fitness program. Assessment instruments in Chapters 4, 5, 6 and 8 will evaluate your cardiorespiratory endurance, muscular strength and muscular endurance, flexibility, and body composition.

Goal Setting

After completing the assessments in the laboratories in Chapters 4, 5, 6 and 8, you will have the information needed to establish a set of short-term and long-term goals related to each health-related physical fitness component. Short-term goals are small steps taken in order to achieve long-term goals and can be rewritten or changed to reflect progress. Even though you are developing goals for each area of physical fitness, the ultimate goal should be the same of every health-related fitness program—wellness that lasts a lifetime.

Activity Selection

The **physical activity pyramid** (see **Figure 3.1**) is a good way to illustrate different types of activities and how each contributes to the development of health, wellness and physical fitness. It consists of four different levels. Each level consists of one or two types of activities and recommendations of time allotment for each activity to achieve health, wellness, and physical fitness.

The four levels of the pyramid are also based on health benefits obtained from participating in regular physical activity. The base of the pyramid consists of low-intensity activities that require greater frequency than those at higher levels in the pyramid. Activities at this level benefits those who have been inactive and may include such activities as walking a dog, climbing stairs rather than taking an elevator, or doing any other type of exercise as part of your normal daily activities.

The next level consists of moderate intensity activities, such as jogging, biking, playing tennis, basketball, swimming, or performing other cardiorespiratory endurance and sport/recreation activities. It is suggested that these activities should be performed for 2.5 hours at a moderate intensity or 75 minutes at a vigorous intensity for most days of the week. (Training for cardiorespiratory endurance is discussed in Chapter 4.)

The next level includes exercises for muscular strength and endurance, and flexibility. Muscular strength and endurance exercises should be performed two to three days a week on all major muscle groups and can be developed through resistance training. (Training for muscular strength and endurance is discussed in Chapter 5.) Stretching exercises are used to develop flexibility in all major muscles and joints and should be performed two or more days per week (Flexibility is discussed in Chapter 6).

The tip of the activity pyramid addresses rest and sedentary activities. These activities are included in the pyramid because they are unavoidable. Rest is important if you are ill or injured. Many people choose sedentary activities such as watching television, reading, and working on the computer during their leisure time over health-related physical fitness activities, but too much inactivity leads to low fitness as well as poor health.

The physical activity pyramid is a useful model for describing different types of activity and their benefits. It is also useful in summarizing the FIT formula for each of the different benefits of activity. The following guidelines for using the pyramid should be considered: (1) No single activity provides all of the benefits; (2) In some cases, one type of activity can substitute for another; (3) Something is better than nothing; (4) Activities from level 3 are useful even if you are limited in performing activities at other levels; and (5) Good planning will allow you to schedule activities from all levels in a reasonable amount of time.

PHYSICAL ACTIVITY PYRAMID

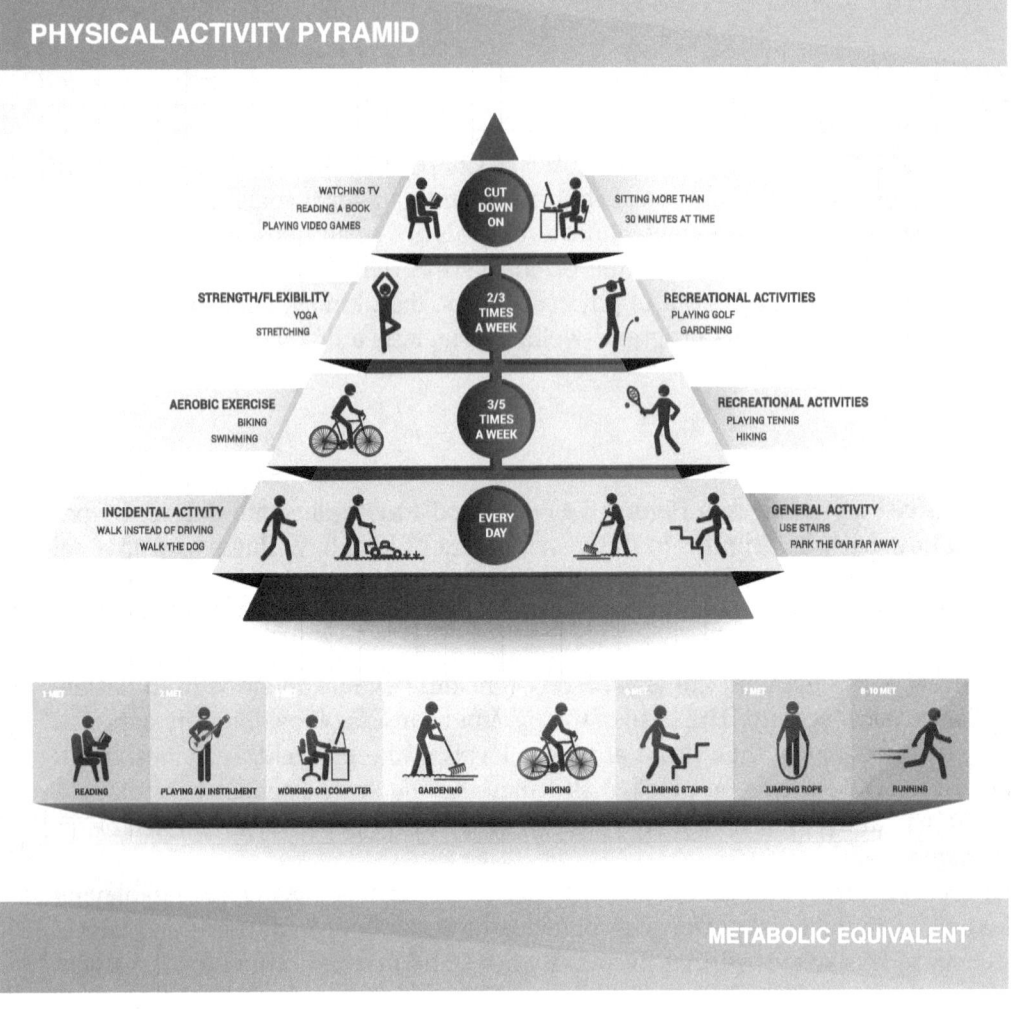

Figure 3.1 The Activity Pyramid.
© elenabsl/shutterstock.com

The basic elements of a physical fitness or exercise session should include the warm-up, workout and cool-down (see **Table 3.2**).

Training Guidelines

In order to make your exercise program more effective, you need to adhere to the following guidelines.

1. **Warm up before exercising.** Warming up prepares the cardiovascular system for more strenuous activity. It reduces injuries, increases blood flow, and contributes to the efficiency of oxygen and fuel being delivered to working muscles. Warming up also provides a transition from rest to exercise, which decreases muscle soreness.

2. **Cool down after exercising.** Cooling down after exercising allows circulation to return to a normal resting state. An inadequate cool down may involve standing or stopping quickly after exercising, which causes blood to pool in your lower extremities and not return to the heart. Gradually cool down by continuing to exercise but with less intensity. Always include stretching exercises as a part of your cool down.

Table 3.2 Basic Elements of a Physical Fitness or Exercise Session

Warm-up
- Prepares cardiovascular system for work
- Increases muscle temperature
- Reduces injury and soreness
- Increases blood flow, which contributes to increase oxygen and fuel to the muscles
- Light stretching of tendons and muscles
- Should range from 10–15 minutes

Workout
- Twenty to sixty minutes of moderate to vigorous activity
- Adhere to the FITT principles (frequency, intensity, time, type)
- Maintain exercise heart rate (monitor heart rate during cardiovascular work-out)
- Specific to selected activity (weight training, aerobics, swimming)

Cool-down
- Allows circulation to return to normal
- Gradual slow down (5–10 minutes)
- Static stretching
- Check heart rate

---

3. **Train the way you want your body to change.** Overload the areas of the body in which you want to see changes. To improve flexibility, perform stretching exercises; to tone your body, lift weights.

4. **Train your mind.** Develop a mind-set about improving your fitness level. This mind-set requires patience, discipline and commitment in order to reach your fitness goals.

5. **Get in shape gradually.** To meet long term goals, an exercise program must consist of three phases: The **beginning phase** of training focuses on gradually starting an exercise program, which allows the body to adapt to new activities. The **progression phase** emphasizes the progressive overload principle. The **maintenance phase** stresses maintaining your current program rather than constantly increasing intensity, duration, or frequency.

6. **Train on a regular basis.** Don't be a weekend warrior. Exercising regularly is the key to developing or enhancing your fitness level.

7. **Listen to your body.** Don't overdo it. Your body provides signals and signs to let you know when to slow down or speed up.

8. **Keep your exercise program in perspective.** Balance your daily activities to include all parts of your life.

9. **Train with a friend.** A partner can encourage you when your spirits are low, as well as observe your exercise techniques.

10. **Positive self-talk.** Use positive self-talk to motivate yourself to achieve your goals. Recite expressions such as "what I believe, I can achieve," I have the power to change my body and the will to become all I can be physically, mentally, and intellectually.

Exercise Precautions

If you are a male and less than forty years old, or a female and less than fifty and in good health, exercise is probably safe for you. If you are over these ages or have health problems, such as obesity, high blood pressure, muscle or joint problems, or heart disease, see a physician before starting a vigorous exercise program. The Physical Activity Readiness Questionnaire (PAR-Q) is an assessment instrument that evaluates one's need to consult a physician before becoming physically active **(Lab 3.1)**. Completing the PAR-Q will help determine if there are potential problems which must be addressed before starting an exercise program. An exercise stress test (EXT) may be recommended by a physician if he or she is not sure whether exercise is safe for you. **Lab 3.2**, the Medical/Health Questionnaire will also help you determine your pre-participation medical history.

Summary

Important concepts that you have learned in this chapter include the following:

- Physical fitness is an essential component of wellness, and it is promoted through physical fitness.
- The health-related components of physical fitness are cardiorespiratory endurance, muscular strength, muscular endurance, flexibility, and body composition.
- Exercising moderately on a regular basis contributes to good health.
- The progressive-overload principle explains how the body adapts to exercise training or physical stress.
- The specificity-of-training principle describes how the body changes as it adapts to the specific type of exercises or training being performed.
- The reversibility-of-training principle describes how the body loses fitness when physical training is lower or discontinued.
- The individual difference principle explains how people deviate in the greatest level of fitness they can accomplish.
- Assessing your current level of fitness, setting realistic goals, and choosing appropriate activities that enhance the components of health-related physical fitness should be addressed when designing an exercise program.
- Adhering to training guidelines can help ensure an effective and successful exercise program.
- If you presently lead a physically active lifestyle, you can enhance your benefits greatly by increasing the intensity or duration of your activities.
- Each training program has a beginning, progressive, and maintenance phase.
- Individuals without health problems can start a moderate to vigorous exercise program without an exercise stress test or doctor's approval.

References

Belin, L.J. (1999). Lifestyle and hypertension—An overview. *Clinical and Experimental Hypertension,* 21:749–762.

Corbin, C.B., Welk, G.J., Corbin, W.R., & Welk, K.A. (2008). *Concepts of Fitness and Wellness,* 7th ed., New York, NY: McGraw Hill.

Fahey, T.D., Insel, P.M., and Roth, W.T. (2008). *Fit and Well: Core concepts and labs in physical fitness and wellness,* 6th ed., California: Mayfield Publishing Company.

Hales, Dianne (2008). *An Invitation to Fitness and Wellness.* Canada: Wadsworth Publishing Company.

McArdle, W.D., Katch, F.I. and Katch, V.L. (2010). Essentials of Exercise Physiology 4th ed. Baltimore, MD: Williams & Wilkins.

Shephard, R.J. (1999). How much physical activity is needed for good health? *International Journal of Sports Medicine,* 20:23–27.

Williams, C.S., Harageones, E.G., Johnson, D.J., & Smith C.D. (2005). *Personal Fitness,* Dubuque, IA: Kendall/Hunt Publishing Company.

Internet Sources

www.ascm.org

www.usda.gov

Lab 3.1
PAR-Q: The Physical Activity Readiness Questionnaire

Name: _____   Date: _____

Regular physical activity is fun and healthy, and increasingly more people are starting to become more active every day. Being more active is very safe for most people. However, some people should check with their doctor before they start becoming much more physically active.

If you are planning to become much more physically active than you are now, start by answering the seven questions in the box below. If you are between the ages of 15 and 69, the PAR-Q will tell you if you should check with your doctor before you start. If you are over 69 years of age, and you are not used to being very active, check with your doctor.

Common sense is your best guide when you answer these questions. Please read the questions carefully and answer each one honestly: check YES or NO.

YES	NO	
☐	☐	1. Has your doctor ever said that you have a heart condition *and* that you should only do physical activity recommended by a doctor?
☐	☐	2. Do you feel pain in your chest when you do physical activity?
☐	☐	3. In the past month, have you had chest pain when you were not doing physical activity?
☐	☐	4. Do you lose your balance because of dizziness or do you ever lose consciousness?
☐	☐	5. Do you have a bone or joint problem that could be made worse by a change in your physical activity?
☐	☐	6. Is your doctor currently prescribing drugs (for example, water pills) for your blood pressure or heart condition?
☐	☐	7. Do you know of *any other reason* why you should not do physical activity?

If you answered

YES to one or more questions

Talk with your doctor by phone or in person BEFORE you start becoming much more physically active or BEFORE you have a fitness appraisal. Tell your doctor about the PAR-Q and which questions you answered YES.

- You may be able to do any activity you want—as long as you start slowly and build up gradually. Or, you may need to restrict your activities to those which are safe for you. Talk with your doctor about the kinds of activities you wish to participate in and follow his/her advice.
- Find out which community programs are safe and helpful for you.

NO to all questions

If you answered NO honestly to *all* PAR-Q questions, you can be reasonably sure that you can:
- start becoming much more physically active—begin slowly and build up gradually. This is the safest and easiest way to go.
- take part in a fitness appraisal—this is an excellent way to determine your basic fitness so that you can plan the best way for you to live actively.

DELAY BECOMING MUCH MORE ACTIVE:
- if you are not feeling well because of a temporary illness such as a cold or a fever—wait until you feel better, or
- if you are or may be pregnant—talk to your doctor before you start becoming more active.

Please note: If your health changes so that you then answer YES to any of the above questions, tell your fitness or health professional. Ask whether you should change your physical activity plan.

Informed Use of the PAR-Q: The Canadian Society for Exercise Physiology, Health Canada, and their agents assume no liability for persons who undertake physical activity, and if in doubt after completing this questionnaire, consult your doctor prior to physical activity.

> You are encouraged to copy the PAR-Q but only if you use the entire form.

Note: If the PAR-Q is being given to a person before he or she participates in a physical activity program or a fitness appraisal, this section may be used for legal or administrative purposes.
   I have read, understood and completed this questionnaire. Any questions I had were answered to my full satisfaction.

NAME _____
SIGNATURE _____   DATE _____
SIGNATURE OF PARENT _____   WITNESS _____
or GUARDIAN (for participants under the age of majority)

Source: Physical Activity Readiness Questionnaire (PAR-Q) © 2002. Used with permission from the Canadian Society for Exercise Physiology www.csep.ca.

Lab 3.2
Screening Questionnaire

Name: _____   Date: _____

Assess your health needs by marking all **true** statements.

History

You have had:
- ❏ a heart attack
- ❏ heart surgery
- ❏ cardiac catheterization
- ❏ coronary angioplasty (PTCA)
- ❏ pacemaker/implantable cardiac
- ❏ defibrillator/rhythm disturbance
- ❏ heart valve disease
- ❏ heart failure
- ❏ heart transplantation
- ❏ congenital heart disease

Other health issues:
- ❏ You have musculoskeletal problems.
- ❏ You have concerns about the safety of exercise.
- ❏ You take prescription medication(s).
- ❏ You are pregnant.
- ❏ You have diabetes
- ❏ You have asthma or other lung disease
- ❏ You have burning or cramping in lower legs when walking

Recommendations

*If you marked any of the statements in this section, consult your healthcare provider before engaging in exercise. You may need to use a facility with a **medically qualified staff**.*

Symptoms

- ❏ You experience chest discomfort with exertion.
- ❏ You experience unreasonable breathlessness.
- ❏ You experience dizziness, fainting, blackouts.
- ❏ You take heart medications.

Cardiovascular risk factors

- ❏ You are a man older than 45 years.
- ❏ You are a woman older than 55 years or you have had a hysterectomy or you are postmenopausal.
- ❏ You smoke.
- ❏ Your blood pressure is greater than 140/90 mm Hg.

Recommendations

*If you marked two or more of the statements in this section, you should consult your healthcare provider before engaging in exercise. You might benefit by using a facility with a **professionally qualified staff** to guide your exercise program.*

Lab 3.2—Cont'd
Screening Questionnaire

Name: _____   Date: _____

- ❑ You don't know your blood pressure.
- ❑ You take blood pressure medication.
- ❑ Your blood cholesterol level is >200 mg/dl.
- ❑ You don't know your cholesterol level.
- ❑ You have a blood relative who had a heart attack before age 55 (father/brother) or 65 (mother/sister).
- ❑ You are diabetic or take medicine to control your blood sugar.
- ❑ You are physically inactive (i.e., you get less than 30 minutes of physical activity on at least 3 d/wk).
- ❑ You are more than 20 pounds overweight.

- ❑ **None of the above is true.**   *You should be able to exercise safely without consulting your healthcare provider.*

From *Fitness and Your Health*, Seventh Edition, by David C. Nieman. Copyright © 2015 by Kendall Hunt Publishing Company. Reprinted by permission.

Lab 3.3
Health-Related Fitness Goals

Name: _____   Date: _____

Purpose: To define the health related fitness goals and specify your personal health-related fitness goals.

Instructions: Define each health-related fitness component and state a specific goal that is achievable and measurable.

1. Cardiorespiratory endurance

    Define: _____

    Your goal: _____

2. Muscular endurance

    Define: _____

    Your goal: _____

3. Muscular strength

    Define: _____

    Your goal: _____

4. Body Composition

    Define: _____

    Your goal: _____

5. Flexibility

    Define: _____

    Your goal: _____

Chapter 4

Cardiorespiratory Endurance

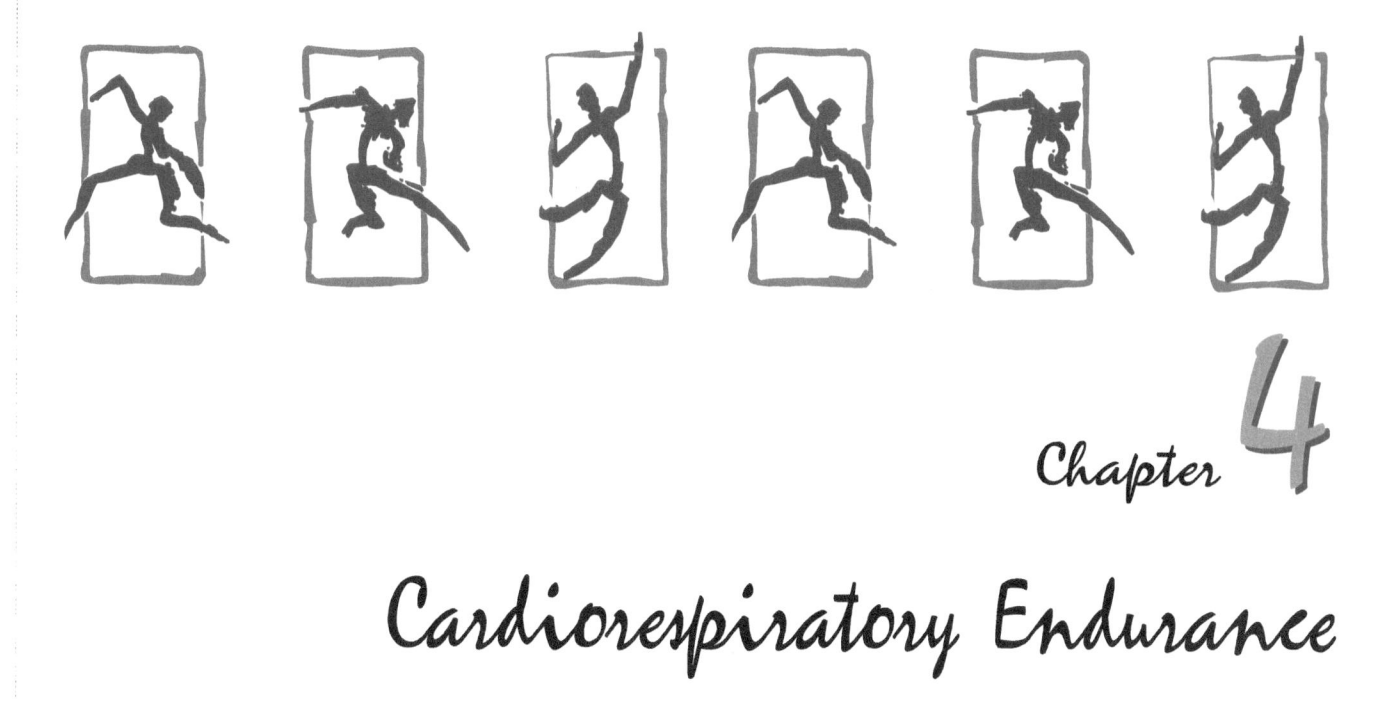

Objectives
Introduction
Understanding the Cardiorespiratory System
The Energy Systems
The Physiological Benefits of Improved Cardiorespiratory Endurance
Cardiorespiratory Endurance Program Design
Training Principles

Summary
References
Lab 4.1: Your Resting Heart Rate
Lab 4.2: Target Heart Rate Zone
Lab 4.3: Cardiorespiratory Endurance Program

Objectives

Upon completion of this chapter, the student will be able to:

1. Define cardiorespiratory endurance.
2. Discuss acute and chronic responses to aerobic exercise.
3. Describe the basic functions and structure of the cardiorespiratory system.
4. Discuss the energy systems utilized during exercise.
5. Discuss the benefits of cardiorespiratory endurance in maintaining health and well-being.
6. Plan a personalized cardiorespiratory endurance fitness program.
7. Describe the importance of warm-up and cool-down.
8. Explain how the training principles are applied to improve cardiorespiratory endurance.

Introduction

Cardiorespiratory endurance is defined as the ability of the heart, lungs, and blood vessels to deliver adequate amounts of oxygen to the body during extended periods of physical activity. The greater your cardiorespiratory endurance, the longer and harder you can exercise before becoming fatigued. Modern-day technological advances have resulted in the adoption of a sedentary lifestyle by many Americans and an increase in chronic conditions such as cardiovascular diseases, low back pain, and obesity.

Cardiorespiratory endurance can improve with regular participation in aerobic exercise. Aerobic exercise is any activity that can be performed for a prolonged time period, is rhythmic, and uses a large amount of muscle mass. Examples of aerobic exercise activities include walking, jogging/running, cycling, swimming, rope skipping, stair climbing, and aerobic dance.

Understanding the Cardiorespiratory System

The cardiorespiratory system is comprised of the heart, lungs and blood vessels. The function of the heart is to circulate blood throughout the body—to provide blood and nutrients to all cells. The heart consists of two upper chambers known as the **atria** and two lower chambers known as the **ventricles.** The heart has four valves that function to ensure that blood flows only in the forward direction. The left AV or mitral valve is located between the left atrium and left ventricle. The left AV valve prevents backward blood flow into the left atrium from the left ventricle. The right AV or tricuspid valve is located between the right atrium and the right ventricle. It prevents the backward flow of blood into the right atrium from the right ventricle. The aortic valve is located between the left ventricle and the aorta and prevents the backward flow of blood into the left ventricle from the aorta. The pulmonary valve is located between the right ventricle and the pulmonary artery and prevents the backward flow of blood into the right ventricle from the pulmonary artery. The blood flow pathway is a closed circuit such that the circulation of blood can be traced from any starting point in the heart, circulated throughout the heart and body and returned to the original starting point. The right atrium receives blood low in oxygen and high in carbon dioxide content from the body through the superior and inferior vena cava to the right atrium. The blood then travels through other structures on the right side of the heart (right AV or tricuspid valve, right ventricle, and pulmonary valve) through the pulmonary arteries to the lungs, where it receives rich, oxygenated blood to circulate to all the body's cells. This rich, oxygenated blood returns via the pulmonary veins to the left atrium, and then passes through other structures on the left side of the heart (left AV or mitral valve, left ventricle, aortic valve) through the aorta, to all the body's cells. The circulation of blood through the heart leading to the rest of the body is depicted in **Figure 4.1.**

The heart is a muscle and requires adequate oxygen supply and nutrients. The **coronary arteries** function to supply the heart muscle with needed oxygen and nutrients. The coronary arteries are located on the outside of the heart and supply the heart with oxygen and nutrients. These vessels can become narrowed over time due to **atherosclerosis,** which is the build up of cholesterol and other fatty deposits inside the blood vessel, reducing the amount of oxygen available to the heart (see **Figure 4.2**), thus increasing the risk of heart attack. This can result in chest pain (angina) or in severe cases, a heart attack. Atherosclerosis is associated with a sedentary lifestyle; poor dietary practices, smoking, elevated cholesterol levels, hypertension and obesity. Regular participation in a cardiorespiratory endurance program can reduce the atherosclerosis, angina and the heart attack.

The pathway of blood flow through the heart

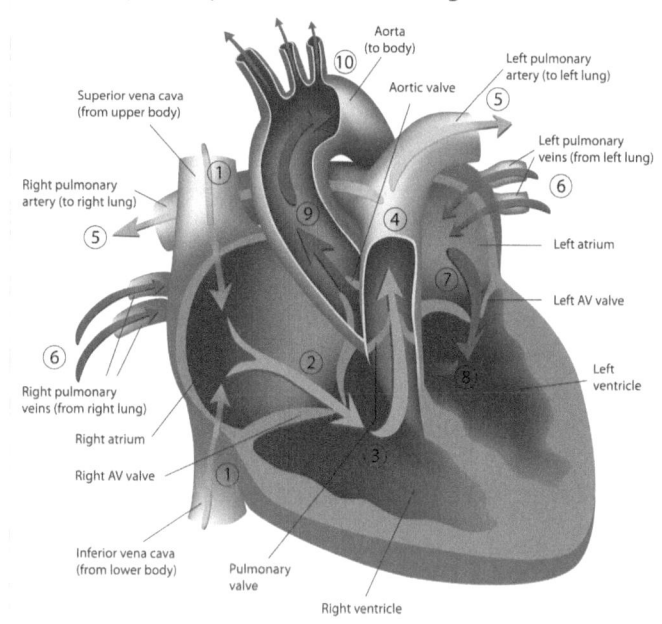

Figure 4.1 Blood flow through the heart.
Deoxygenated (carbon dioxide–enriched) blood (light arrows) flows into the right atrium from the systemic circulation and is pumped into the right ventricle. The blood is then pumped from the right ventricle into the pulmonary artery, which delivers it to the lungs. In the lungs, the blood releases its carbon dioxide and absorbs oxygen. Reoxygenated blood (dark arrows) is returned to the left atrium, then flows into the left ventricle, which pumps it to the rest of the body through the systemic circuit.
© Alila Medical Media/Shutterstock.com

ATHEROSCLEROSIS

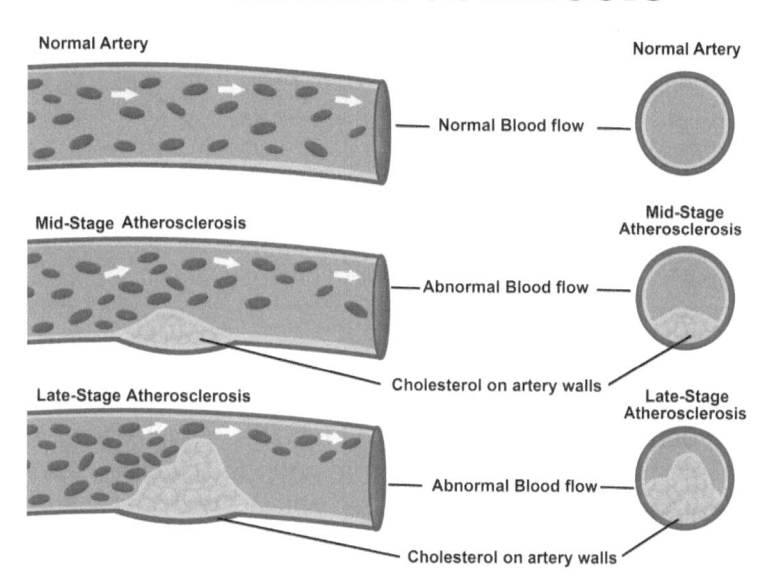

Figure 4.2 Atherosclerosis is an accumulation of plaque (cholesterol and other deposits) inside the lining of arteries. This sequence of drawings illustrates a gradual build-up of atherosclerotic plaque, which, in the long term reduces circulation of blood. This increases the risk of heart attack, stroke, and other serious heart diseases.
© ducu59us/Shutterstock.com

Heart rate is commonly used to determine and monitor exercise intensity. The **resting heart rate** (RHR) is the number of times the heart contracts each minute under resting conditions. The resting heart rate is measured by palpation of the carotid artery in the neck or the radial artery in the wrist (see **Figures 4.3** and **4.4**) for ten seconds and multiplying the result by six. Other methods to determine resting heart rate include palpating the pulse for thirty seconds and multiplying the result by two or palpating the pulse for sixty seconds. Your RHR will be measured using **Lab 4.1**. The normal resting heart rate typically ranges from 60–100 beats per minute. During exercise the heart rate increases significantly to meet the body's greater need for oxygen. The amount of blood pumped by the heart at rest each minute is **cardiac output.** The heart pumps approximately 5 to 6 liters of blood per minute at rest. The amount of blood pumped by the heart on each beat is the **stroke volume.** During exercise body the need for oxygen and blood flow is greater, therefore, cardiac output and stoke volume increases to provide the extra oxygen and blood flow required. Cardiac output and stroke volume can be improved with cardiorespiratory endurance training making the heart stronger and more efficient as well as decrease the risk of heart attack and lowering elevated blood pressure.

Figure 4.3 Pulse Palpation: Carotid.
Source: *Concepts of Health-Related Fitness.* Author: Thomas M. Adams II. Reprinted with permission.

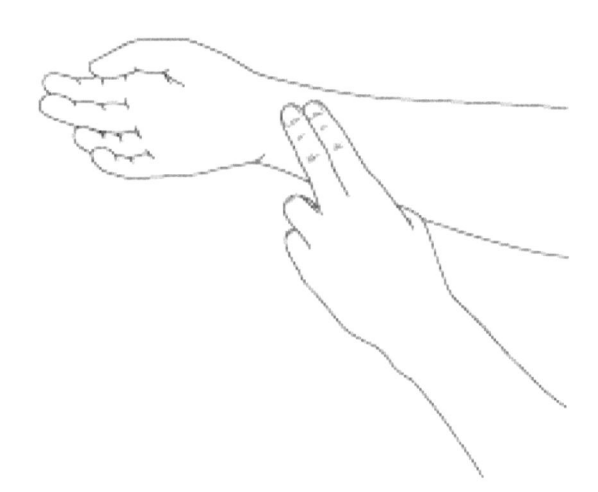

Figure 4.4 Pulse Palpation: Radial.
Source: *Concepts of Health-Related Fitness.* Author: Thomas M. Adams II. Reprinted with permission.

The Energy Systems

The body requires energy to perform any type of work. You obtain this energy from the foods you eat. When you eat food, the body transforms the food into chemical energy known as **adenosine triphosphate** (ATP). ATP is a high-energy compound that releases energy when broken down by the body in order to power its cells. The muscles' cells then convert chemical energy of ATP into mechanical energy to produce movement. There are three energy systems that produce ATP: the **immediate** or phosphagen system, the **short-term** or glycolytic, and the **long-term** or aerobic system. The immediate and short- term systems produce ATP via anaerobic metabolism which does not require oxygen, while the aerobic system produces ATP via aerobic metabolism which requires large amounts of oxygen to operate. **Table 4.1** summarizes the primary attributes of each energy system.

The immediate system produces ATP the fastest of the three systems, but in very small quantities. This system stores minute quantities directly in the muscle cell. The energy in the

Table 4.1 Summary of Energy Systems

Energy System	Rate ATP Produced	Amount ATP Produced	Fuel Source	Exercise Intensity (Sample activity)
Immediate	Fastest	Very small	Creatine phosphate	Very high (100 meter sprint)
Short-term	Fast	Small	Glycogen/glucose	High (400 meter run)
Long-term	Slow	Unlimited	Carbohydrate Fat, Protein	Low (3 mile jog)

immediate system functions get you started, especially during very high-intensity short duration exercise. The immediate system predominates during activities lasting ten seconds or less, such as a 100 meter sprint, a volleyball spike, basketball dunk, or a maximal lift in weight training. As ATP is broken down to produce energy for the body's cells, it is also rapidly restored by another high-energy compound, creatine phosphate, which is also stored in the muscle cell in small quantities. The immediate energy system provides the energy needed to initiate all movements, particularly explosive, all-out maximal efforts. The chemical reactions for this system occur in the cytoplasm of the cell. Therefore, ATP is provided the fastest compared to the short term and long term systems. When the exercise intensity is reduced to less than all-out maximal efforts, yet remains at a high level and duration increased, the immediate energy system can no longer supply enough ATP to meet the body's demand. Therefore, the body must now rely on the short-term energy system to supply needed ATP.

The short-term energy system supplies more total ATP than the immediate system, but not as quickly. This system, like the immediate energy system, operates via anaerobic metabolism and it's chemical reactions occur in the cytoplasm (the liquid portion of the body's cells). The short-term energy system produces ATP using a process known as glycolysis, the breakdown of glycogen stored in the muscles or glucose located in the bloodstream. Glycolysis can occur rapidly when ATP is needed for high intensity exercise lasting up to approximately two minutes as in a four hundred meter run sprint, performing multiple repetitions with a heavy load during weight training, or a highly competitive rally during a racquetball game. This high intensity anaerobic performance results in the accumulation of lactic acid in the muscle. Lactic acid is a by-product of anaerobic metabolism which leads to muscle fatigue and reduced exercise duration. Glycolysis can occur at a slow rate when exercise intensity is low or moderate such that sufficient amounts of oxygen are available to working muscles in the body. Glycolysis produces pyruate when adequate amounts of oxygen are available, and exercise intensity and duration are not reduced and lactic acid is not accumulated causing muscle fatigue. Now the long term energy system can assume the role of supplying ATP for exercise during low to moderate intensities and longer exercise duration.

The long term system dominates ATP energy production during prolonged, low to moderate intensity exercise. The long term system provides ATP by breaking down carbohydrates, fats, and to a lesser degree proteins in the presence of large amounts of oxygen, thus employing aerobic metabolism, unlike the immediate and short term energy systems. Carbohydrates and fats provide ATP at rest and during low to moderate physical activity, however the relative contribution of each varies according to the intensity of activity. At rest carbohydrates provide approximately 30% of the ATP produced, while 70% is produced by fats. The onset of physical activity causes a shift such that there is a greater preference for carbohydrates than fats. During high intensity aerobic physical activity carbohydrates provide approximately 100% of ATP production for energy. However, during less than maximal (submaximal) activity where the demand for energy is equal to that supplied, a gradual shift from carbohydrates to fats and protein occurs.

Protein typically plays a minor role in providing ATP, unless carbohydrates are unavailable due to long term starvation or during exercise bouts exceeding ninety minutes. The long-term system provides ATP at a much slower rate compared to the short-term or immediate systems. However, it produces large quantities of ATP. Chemical reactions for the long term system occur in the mitochondria, the energy-generating component of the body's cells.

The intensity and duration of exercise determines which energy system will dominate ATP production during exercise. One system usually dominates ATP production during exercise, with varying contributions from the other systems. For example, during a three-mile brisk walk, the aerobic system will provide approximately 99 percent of the required ATP. During a 200-meter race the immediate and short-term systems will provide approximately 90 percent of the required ATP. When an activity is referred to as "aerobic", the majority of the energy is supplied by aerobic metabolism.

Training adaptations that occur as a result of anaerobic and aerobic training differ. In anaerobic training the immediate and short-term systems' ability to provide ATP is increased. This allows the physically trained individual to exercise at a high-intensity level for a longer time period before becoming fatigued. In aerobic training the capacity of the aerobic system to provide ATP is elevated. This allows the physically trained individual to work at a low to moderate level for an extended time period (at least twenty minutes) before becoming fatigued. Understanding how each system operates can help you design an effective program to help you reach your fitness goals.

The Physiological Benefits of Improved Cardiorespiratory Endurance

The best indicator of one's level of cardiorespiratory endurance is maximal oxygen uptake or VO_2 max. **Maximal oxygen uptake** is the greatest amount of oxygen the body is able to use during intense physical activity. Regular participation in aerobic activities can increase your maximal oxygen uptake level. Regular participation in activities such as brisk walking, swimming, jogging, cycling, or rope skipping performed at the appropriate intensity, duration, and frequency increase max VO_2. Oxygen uptake and heart rate are closely related. The heart rate increases during physical activity. Therefore, the harder you exercise the higher your heart rate. As your heart rate increases your oxygen uptake also increases. The best method to evaluate maximal oxygen uptake is to measure VO_2 in a laboratory setting with expensive equipment that measures the amount of oxygen one uses during physical activity with exercise intensity increasing at regular intervals until heart rate no longer increases as exercise intensity increases. The 1.5 mile walk/run field test **(Lab 4.3)** can be used to determine maximal oxygen consumption. The goal is to complete the 1.5 mile distance as fast possible. Your completion time will serve as an appropriate estimate of your maximal oxygen uptake. The Rockport Walking Field Test can also be used to estimate maximal oxygen uptake in adult men and women. The Rockport Walking field test is most applicable to individuals with risk factors for heart disease, those over thirty years of age or poorly conditioned. The goal, like that of the 1.5 mile walk/run test, is to walk at a brisk pace for one mile as quickly as possible. The formula to estimate maximal oxygen uptake is as follows:

$$VO_2 max\ (ml/kg/min) = 132.853 - (0.0769 \times BW) - (0.3877 \times age) + (6.315 \times gender) - (3.2649 \times time) - (0.1565 \times HR)$$

BW = body weight in pounds   Age = age in years   Time: 1.0 mile walk time
HR = heart rate bpm   Gender: 1 for males & 0 for females

The higher the VO₂ max, the longer and harder an individual can exercise before becoming fatigued. Regular aerobic exercise causes acute and chronic positive responses to take place in the body.

Acute Responses

Acute responses refer to changes in various physiological parameters during exercise. During exercise, heart rate, stroke volume, cardiac output, systolic blood pressure and ventilation all increase. These changes occur to help supply the additional energy required during exercise. The body produces this additional energy by altering the blood flow within the body. Blood flow to the body's active areas (working muscles) is increased, while blood flow to the body's inactive areas (stomach, liver, gastrointestinal tract) is reduced. The heart rate must increase during exercise to meet the additional demands imposed by exercise. Changes in stroke volume and cardiac output also occur to meet these additional demands. Stroke volume increases during exercise because more blood is returned to the right atrium of the heart via the superior and inferior vena cava a producing a blood filled chamber that has been stretched to accommodate greater amounts of blood flow (similar to a balloon filled with water) and contract more forcefully. This enhances the heart's ability to eject more blood from the left ventricle through the aorta to the rest of the body. Cardiac output is the product of stroke volume and heart rate. Therefore, an increase in stroke volume and heart rate will cause an increase in cardiac output. Ventilation must also increase to supply the additional oxygen needed by the working muscles. Systolic blood pressure increases as a result of increased heart rate, heart contractility, and dilation of various blood vessels in the body to provide greater blood volume to working muscles.

Chronic Responses

Chronic responses refer to changes in various physiological parameters due to regular participation in aerobic activities for extended time periods (weeks or months) resulting in improved, cardiorespiratory endurance, and decreased risk of disease. The size and strength of the heart is increased due to an enlarged ventricular cavity and a small increase in the thickness of the heart wall. This enlarged cavity allows the heart to hold a greater volume of blood that can be pumped to the body's cells. The increased wall thickness allows the heart to contract more forcefully, pumping greater amounts of blood at rest, and during submaximal and maximal tasks to the body. Cardiac output and stroke volume increase with chronic aerobic physical activity while the resting heart rate decreases. The greater the cardiac output and stroke volume, the more efficient the heart will be; therefore, the resting heart rate decreases due to chronic physical activity. The total amount of hemoglobin increases as a result of aerobic training. Hemoglobin transports oxygen in the blood. Increased hemoglobin allows more oxygen to be carried in the blood. This is especially important during high-intensity exercise when large quantities of oxygen are required. Blood volume is also increased as a result of chronic physical activity allowing blood to flow through vessels with less resistance. The number and size of mitochondria are increased. The mitochondria produce energy needed for cellular activity. The body's ability to burn fat as a fuel is enhanced as well. Therefore performing aerobic activities on a regular basis can help you achieve and maintain your ideal body weight. Maximal oxygen consumption and ventilation are increased with aerobic training. Ventilation, the amount of air inhaled and exhaled each minute increases with regular aerobic training. This allows the body to move more air in and out of the lungs resulting in greater maximal oxygen consumption. Chronic exercise also slows the aging process. **Table 4.2** depicts some chronic and acute responses to exercise.

Table 4.2 Acute and Chronic Exercise Responses

Physiological Parameter	Acute Response	Chronic Response
Cardiac output	Increase	Increase
Stroke volume	Increase	Increase
Hemoglobin	Increase	Increase
Resting heart rate	Increase	Decrease
Systolic blood pressure	Increase	Decrease (only if elevated)
Blood volume	Increase	Increase
Ventricle chamber size	Unchanged	Increase
Max VO$_2$	Increase	Increase
Heart contractility	Increase	Increase
Ventilation	Increase	Increase
Mitochondria	Unchanged	Increase
Fat metabolism	Increase (intensity related)	Increase

Cardiorespiratory Endurance Program Design

Setting realistic, obtainable goals is essential in designing a program to improve cardiorespiratory endurance. The key to reaching your cardiorespiratory fitness goals is to develop a program to meet your specific needs. In order to promote adherence to your program, you should start by assessing cardiorespiratory endurance. This will enable you to develop a program based on your current level of cardiorespiratory endurance and determine how you should apply the training principles to meet your goals. Cardiorespiratory endurance can be assessed via the time it takes one to walk or run 1.5 miles. Your personalized program to improve cardiorespiratory endurance consists of three parts: the warm-up, aerobic workout, and cool-down.

Warm-up

The purpose of the warm-up is to prepare the body's muscles and the cardiorespiratory endurance for the up-coming physical activity. An adequate warm-up gradually increases body temperature and elevates the heart rate. This allows the body time to make the necessary adjustments in circulation to meet the increased demand for oxygen needed during exercise. The warm-up may consist of general activities such as walking or jogging for five to ten minutes or sport-specific activities such as hitting forehand and backhand shots in tennis at a slow pace gradually increasing to a brisk pace. The increased body and muscle temperature may also reduce the chance of injury.

Your Aerobic Workout

Your cardiorespiratory endurance improves when workout intensity, duration, and frequency are appropriate for you. Your **target heart rate** (THR) zone is the safe and effective level at which you should performed any cardiorespiratory physical activity. Your THR zone can be determined using your heart rate or maximal oxygen uptake.

There are two heart rate methods that can be used to determine your exercise intensity: the heart rate reserve method and age-predicted maximal heart rate method. The **heart rate reserve** is the difference between the maximal heart rate and the resting heart rate. You should exercise at 50% to 85% of your heart rate reserve or 70% to 85% of your age-predicted maximal heart rate. **Labs 4.1** and **4.2** will help you determine your resting heart rate, age-predicted maximal heart rate, and heart rate reserve. The heart rate reserve method utilizes the Karvonen formula to determine exercise intensity. **Lab 4.2** illustrates how to determine your THR zone using the Karvonen formula. When the oxygen uptake method is used your target intensity should correspond to 55% to 75% of your maximal oxygen uptake. Exercise at lower percentage levels if you are new to exercise and the higher intensities if you are already well-trained.

According to the Physical Activity Guidelines for Americans published by the U.S. Department of Health and Human Services adults should perform two and one-half hours of moderate intensity exercise or seventy-five minutes of vigorous intensity exercise each week. Cardiorespiratory exercise may be performed in segments of at least ten minutes distributed over several times per week. Additional health benefits such as lower risk of heart disease, stroke, hypertension, obesity, depression, adverse lipid profile, and colon and breast cancers can be obtained by increasing to five hours a week of moderate intensity exercise and two and one-half hours of vigorous intensity exercise.

The type of activity you select should elevate the heart rate and breathing, utilize large muscle groups such as the legs, be rhythmic in nature (performed continuously without stopping), and be performed for an extended time period. Examples include cycling, swimming, running, walking, hiking, dancing, and rope skipping.

Cool-down

After completion of the aerobic workout, your exercise session should end with a five to ten minute period of physical activity at a slow pace. The cool-down period is important for returning the body to its pre-exercise state and to prevent blood from pooling in the extremities. The cool-down must be dynamic to help return blood back to the heart after high-intensity exercise, otherwise cardiovascular problems may occur. Dynamic movement is required in the muscles of the legs to pump blood back to the heart.

Training Principles

The **progressive-overload** and **specificity** principles must be addressed in your cardiorespiratory endurance program if your fitness level is to increase. According to the **principle of progressive overload**, the workload must be gradually increased and the body must be exposed to a new higher stimulus as the body adapts, in order for continued improvements in cardiorespiratory endurance to take place. Implementation of the progressive-overload principle may be accomplished by increasing the duration, frequency, or intensity of exercise. Increases in duration should precede increases in frequency and intensity. **Table 4.3** illustrates how you can apply these principles to achieve improved cardiorespiratory endurance. According to the **principle of specificity**, in order to improve cardiorespiratory endurance one must perform movement activities that elevates the heart rate to one's personalized target heart rate range for an extended time periods.

Table 4.3 Progression for Aerobic Fitness Program

Weeks 1 and 2	Walk ½ mile at 50–59 percent of your heart rate reserve on flat terrain.
Weeks 3 and 4	Walk 1 mile at 50–59 percent of your heart rate reserve on flat terrain.
Weeks 5 and 6	Alternate jogging for 1 minute and walking for 4 minutes at 50–59 percent of your heart rate reserve on flat terrain for at least 20 minutes.
Weeks 7 and 8	Jog ¼ mile at 60–65 percent of heart rate reserve and walk ¼ mile at a brisk pace. Repeat at least 3 times.
Weeks 9 and 10	Jog ½ mile at 60–65 percent of heart rate reserve, walk ¼ mile at a brisk pace, jog ⅛ mile at 65–75 percent of your heart rate reserve.

Summary

Important concepts that you have learned in the chapter include the following:

- The cardiorespiratory system is comprised of the heart, lungs, and blood vessels.
- The immediate, short-term and long-term energy systems provide the fuel needed for human movement
- Aerobic exercise yields both health-related and psychological benefits.
- The exercise session should include a warm-up, aerobic activity, and cool-down.
- Perform two and one-half hours of moderate intensity or seventy-five minutes vigorous intensity cardiorespiratory endurance activities weekly at 50% to 85% of your heart rate reserve. Exercise sessions should be distributed over several days per week.
- The progressive-overload and specificity principles must be addressed in your cardiorespiratory endurance program if your fitness level is to increase.

References

American College of Sports Medicine (2013). *ACSM's Guidelines for Exercise Testing and Prescription.* (9th ed.). Baltimore: Williams & Wilkins.

American College of Sport Medicine. (2013). *ACSM's Resources for the Personal Trainer.* (4rd ed.). Baltimore: Williams & Wilkins.

Haff, G., and Triplett, N. eds. (2016). *Essentials of Strength and Conditioning.* (4th ed). Champaign, IL: Human Kinetics.

McArdle, W.D., Katch, F.I., & Katch, V.L. (2005). *Essentials of Exercise Physiology.* (3rd ed.). Baltimore: Williams & Wilkins.

Internet Resources

www.acsm.org

www.nsca.com

Lab 4.1
Your Resting Heart Rate

Name: _____   Date: _____

Directions: Take your resting heart rate (RHR) after sitting quietly for five minutes. Place the index and middle finger of one hand to palpate the carotid artery in the neck as shown in **Figure 4.3** or the radial artery as shown in **Figure 4.4**. Apply light to medium pressure to the artery for 10 seconds and multiply the result by six to determine your resting heart rate. Repeat this procedure two more times and record them below. Calculate the average of the three readings.

Reading 1

RHR = _____ × 6 = _____
 \# heart beats in 10 seconds

Reading 2

RHR = _____ × 6 = _____
 \# heart beats in 10 seconds

Reading 3

RHR = _____ × 6 = _____
 \# heart beats in 10 seconds

Average RHR = RHR1 _____ + RHR2 _____ + RHR3 _____ = _____ ÷ 3 = _____

Lab 4.2
Target Heart Rate Zone

Name: _____   Date: _____

A. Your current age _____

   Record your average resting heart rate (RHR) (see **Lab 4.1**). _____

B. Determine your estimated maximal heart rate (MHR).

   (MHR) = 207 − (0.7 × age _____) = _____

C. Determine your heart rate reserve (HRR).

   HRR = (MHR) − (RHR) = _____

   _____

D. Apply the Karvonen Formula to determine your target heart rate (THR) zone. Select your exercise intensity (EI) level

   a. Vigorous physical activity range: 80%–90% (express as decimal)
   b. Moderate physical activity range: 70–79% of HRR (express as a decimal)
   c. Sedentary/poorly conditioned persons: 60–69% (express as a decimal)

   1. (Lower EI × HRR) + RHR = Lower target heart rate limit
      (_____ × _____) + _____ = _____

   2. (Upper EI × HRR) + RHR = Upper target heart rate limit
      (_____ × _____) + _____ = _____

THR Zone _____ to _____
         Lower THR Limit   Upper THR Limit

This is the safe and effective zone you should achieve during your cardiorespiratory exercise session. See sample calculation on the next page.

Lab 4.2—Cont'd
Target Heart Rate Zone

Name: _____   Date: _____

Sample THR Calculation

A. Your current age: 20

   Your average resting heart rate (RHR): 60

B. Determine your estimated maximal heart rate (MHR).

   1. MHR = 207 − (0.7 × 20) = 193

C. Determine your heart rate reserve (HRR).

   1. MHR − (RHR) = HRR
       193 −   60   = 133

D. Apply the Karvonen Formula to determine your target heart rate (THR) zone.

   1. (Lower EI × HRR) + RHR = Lower target heart rate limit
      (.70 × 133) + 60 = 153

   2. (Upper EI × HRR) + RHR = Upper target heart rate limit
      (.85 × 133) + 60 = 173

   THR Zone   153   to   173
                Lower THR Limit   Upper THR Limit

Lab 4.3
Cardiorespiratory Endurance Program

Name: _____   Date: _____

Purpose: To develop your personalized cardiorespiratory endurance program

Step 1: State your long term cardiorespiratory endurance goal, including a date of completion.

Long term goal: _____
_____

Describe specifically how you will warm-up before each exercise session.
_____
_____

Step 2: Prepare an action plan: Develop your personalized cardiorespiratory endurance program which will permit you to accomplish your goal stated in step one. List the specific cardiorespiratory endurance activities you will perform each week, how often activities will be performed each week (frequency) and how long you will exercise (duration)

Age: _____   Body Weight: _____   Target Heart Rate: _____ (see lab 4.2)

Week	Cardiorespiratory Activities	Frequency	Duration
Week 1			
Week 2			
Week 3			
Week 4			
Week 5			
Week 6			

Describe specifically how you will apply the progressive overload principle to your cardiorespiratory program relative to how much you will alter training intensity on a weekly basis.
_____
_____

Lab 4.3—Cont'd

Cardiorespiratory Endurance Program

Name: _____   Date: _____

Describe two strategies you will use to motivate yourself to participate in a cardiorespiratory endurance program consistently.

1. _____

   _____

2. _____

   _____

Chapter 5

Muscular Strength and Endurance

Objectives
Introduction
Skeletal Muscle Structure
Benefits of Resistance Training
Factors Influencing Strength Production
Resistance Training Program Design
Resistance Training Methods
Resistance Training Guidelines and Safety Tips

Upper Body Exercises
Lower Body Exercises
Summary
References
Internet Source
Lab 5.1: Muscular Strength and Endurance Program

Objectives

Upon completion of this chapter, you will be able to:

1. Distinguish between muscular strength and endurance.
2. Describe the skeletal muscle structure.
3. Describe the three types of muscle fibers.
4. Describe factors that influence muscular force development.
5. Design a personalized muscular strength and endurance program.
6. Discuss the importance of lifelong improved muscular strength and endurance.
7. Discuss the benefits of resistance training.
8. Describe various methods of resistance training.
9. Know how to execute various resistance training exercises and the major muscles involved.
10. Discuss muscular soreness.

Introduction

Muscular strength is defined as the maximum amount of force that a muscle or muscle group can generate in a single effort. **Muscular endurance** is defined as the ability of a muscle or muscle group to contract repeatedly. Muscular strength and endurance are not completely separate entities—they exist on a continuum. Exercises that increase muscular strength also increase muscular endurance. Adequate muscular strength and endurance are important for all activities of daily living. Anyone can increase muscular size by participating in a well-designed muscular strength and endurance program and consuming an appropriate diet. This chapter will examine muscle structure, the benefits of resistance training (also known as weight training), training methods, and program development. **Figures 5.1** and **5.2** illustrate the various muscles of the body that are strengthened in resistance training.

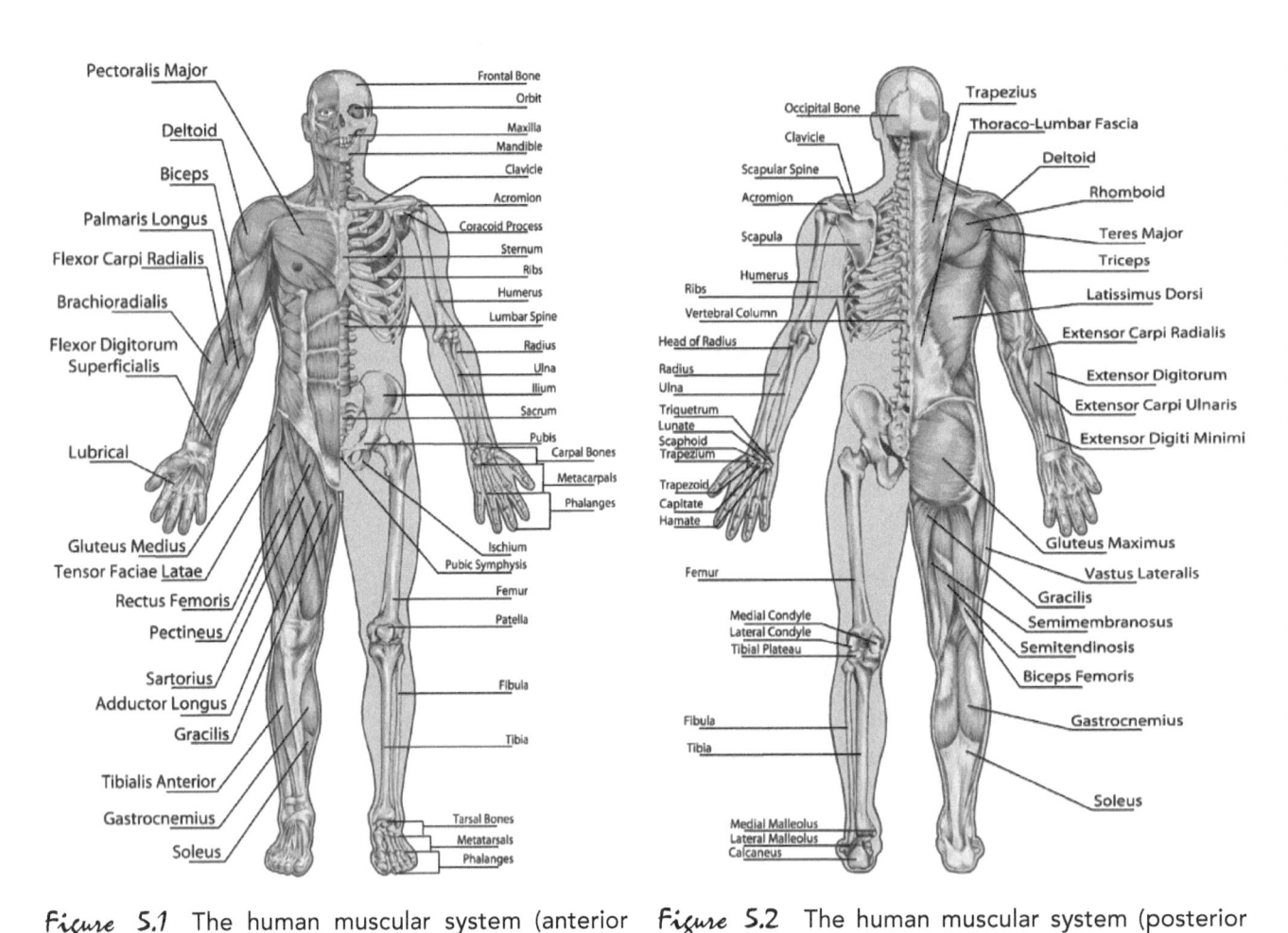

Figure 5.1 The human muscular system (anterior view).
© stihii/Shutterstock.com

Figure 5.2 The human muscular system (posterior view).
© stihii/Shutterstock.com

Figure 5.3 Tendons attach to muscles and bones.
(Adapted from *Steps to Weight Training—Steps to Success*.) From *Weight Training: A Practical Approach to Total Fitness*, 2nd edition by Richard Trestrail. Copyright © 1999 by Kendall/Hunt Publishing Company. Reprinted by permission.

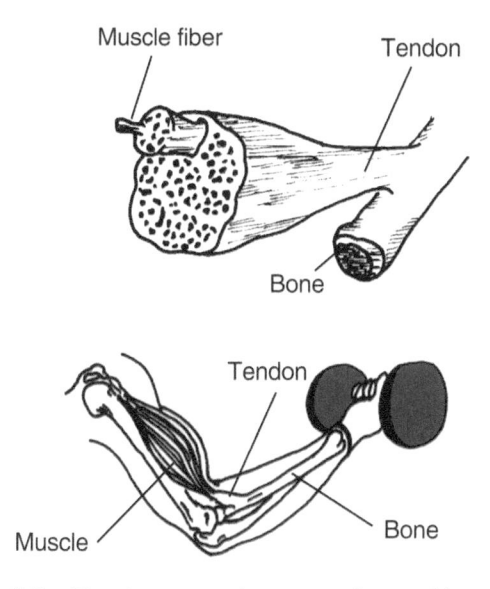

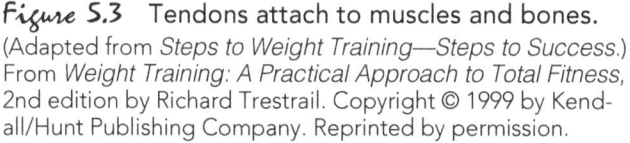

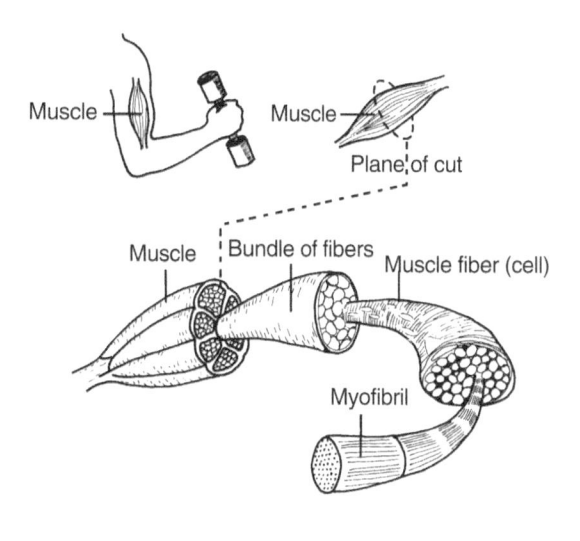

Figure 5.4 Skeletal muscle tissue components.
From *Weight Training: A Practical Approach to Total Fitness*, 2nd edition by Richard Trestrail. Copyright © 1999 by Kendall/Hunt Publishing Company. Reprinted by permission.

Skeletal Muscle Structure

Muscular Coverings and Connective Tissues

The contraction of skeletal muscles make human movement possible. Muscles are covered by layers of connective tissue. Each muscle is composed of bundles of muscle tissue known as **fasciculi** and cells known as muscle fibers. The **epimysium** is connective tissue that covers the entire muscle. The **perimysium** is connective tissue that covers the fasciculi and **endomysium** covers each muscle fiber. These three tissues come together to form tendons. **Tendon**s are tough connective tissues that attach muscles to bones making movement possible (see **Figure 5.3**). **Ligaments** are connective tissues that connect one bone to another bone. The muscle fiber is subdivided into smaller units known as **myofibrils** (see **Figure 5.4**). Myofibrils are long threadlike structures made up of thick and thin protein myofilaments that produce muscle contraction through a mechanism known as the sliding filament theory of muscle contraction. The thick filament is primarily made up of protein known as **myosin.** The thin filament consists mainly of a protein known as **actin** (see **Figure 5.5**). According to this theory the thick and thin filaments slide across each other resulting in muscle fiber shortening and contracting.

Muscle Fibers

Muscle fibers are generally of three types: **slow oxidative (SO), fast oxidative glycolytic (FOG), and fast glycolytic (FT).** Slow oxidative muscle fibers are characterized by a slow contraction speed and low force development. They rely on the long term energy system to supply needed fuel for physical activity. SO muscle fibers are highly resistant to fatigue due to the large blood supply, and are recruited primarily for endurance activities such as

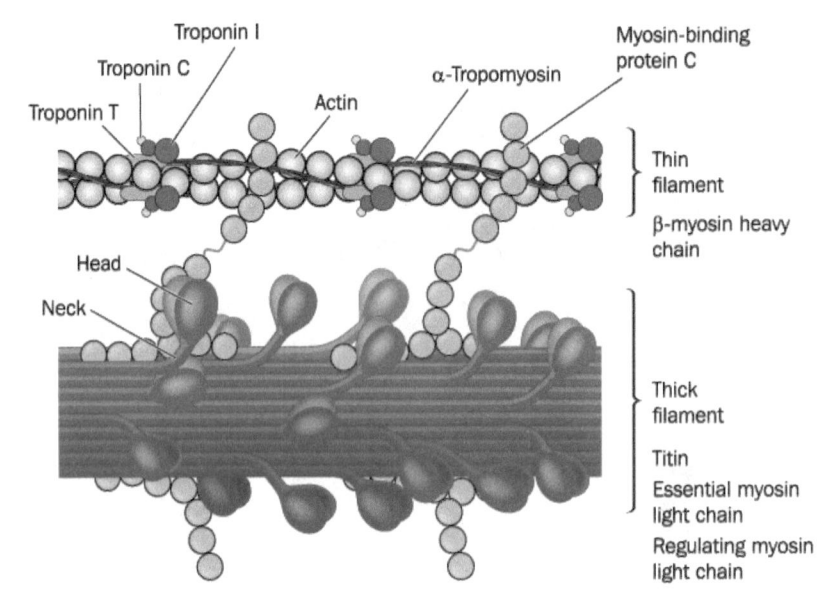

Figure 5.5 Illus muscle fiber Actin myosin.
© Blamb/Shutterstock.com

Table 5.1 Muscle Fiber Characteristics

Characteristic	Slow Oxidative	Fast Oxidative Glycolytic	Fast Glycolytic
Force production level	Low	High	High
Speed of contraction	Slow	Fast	Fast
Blood supply level	High	Medium	Low
Muscle fiber color	Red	Red/White	White
Muscle fiber size	Small	Medium	Large
Dominant energy system	Long term	Short term	Immediate
Fatigue resistance level	High	High/Medium	Low
Power Output	Low	High	High
Aerobic enzymes	High	Medium/low	Low
Anaerobic enzymes	Low	High	High
Endurance	High	Medium/low	Low
Mitochondria density	High	Medium	Low

jogging, cycling, or other activities requiring the low muscular force production for an extended period of time. SO fibers also have a large supply of mitochondria and mitochondrial enzymes (substances that speed up chemical processes in cells) producing its high aerobic metabolic capabilities in these fibers. Slow oxidative muscle fibers are known as type I, red, or slow twitch. FOG muscle fibers are characterized by a moderate fatigue resistance, fast contraction speed, and moderate to high force production. Fast oxidative glycolytic fibers are also known as type IIa, muscle fibers. Fast glycolytic muscle fibers fatigue quickly, produce the highest level of force in a short time period and are white in appearance due to their small blood supply. Fast oxidative glycolytic and FG fibers possess high levels of anaerobic enzymes (substances that control the speed of chemical reactions in a cell). FG muscle fibers are recruited for activities such as a volleyball spike, basketball dunk, or other activities requiring an explosive power. **Table 5.1** summarizes the characteristics of each muscle fiber.

Benefits of Resistance Training

A moderate to high level of muscular strength and endurance are important for all activities of daily living, such as carrying books, or lifting objects. Increased muscular strength and endurance can also enhance one's enjoyment of recreational activities by elevating performance level during participation in activities such as tennis, basketball, racquetball and other activities. Improvements in muscular strength and endurance gained through resistance training can enhance your quality of life in various ways.

Increased Lean Body Mass and Reduced Body Fat

Resistance training increases muscle mass by increasing the contractile proteins (actin and myosin), and the number and size of myofibrils within the muscle. This increase in muscle mass or size is known as **hypertrophy**. Hypertrophy is typically not measureable until approximately eight weeks after the initiation of resistance training. The greater the amount of muscle mass an individual possesses the greater his/her force and power production capability will be during physical activity as well as metabolic rate resulting in positive body composition changes. Because muscle is metabolically active tissue that burns calories, body fat levels are reduced with long-term consistent resistance training. Prolonged resistance training also increases the number of capillaries serving a given muscle which significantly increases the amount of blood flow to muscle. This increased blood flow to working muscles allows one to train even harder to produce benefits.

Improved Psychological Well-Being

Enhanced muscular strength and endurance improves self-image by producing a more defined, attractive, healthy and toned physique. The positive external transformation in physical appearance causes you to feel better about yourself internally, thereby elevating your self-esteem and self-confidence. In addition one can easily recognize the accomplishment of measurable objectives such as increases in the amount of weight lifted or repetitions performed.

Injury Prevention

Greater muscular strength and conditioning helps maintain proper posture and body mechanics during activities such as walking, and carrying or lifting objects. Resistance training not only strengthens muscles but tendons and ligaments as well. This allows the body to withstand additional strain to become more injury resistance.

Improved Muscle and Bone Health

Muscle mass begins to decline after age 30 in the general population in adults who do not engage in resistance training consistently. This phenomenon is known as **sarcopenia.** Regular participation in a resistance training program throughout adulthood at an appropriate intensity can greatly diminish the loss of lean body mass related to aging and physical inactivity. Resistance training also increases bone mineral density, resulting in stronger bones and decreasing the risk of osteoporosis.

Improved Physical Performance

Improved muscular strength and endurance increases the storage capacity of fuel required for muscle contraction, increasing your energy level during physical activity, delaying fatigue, and allowing faster recovery during rest periods of workout sessions. The hypertrophy caused by resistance training increases the muscle's force and power production capabilities translating into greater work output and improved performance during physical activity. Relative to FOG and FT muscle fibers, resistance training can cause conversion of FOG fibers to FG fibers due to greater enzyme activity. This can also lead to greater work output and improved movement performance. Current research does not support a shift from SO to FG or from FG to SO fibers.

Other Benefits

Other benefits of improved muscular strength and endurance include relief of low back pain, greater work efficiency, decreased serum cholesterol levels, increased metabolic rate, improved physical appearance, and decreased resting blood pressure.

Factors Influencing Strength Production

Motor Unit Activation

The motor unit is the fundamental component of the neuromuscular system consisting of a single motor neuron and the muscle fibers it stimulates. Muscular force production increases as the number of motor units recruited increases during a contraction. Muscle fiber types are sometimes referred to as motor units because all muscle fibers must possess nerve stimulation in order for contraction for occur. FOG and FG fibers generate more force than SO fibers. Large muscles (hamstrings) generate more force than small muscles (biceps, brachials). A muscle twitch is produced when a single stimulus is applied to a motor unit. The motor unit responds by contracting very briefly then relaxing. When a motor unit is stimulated repetitively such that it cannot completely relax from the previous stimulus, the twitches have an additive effect resulting in greater force production.

Leverage

Our bodies move as a result of tendons that attach to and pull on bones when the muscles shorten during contraction. The position of tendon attachment on the bone varies during movement throughout a given range of motion, such that the amount of force developed changes as the muscle's joint angle changes. These joint angle changes provide a leverage advantage, such that the muscle exerts less force, at joint angles, where the leverage advantage is present and more force, where the leverage advantage is absent. Thus, the greatest amount of force is produced when the joint angle of the muscle tendon's pull is ninety degrees to the bone. The least amount of force is generated when the joint angle of the muscle tendon's pull is significantly less than or greater than 90 degrees. This variation in force production causes maximal force to be generated only at the weakest point in the range of motion.

The Length-Tension Relationship

The length of the muscle influences the amount of force a muscle can generate. According to the length-tension relationship, the greatest force is generated when the muscle is elongated, such that there is optimal interaction between actin and myosin. When the muscle length is too long, the interaction between actin and myosin is insufficient for maximal force production. When the muscle length is too short, actin and myosin overlap each other, such that maximal force production is not possible.

Age

Research has repeatedly demonstrated that resistance training increases muscle mass, bone strength, and mobility in older adults just as in younger individuals. This translates into reduced injury potential and a greater ability to carry out activities of daily living, such as walking up steps, carrying groceries, and completing domestic chores with minimal assistance from others. A resistance training program designed specifically to meet the needs of older individuals, yields strength gains similar to or greater than those young individuals experience. Even though you won't have the same level of muscular strength and endurance at age fifty compared to that at age twenty, resistance training to improve muscular strength and endurance should be a part of your weekly exercise regimen throughout your lifetime. This is critical to retard the loss of muscle mass associated with aging and physical inactivity and maintain functional independence to perform normal activities of daily living during your golden years.

Resistance Training Program Design

The type of program most beneficial for developing muscular strength and endurance will depend on your specific goals. In order to understand program design, the following terms must be defined: repetition (rep), set, repetition maximum (RM), and rest interval. A **repetition** is the number of times a specific exercise is performed. A **set** is a group of repetitions for a particular exercise. A **RM** is the execution of a given number of consecutive repetitions, such that the final repetition is the last rep that can be completed using correct technique. For example, a 10 RM of 150 pounds means that the 150 pound weight can be lifted 10 times but not 11 times. The **rest interval** is the amount of time taken for recovery between sets. The guidelines below may be used to create your own personalized resistance training program.

1. Assess your current muscular strength and endurance status (see **Appendix B**)
2. Apply the specificity, and progressive overload principles at the appropriate intensity, frequency, and duration. Exercise intensity is a function of the amount of weight lifted and the number of reps and sets performed. Your current muscular fitness level will determine **load** (amount of weight) and **volume** (reps & sets) you can tolerate. In order to determine the starting weight for your program, select a weight for a given exercise that you can lift only ten times (10RM) and perform ten repetitions. Inexperienced lifters should start with the lightest poundage on the weight stack and perform ten repetitions. If that weight is easy to lift ten times, increase the weight by five pounds and perform ten repetitions for a second set. Repeat the procedure for a third set if needed, however do not exceed three sets. Allow a one to three minute rest period between sets.

The following guidelines will assist you in modifying the intensity of your resistance training program. Beginners may increase the weight load by 2.5 to 5 pounds for multi-joint upper body exercises such as the bench press and shoulder press and increase by 1 to 2.5 pounds for single joint exercises such as bicep curl and triceps extension. Beginners may increase by 10 to 15 pounds for multi-joint lower body exercises such as leg press and squats and by 5 to 10 pounds for single joint lower body exercises such as leg curl and leg extension. Experienced lifters may increase by 5 to 10 pounds for upper body multi-joint and single-joints exercises. Experienced lifters may increase by 10 to 20 pounds for lower body multi-joint exercises and by 10 to 15 pounds for single joint exercises. When you can perform two or more repetitions in the last set for two consecutive workouts for a given exercise, weight should be added to that exercise for the next workout. Exercise intensity may also be varied by changing the duration of the rest interval between sets, the number of repetitions and/or sets performed. The American College of Sports Medicine recommends a training frequency of two to three days a week for each major muscle group for two to four sets per workout and a rest interval of two to three minutes between sets. The following suggested guidelines are based on desired training outcomes (strength, hypertrophy, endurance).

Strength program: A program of low reps and high resistance will develop muscular strength to a greater degree compared to muscular endurance.

Strength: Perform 2 to 6 sets of six or less reps at a load that is relatively heavy for you to lift.

Frequency: at least 2 days per week on nonconsecutive days for a body parts/major muscle group.

Rest interval: 2 to 5 minutes

Muscle hypertrophy (size): Perform 3 to 6 sets of 6 to 12 reps at a load moderately heavy for you to lift.

Frequency: at least 2 days per week on nonconsecutive days for each body part or muscle group body parts/major muscle group.

Rest interval: 45 seconds to 1.5 minutes

Endurance program: A program of high reps and low resistance will develop muscular endurance strength to a greater degree.

Endurance: 2 to 3 sets at a load that allows you to perform 12 or more repetitions

Frequency: at least 2 days per week on nonconsecutive days for each body part or muscle group body parts/major muscle group.

Rest interval: 30 seconds or less

3. **Choice of exercise:** Your selection of exercises will be determined by your goals, equipment availability, and resistance training experience. Beginners may select one to two exercises per muscle group (chest, upper/middle back, lower back, shoulders, thighs, biceps, triceps, abdominals, and calves). See **Table 5.2** for exercises. Experienced lifters may select two or more exercises per muscle group. Your program should include multi-joint (involves movement occurring at two or more joints) exercises that use large muscle areas such as the chest, shoulders, upper/middle back, and thighs and single-joint (movement at only one joint) exercises that use small muscle areas such as the biceps, triceps, calves, lower back, forearms, and abdominals.

4. **Exercise order:** Exercise order can have a significant impact on exercise intensity, especially for beginners. Perform multi-joint, large muscle exercises (leg press, squat, bench press, lat pull-down) before single-joint, small muscle exercises (abdominal curl, bicep curl, triceps extension, calf raises). Select exercises utilizing both machines and free weights (barbells and dumbbells) and perform different variations of exercises approximately every four weeks. This will provide muslces with sufficient variety to

permit maximal training adaptations to occur, prevent boredom and achieve consistent gains in muscular strength and endurance.

5. **Frequency:** Beginners may lift two to three times per week, while experienced lifters may workout four to six times per week. Allow at least 48 hours of rest between workout sessions for each body segment or muscle group to fully recover. Training adaptations that produce gains in muscular fitness occur during recovery. Therefore, complete muscle recovery between workouts is essential to achieving your resistance training goals.

6. **Resistance training systems:** A variety of training systems can be utilized to achieve your muscular fitness training goals.
   (1) *Upper/Lower body alternation:* Perform an upper body exercise and then follow with a lower body exercise. For example, perform a seated row then follow with a leg press
   (2) *Opposing muscle group:* Perform an exercise for one body segment or muscle group and follow with an exercise opposing the first. For example, perform a bench press for the chest then follow with a lat pull-down for the back.
   (3) *Straight sets:* Perform two or more sets of the same exercise for one body segment or muscle group, then move to another body segment or muscle group and repeat.
   (4) *Push/pull alternation:* Perform push exercise (bench press, shoulder press) then follow with a pull exercise (lat pulldown, upright row).
   (5) *Supersets and compound sets:* A superset involves performing two exercises for opposing body segment(s) or muscles (biceps curl followed by triceps extension). A compound set involves performance of two different exercises for the same muscle group consecutively (cable biceps curl, dumbbell bicep curl, hammer curl).

Resistance Training Methods

You can use a variety of resistance training methods to develop muscular strength and endurance or muscular fitness. These methods include dynamic training, isometric training, and isokinetic training.

Dynamic resistance training methods involve performing dynamic contractions using variable resistance devices, constant resistance devices, and circuit training activities. Dynamic muscle contractions entail force-development with a change in the length of the muscle. Dynamic contractions are of two types: **concentric** and **eccentric.** A concentric contraction is a dynamic contraction in which the muscle shortens as force is developed. An eccentric contraction is a dynamic contraction in which the muscle lengthens as force is developed. Dynamic concentric and eccentric contractions occur when using variable and constant resistance devices.

Variable resistance training involves the use of machines designed to provide near maximal force-development throughout the entire range of motion. This allows an individual to generate greater muscular tension at positions in the range of motion, where the individual has better leverage and thus, has the capacity to exert more force, due to the muscle's angle of attachment to the bone and the length of the muscle (length-tension relationship).

Free weights such as barbells and dumbbells are examples of constant resistance-training devices. When a barbell/dumbbell is lifted the load (weight) is constant. However, the amount of force that the muscle exerts to move the load (weight) is not constant. The force exerted by the muscle varies at different points in the range of motion, due to variations in leverage during the exercise. As a result the muscle develops maximal force at the weakest point in the range of motion when using free weights. This weak point is referred to as the **sticking point.** This is a limitation when using free weights because the amount of weight the person can lift is limited by the sticking point in the range of motion. Variable-resistance machines were developed in an effort to solve this problem. However, variable-resistance machines did not completely eliminate the sticking point. Variable-resistance machines such as Nautilus, utilizes kidney shaped cams to vary the amount of force the muscle must exert, such that maximal or near maximal force can be generated throughout the full range of motion.

Circuit resistance training consists of performing a series of sequential resistance exercises with short rest intervals between work stations. The objective is to move from one exercise to another within a specified time period. The circuit uses a series of exercises that can be completed in 30 to 60 minutes.

Isometric training requires little or no equipment, and can be performed almost anywhere. An isometric contraction is a contraction in which force is developed, but the length of the muscle does not change, as when pushing against an immovable object such as a wall. Isometric training is joint-angle specific. Therefore, increases in strength and endurance are limited to the joint-angle position trained. Isometric training results in greater muscle soreness, compared to dynamic training and a significant sudden spike in blood pressure. This can initiate the Valsalva maneuver, resulting in greater intrathoracic pressure that elevates blood pressure very quickly, such that one becomes dizzy while lifting. However, isometric training can be used to help overcome weak points in a lifter's range-of-motion and for rehabilitative purposes.

Isokinetic training requires special machines that control the speed of movement, such that the muscle develops maximal or near maximal contraction at each point in the movement. In an isokinetic contraction maximal tension develops over the full range of motion, as the muscle shortens by maintaining constant speed. The isokinetic machine matches the muscular force generated by the lifter, by exerting a resistive force equal to that of the muscular force. This feature in isokinetic training equipment is referred to as accommodating resistance.

The following strategies will assist you in maximizing strength gains.

(1) Train at a high intensity level. This will stimulate your muscles to the highest degree allowing you to train each muscle to its full capabilities to produce the greatest benefits for the muscle.

(2) Track your progress weekly using a training log. In order to make consistent gains in hypertrophy and strength, you must be attentive to the progress you achieve each week. Try to increase your sets, reps, or load (weight) each workout session.

(3) Eat more often and increase your water intake. Proper nutrition is just as important in gaining muscle mass as resistance training. You should consume 5 to 7 small meals each day, every 2 to 3 hours, consisting of high-quality protein (1–1.2 grams per pound of body weight) such as poultry, fish, eggs, and complex carbohydrates (vegetables, milk, whole grains) to keep your muscles continually fueled for training.

Resistance Training Guidelines and Safety Tips

1. Get a medical clearance before starting your program.
2. Always warm-up before and cool-down after your workout.

3. Wear clothing that allows perspiration to escape from the body and permit free movement.

4. Always lift loads within your capacity and use spotters with heavy free weights.

5. Always use collars on plate-loading equipment.

6. Always breathe when lifting, exhale as the weight is being lifted and inhale when lowering the weight.

7. Do not bounce weights off your body (Example: Bouncing the barbell on the chest during the bench press exercise).

8. Always emphasize correct form over lifting heavier weight.

9. Apply the progressive overload principle according to your unique capabilities, goals and the aforementioned guidelines. Start slowly and gradually increase the weight, repetitions, or sets as your muscular fitness level improves.

10. Perform all exercise through the joint's full range of motion. This will result in increased muscular fitness and flexibility in a properly designed resistance training program.

Muscular Soreness

Muscle soreness is experienced under a variety of circumstances, such as during exercise, following exercise by a person is unaccustomed to it, after extended layoffs from exercise, or due to overexertion during exercise. Muscle soreness can cause pain, acute inflammation, and muscle spasms. The precise mechanism which causes muscular soreness is unknown, however various theories have been proposed. The muscle spasm theory proposes that muscular soreness is the result of reduced blood flow to the muscle during exercise due to the accumulation of a pain causing substance in the muscle. The skeletal muscle damage theory proposes that tears in muscle fibers cause muscle soreness. The connective tissue damage theory proposes that damage to connective tissues (tendons, sarcolemmna) cause muscle soreness. Acute muscle soreness occurs during or immediately following the performance of exercise. Acute muscle soreness may last for up to an hour following exercise and then dissipate. Acute muscle soreness may be due to the build-up of lactic acid and reduced blood flow in the muscle. Delayed muscle soreness (DOMS) occurs twenty-four to seventy-two hours after exercise. It occurs when muscle tears and damage to connective tissues develops as a result of exercise. Eccentric muscle contractions such as those that occur during downhill running or when slowly lowering the weight during resistance training produces greater levels of DOMS compared to concentric muscle contractions. Muscle soreness can be prevented or reduced by always warming up before exercise; beginning your exercise program at a low intensity level with gradually increasing intensity, duration, and frequency; and limiting the amount of eccentric type contractions performed.

The resistance training exercises in this section can be performed using free weights, as well as machines. Resistence training can also be performed using resistance bands.

Upper Body Exercises

Chest

Figure 5.6 Bench Press.
Primary muscles: Pectorals, triceps, front or anterior deltoids © VHI, Inc.

Figure 5.7 Vertical Fly.
Primary muscles: Pectorals, front/anterior deltoid © VHI, Inc.

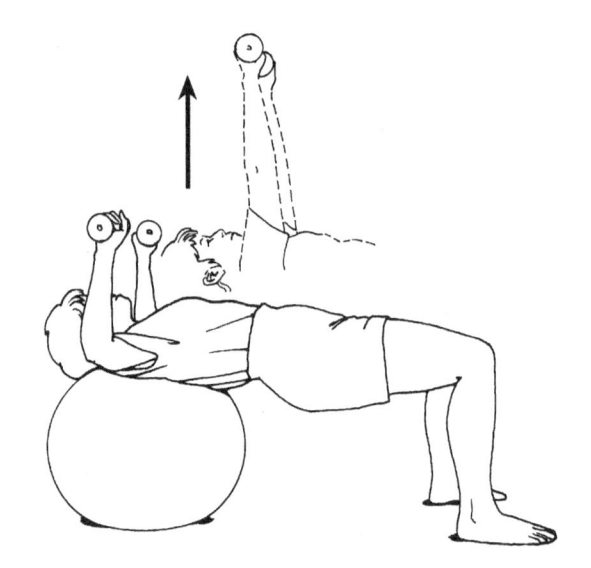

Figure 5.8 Swiss Ball Bridge Chest Press.
Primary muscles: Pectorals, front/anterior deltoid, triceps, erector spinae © VHI, Inc.

Back

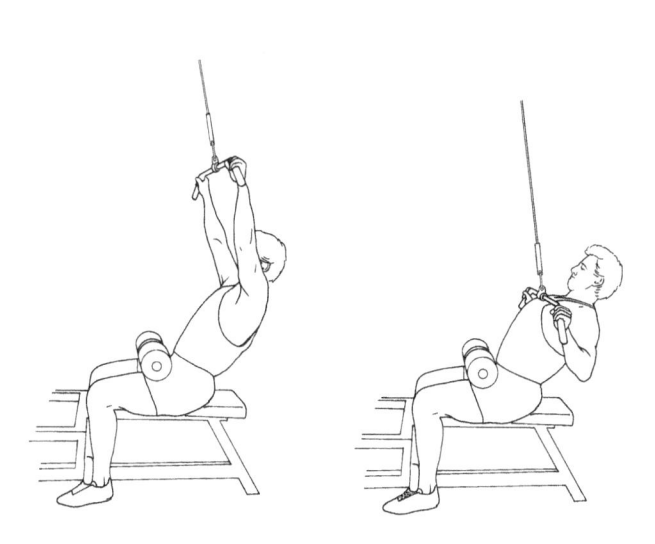

Figure 5.9 Lat Pulldown.
Primary muscles: Latissimus dorsi, middle trapezius, rhomboids, teres major © VHI, Inc.

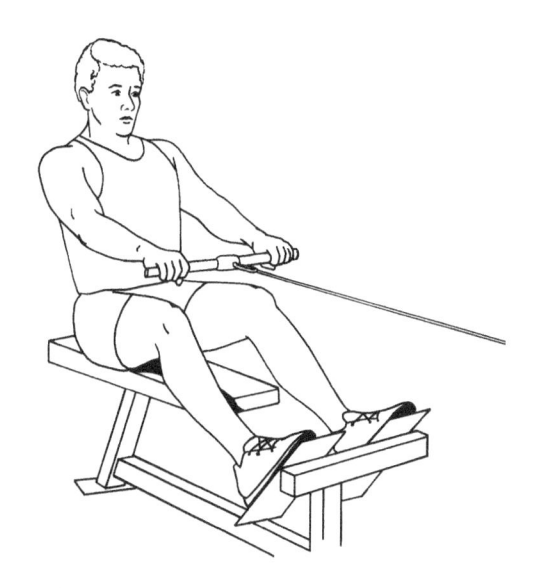

Figure 5.10 Seated Row.
Primary muscles: Latissimus dorsi, middle trapezius, rhomboids, teres major © VHI, Inc.

Figure 5.11 Swiss Ball Bridge Pullover.
Primary muscles: Latissimus dorsi, erector spinae, deltoid © VHI, Inc.

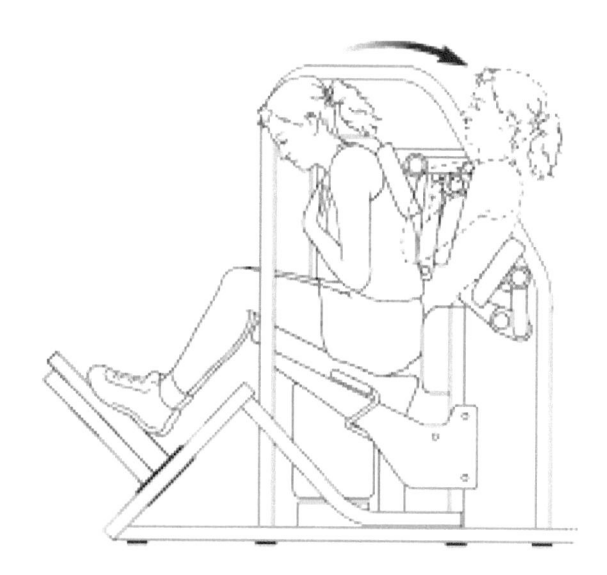

Figure 5.12 Back Extension.
Primary Muscles: Erector spinae Source: *Concepts of Health-Related Fitness*. Author: Thomas M. Adams II. Reprinted with permission.

Shoulders

Figure 5.13 Dumbell Overhead Raise.
Primary muscles: Front/anterior & side/lateral deltoids © VHI, Inc.

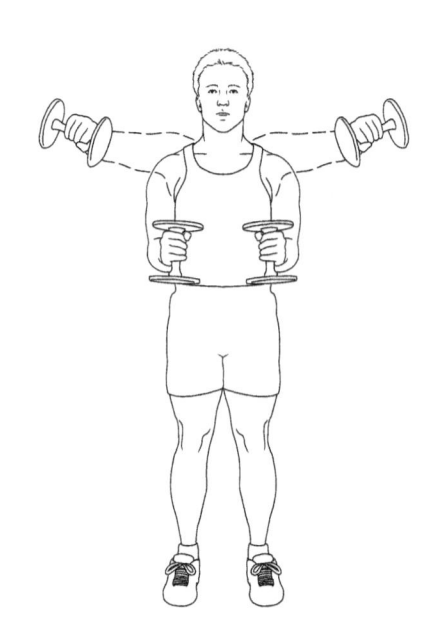

Figure 5.14 Side/Lateral Raise.
Primary muscles: Side/lateral deltoid © VHI, Inc.

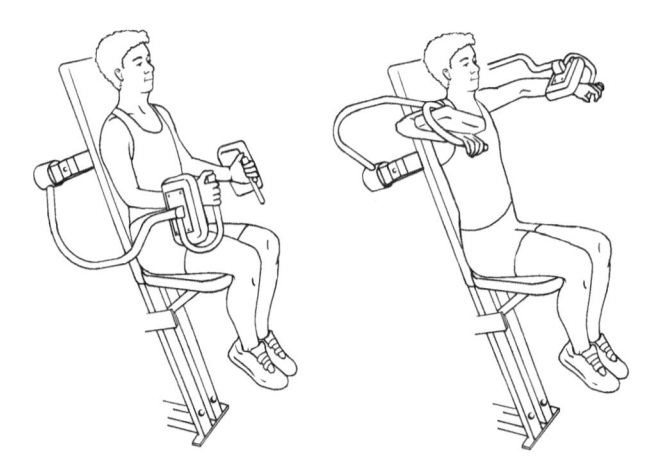

Figure 5.15 Seated Rear Deltoid.
Primary muscles: Rear/posterior deltoid © VHI, Inc.

Abdominals

Figure 5.16 Swiss Ball Crunches.
Primary muscles: Rectus abdominis © VHI, Inc.

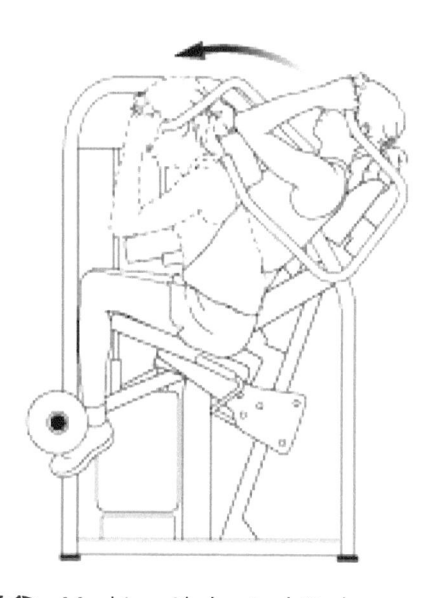

Figure 5.17 Machine Abdominal Curl.
Primary muscles: Rectus abdominis Source: *Concepts of Health-Related Fitness.* Author: Thomas M. Adams II. Reprinted with permission.

Triceps

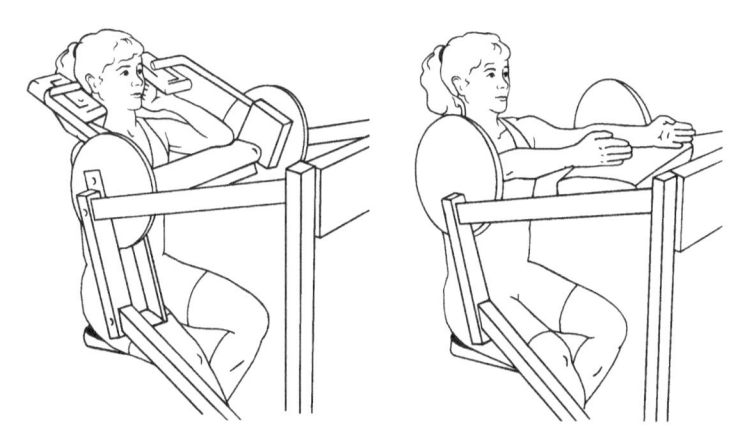

Figure: 5.18 Seated Triceps Extension.
Primary muscles: Triceps brachii (posterior arm) © VHI, Inc.

Arm Curls

Figure: 5.19 Standing Cable Arm Curls.
Primary muscles: Biceps brachii (anterior arm), brachialis (anterior arm), brachioradialis (forearm) © VHI, Inc.

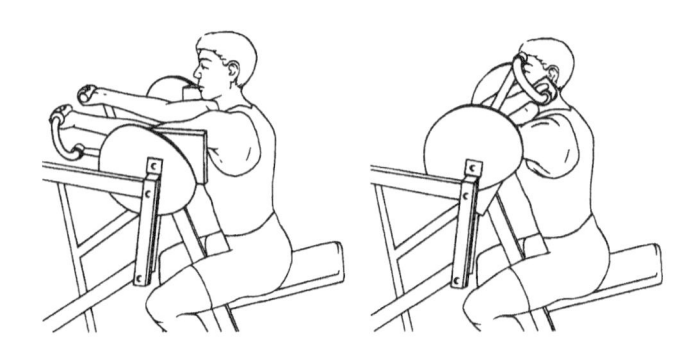

Figure: 5.20 Seated Arm Curls.
Primary muscles: Biceps brachii, brachialis, brachioradialis © VHI, Inc.

Dips

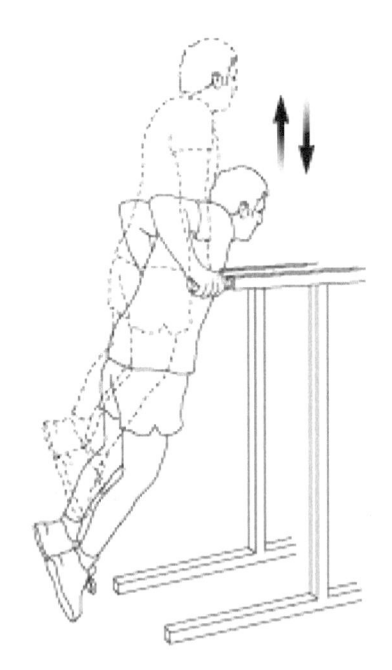

Figure: 5.21 Dips.
Primary muscles: Pectorals, triceps, anterior deltoid, latissimas dorsi Source: *Concepts of Health-Related Fitness*. Author: Thomas M. Adams II. Reprinted with permission.

Wrists

Figure: 5.22 Wrist Curls.
Primary muscles: Flexor carpi radialis, flexor carpi, ulnaris © VHI, Inc.

Figure: 5.23 Wrist Extension.
Primary muscles: Extensor carpi radialis, extensor carpi ulnaris
Source: *Concepts of Health-Related Fitness*. Author: Thomas M. Adams II. Reprinted with permission.

Lower Body Exercises

Thighs

Figure: **5.24** Swiss Ball Squats.
Primary muscles: Quadriceps (front thigh), hamstrings (rear thigh) © VHI, Inc.

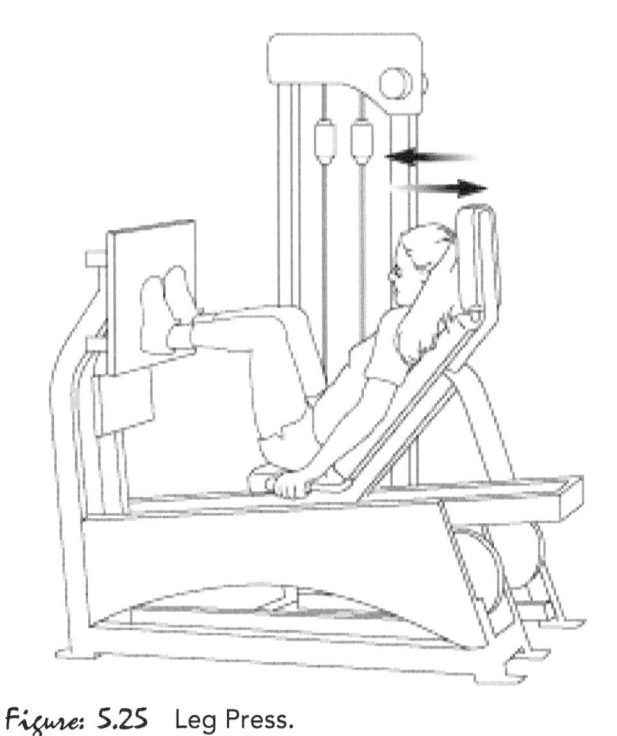

Figure: **5.25** Leg Press.
Primary muscles: Quadriceps and hamstrings Source: *Concepts of Health-Related Fitness*. Author: Thomas M. Adams II. Reprinted with permission.

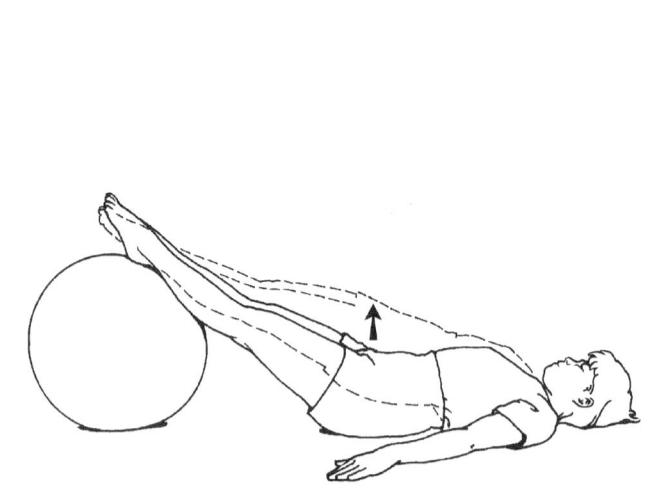

Figure: **5.26** Swiss Bridge with Heels on Ball.
Primary muscles: Gluteals and hamstringss © VHI, Inc.

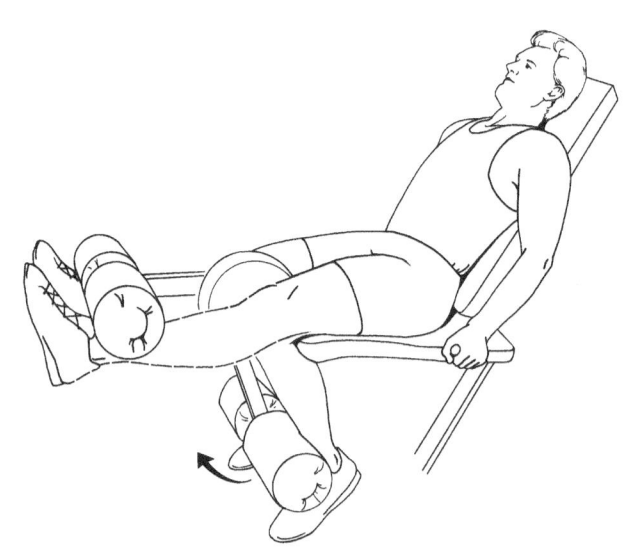

Figure: **5.27** Leg Extension.
Primary muscles: Quadriceps © VHI, Inc.

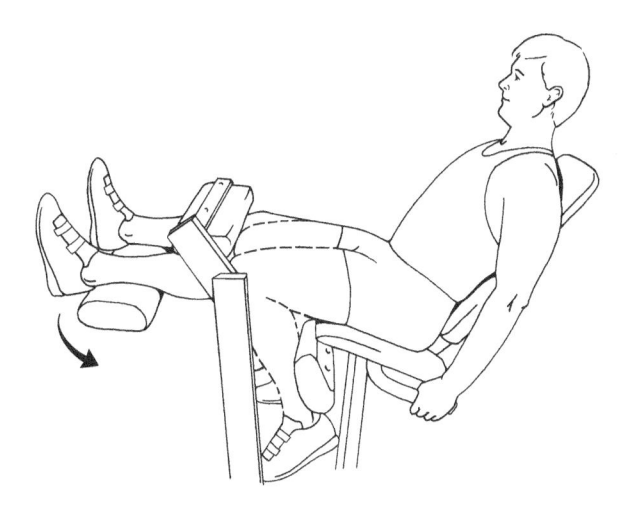

Figure: 5.28 Leg (Knee) Curl.
Primary muscles: Hamstrings © VHI, Inc.

Calf

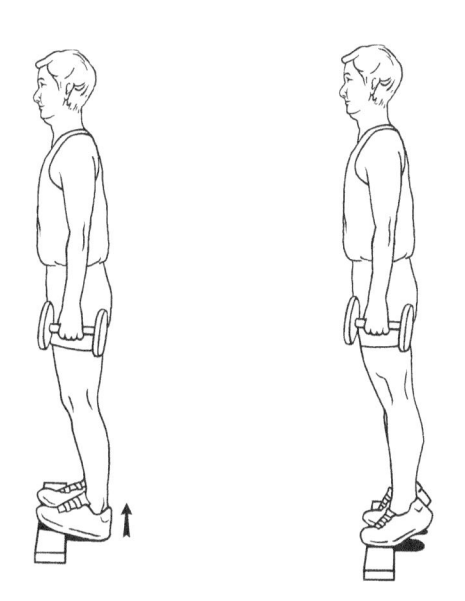

Figure: 5.29 Standing Calf (Heel) Raise.
Primary muscles: Soleus, gastrocnemius © VHI, Inc.

Table 5.2 Muscular Fitness Chart

Body Part	Muscle(s)	Exercise(s)
Upper Anterior (front) arm	Bicep brachii, Brachialis	Arm/bicep curls, hammer curls
Upper Posterior (back) arm	Triceps brachii	overhead triceps extension, triceps pressdown
Chest	Pectoralis major	Bench press, fly, dips, push-ups, pull-ups
Shoulders		
Anterior	Anterior deltoid	Dumbbell overhead press, high pull, push press
Lateral (side)	Lateral deltoid	Lateral raise, high boy row
Posterior	Posterior deltoid	Face pull, one arm dumbbell row
Back		
Upper back	Upper Trapezius	Shoulder shrugs
Middle back	Latissimus dorsi, teres major, Middle trapezius, rhomboids	Lat pulldown, seated row, swiss ball pullover, dips, pull-ups
Lower back	Erector spinae	Back extensions
Abdominals	Rectus Abdominis	Tuck planks, hanging knee/leg raise, crunches, reverse crunches, upper body circle crunches
	External & internal obliques	Starfish crunch, figure 8's, screwdriver
Buttocks	Gluteus maximus	
Thigh		
Anterior	Quadriceps: rectus femoris, vastus medialis, vastus lateralis, vastus intermedius	Lunges, squats, leg press, deadlift
Posterior	Hamstrings: Biceps femoris, Semimembranosus, Semitendinosus	Lunges, squats, leg press, leg curl, deadlift
Inner thigh	Adductors	Hip adduction, squats, lunges
Outer thigh	Abductors	Hip abduction, squats, lunges
Anterior leg (shin)	Tibialis anterior	Ankle dorsiflexion
Posterior leg (calf)	Gastrocnemius, soleus	Calf raises (toes straight, toes in, toes out), calf launchers
Wrist (forearm)		
Wrist flexion	Flexor carpi radialis, flexor carpi ulnaris	Wrist curls
Wrist extension	Extensor carp radialis, extensor carpi ulnaris	Wrist extension

Summary

Important concepts that you have learned in this chapter, include the following:

- ≈ Muscular endurance and muscular strength together constitute muscular fitness.
- ≈ Thick and thin protein filaments slide across each other causing muscle fibers to shorten and contract to produce human movement.
- ≈ Muscle fibers are generally of three types: slow oxidative, fast oxidative glycolytic, and fast glycolytic.
- ≈ Improving muscular fitness can increase lean body mass, reduce body fat, enhance physical performance, and strengthen bones.
- ≈ Designing a muscular fitness program involves assessing current fitness levels, setting realistic goals, and choosing the appropriate equipment and exercises to meet your goals.
- ≈ Resistance training methods used to develop muscular fitness include dynamic, isometric, and isokinetic resistance training.
- ≈ Resistance training must be consistent to maintain the benefits it provides.

References

ACSM (2009). *ACSMs Guidelines for exercise testing and prescription*, 8th Edition. Baltimore: Williams and Wilkins.

Baechle, T.R. & Groves, B.R. (1998). *Weight training steps to success*. Champaign, IL: Human Kinetics.

Beachle, T. & Roger, E. (2008). *Essentials of strength training and condition*. Champaign, IL: Human Kinetics.

Bouchard, C. et al., (2007). *Physical Activity and Health*. Champaign, IL: Human Kinetics.

Evans, E. (1992). Exercise, nutrition, and aging. *Journal of nutrition* 122:796–801.

Fleck, S. & Kraemer, W. (1988). *Designing resistance training programs*. Champaign, IL: Life Enhancement Publications.

Fleck, S. & Kraemer, W. (1988). Resistance training: Physiological responses and adaptations. *Physician and sports medicine*. 16(May):63–76.

Hopp, J. (1993). Effects of age and resistance training on skeletal muscles: A review. *Physical therapy*. 73:361–73.

Komi P.V. (1992). *Strength and power in sport: The encyclopedia of sports medicine*. Oxford, UK: Blackwell Scientific.

Kraus, W. (1994). Skeletal muscle adaptation to chronic low frequency motor nerve stimulation. *Exercise sport sciences reviews*. Baltimore: Williams and Wilkins.

Kreighbaum, E. & Barthels, K. (1996). *Biomechanics: A qualitative approach for studying human movement*. 4th edition. Needham Heights, MA: Allyn & Bacon.

Liemohn, W. & Sharpe G. (1992). "Muscular strength and endurance, flexibility, and low back function." in E.T. Howley and B.D. Frank, *Health fitness instructors handbook*. Champaign, IL: Human Kinetics.

Payne, V.G., et al. (1997). "Resistance training in children and youth: A meta-analysis," *Research quarterly for exercise and sport* 68:1, 80–86.

Powers S. & Howley E. (2009). *Exercise physiology: Theory and application to fitness and performance*, 7th Edition. Dubuque, IA: McGraw-Hill.

Shier, D., Butler, J., Lewis, R. (2007). *Hole's anatomy & physiology.* 11th Edition, Dubuque, IA: McGraw-Hill.

Stone, M. H., Stone M., Sand, W. (2007). *Principle and Practice of Resistance Training.* Champaign. IL: Human Kinetics.

U.S. Department of Health and Human Services (1996). *Physical activity and health: A report of the surgeon general.* Atlanta, GA: U.S. Department of Health and Human Services, Centers for Disease Control and Prevention, National Center for Chronic Disease Prevention and Health Promotion.

Westcott, W.L. (1997). "Strength Training 201" *Fitness management,* 13:7:3–35.

Internet Source

http://www.muscleblitz.com

Lab 5.1
Muscular Strength and Endurance Program

Name: _____   Date: _____

Purpose: To help develop an effective personalized muscular strength and endurance program.

Instructions: Develop your muscular strength and endurance program based on your current fitness level and your personal goals.

Long term goal: Describe your long-term muscular fitness goal. This goal should be specific, achievable and measureable.

1. _____

Date you plan to reach Your long term goal: _____

Short term goals: Your short-term goals should include strategies you will employ to accomplish your long-term goal. List two short-term goals and the target date you plan to reach your short-term goals.

1. _____

(Target Date_____)

2. _____

(Target Date_____)

How many sets will you perform? _____

How many repetitions will you perform? _____

Describe specifically how you will apply the progressive overload principle to modify the exercise intensity relative to load. (See the Resistance Training Program Design section in textbook).

1. _____

_____

_____

_____

List the days per week will you participate in resistance training activity.

_____

Lab 5.1—Cont'd

Muscular Strength and Endurance Program

Name: _____   Date: _____

List two exercises for each body part. See figures 5.6–5.29 and table 5.2.

Body Area	Exercise One	Exercise Two
Upper Body		
Chest		
Upper back		
Lower back		
Abdominals		
Front of arm		
Back of arm		
Forearm		
Lower Body		
Front thigh		
Back thigh		
Inner thigh		
Outer thigh		
Calf		

Create a sample workout consisting of six exercises for three sets for at least two muscle groups. Record the amount of weight and repetitions for each set. .

Legend: Rp = repetitions   Wt = weight

Exercises	Set 1 Rp/Wt	Set 2 Rp/Wt	Set 3 Rp/Wt
1			
2			
3			
4			
5			
6			

Chapter 6

Developing Flexibility

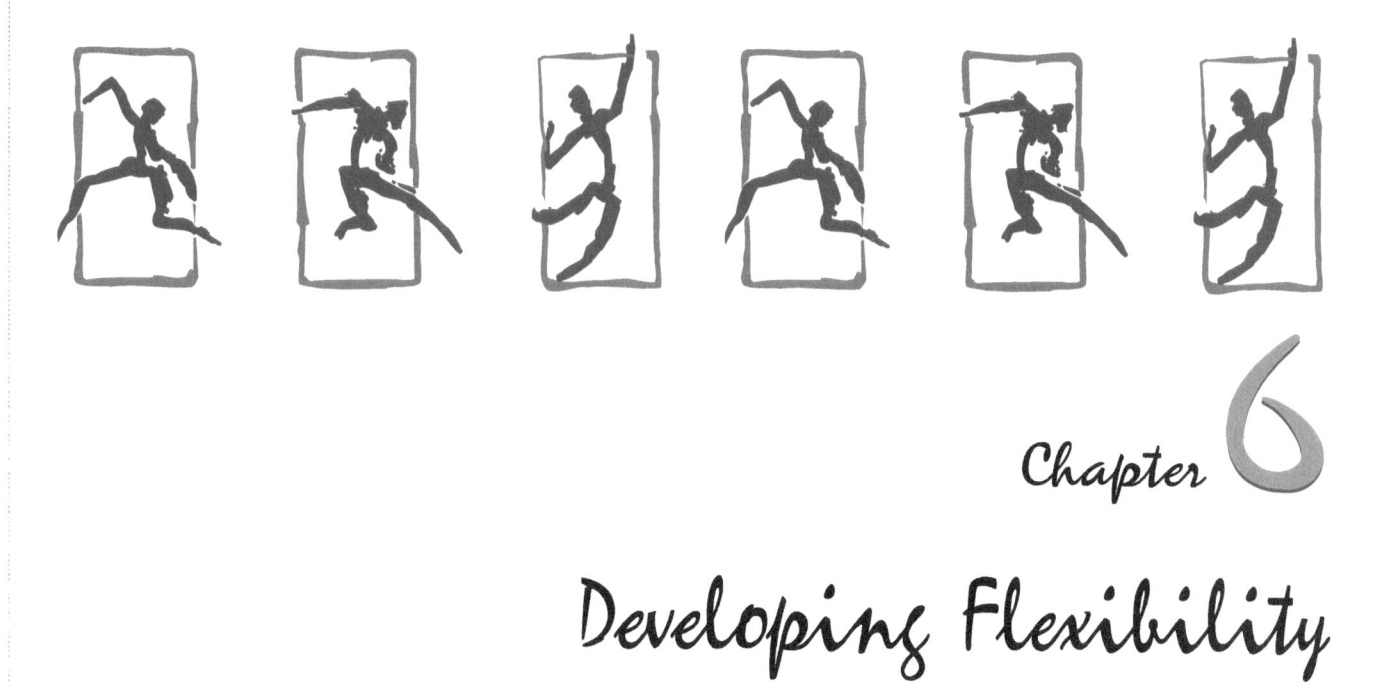

Objectives
Introduction
Benefits of Flexibility
Joint Classifications
Factors Influencing Flexibility
Types of Flexibility Training
Stretching Guidelines
Stretching Exercises

Stretching Exercises to Avoid
Designing a Flexibility Program
Back Health
Summary
References
Lab 6.1: Flexibility Program

Objectives

Upon completion of this chapter, you will be able to:

1. Define flexibility and explain its significance to wellness.
2. Describe the benefits of improved flexibility.
3. Discuss anatomical and mechanical aspects of stretching related to improved flexibility.
4. Describe three stretching techniques.
5. Describe factors that influence flexibility.
6. Discuss parameters that should be considered in the development of a program designed to enhance flexibility.
7. Know specific exercises that improve flexibility.
8. Develop a personalized program to improve flexibility.

Introduction

Flexibility is often a forgotten component of many exercise programs, however, it is just as important as the other health-related fitness components. You should work just as diligently on your flexibility program as your cardiorespiratory endurance and muscular fitness programs. **Flexibility** is the ability of a joint to move through its full range of motion. The amount of flexibility required by each person depends on the type of movements performed and the level of movement proficiency required during the activity. For example, ballet dancing requires greater flexibility than line dancing.

Flexibility is joint specific. Good shoulder flexibility does not imply that hip flexibility is adequate. Flexibility can be improved by participation in a well-designed stretching program containing exercises for all joints in the body.

Benefits of Flexibility

Flexibility is important for effective and efficient participation in daily and recreational activities. Improving and maintaining enhanced flexibility elevates one's quality of life. Poor flexibility is the result of tight muscles that interfere with the ability to move easily. Improved flexibility provides the following benefits:

- It may prevent injuries by maintaining adequate range of motion in a joint.
- It improves posture.
- It reduces muscular soreness and muscle cramps following vigorous physical activity.
- It enhances muscle relaxation and coordination.
- It prevents low back pain.
- It improves performance of movement skills used in competitive and recreational activities.

Joint Classifications

Joints in the body can be classified according to the amount of movement they permit and can be categorized as diarthrodial, amphiarthrodial, and synarthrodial.

Diarthrodial joints are freely movable and have a more complex structure than amphiarthrodial or synarthrodial and are primarily located in the knees, hips, shoulders, and fingers. Most of the joints in the skeletal system are diarthrodial. These joints contain connective tissues such as tendons, ligaments, cartilage, and a joint capsule filled with fluid. The ends of the bones are covered with cartilage tissue acting as a cushion. The joint capsule is a fluid-filled sac made up of fibrous tissue that encloses the ends of the bones. This fluid, known as synovial fluid, lubricates cartilage in the joint.

Amphiarthrodial joints are slightly movable allowing only a limited range of movement. These joints are found in the pubic bone, chest and the vertebrae of the vertebral column in the back. The bone in amphiarthrodial joints are linked together by fibrocartilagenous tissue or ligaments.

Synarthrodial joints are immovable joints. Bones in these joints are separated by a thin layer of connective tissue or cartilage. The bones in the skull that protect the brain are examples of synarthrodial joints.

Factors Influencing Flexibility

The development of flexibility is influenced by the structure of the joint, connective tissue status, core temperature, age, gender, and activity level. Connective tissue status, core temperature, and activity level can be positively altered by implementing a well-designed flexibility program. However, joint structure, age, and gender are factors that cannot be altered by flexibility training.

Structure of the Joint

The structural arrangement of bones within a joint can determine the amount of movement possible at that joint. The bones of the hip and shoulder are arranged, such that one bone with a ball-shaped head is joined to the cup-shaped socket of another bone. The hip and shoulder joints produce a wide variety of movements. For example, the shoulder and hip movements include flexion and extension (forward & backward movement), adduction and abduction (movement toward and away from the center line of the body), circumduction and rotation. The bones in the elbow joint are arranged such that the concave surface of one bone fits into the convex surface of another bone. This bony structural arrangement limits the range of motion in the elbow joint to flexion and extension.

Connective Tissue

Flexibility training focuses on obtaining adaptations to elastic and plastic components in muscles tissues to improve range of motion within a given joint. **Elasticity** refers to the ability of a structure to recoil after being stretched. **Plasticity** is the tendency of a structure to attain a new and greater length after being stretched. Muscle is highly elastic and plastic tissue. Connective tissues such as tendons, ligaments, and the sheaths within and around muscles have both elastic and plastic properties. Connective tissues play a major role in limiting the range of motion possible within a structure. They do not possess the elasticity and plasticity of muscle tissue. Muscle tissue demonstrates greater improvements in range of motion compared to connective tissues and it's elastic and plastic properties are much more responsive to adaptations such as lengthening due to flexibility training.

Core Temperature

Warm muscles stretch more easily than cold muscles. It is important to perform whole body exercises, such as walking or running for five to ten minutes at a low-intensity level to increase core temperature **before** performing stretching exercises. This is known as a general warm-up. Individuals engaging in sport activities may perform a specific warm-up. A specific warm-up consists of movements similar to in athlete's sport (i.e. performing lay-up drills before playing basketball). This will increase the temperature within the muscles and joints; warming synovial fluid that lubricates the joint. Warm muscles relax faster than cold muscles. A relaxed muscle will stretch to a greater, longer length compared to a tense muscle.

Age

Older adults tend to be less flexible compared to younger adults. Flexibility in older adults deceases due to fibrosis. **Fibrosis** is a condition that causes some muscle fibers to degenerate and be replaced by nonelastic connective tissue. This degeneration of muscle tissue is associated with physical inactivity, and there is a tendency to not move joints through available ranges of motion as one advances in age. A well-designed stretching program can reduce the loss of flexibility associated with fibrosis.

Gender

Females tend to be more flexible in the hamstrings and hip joint comparted to males. This can be attributed hormonal influences, wider hips, lower center of gravity, shorter leg length, and to differences in the types of activities that females typically participate in. Females usually participate in activities such as dance and gymnastics that place a premium on flexibility, whereas males tend to participate in strength and power activities. Differences in anatomical structure may also account for this variation. Females tend to be shorter in height and have shorter limbs compared to males.

Activity Level

Physically active individuals tend to have greater flexibility than physically inactive people. Flexibility is particularly greater in active people who perform stretching exercises routinely compared to those who do not. Therefore, stretching exercises are vital to enhancing joint flexibility.

Types of Flexibility Training

Stretching exercises should be performed after whole body, dynamic movements to increase muscle temperature. **Active stretching** takes place when the individual stretching provides the force of the stretch. There are three primary types of flexibility training: **static, dynamic,** and **proprioceptive neuromuscular facilitation** (PNF).

Static stretching is a common technique used to enhance flexibility. Static stretching is the slow, gradual lengthening holding and releasing of a muscle to the point of mild discomfort. The stretched elongated muscle position should be held for approximately thirty seconds. Static stretching is recommended to increase flexibility because it is a safe and

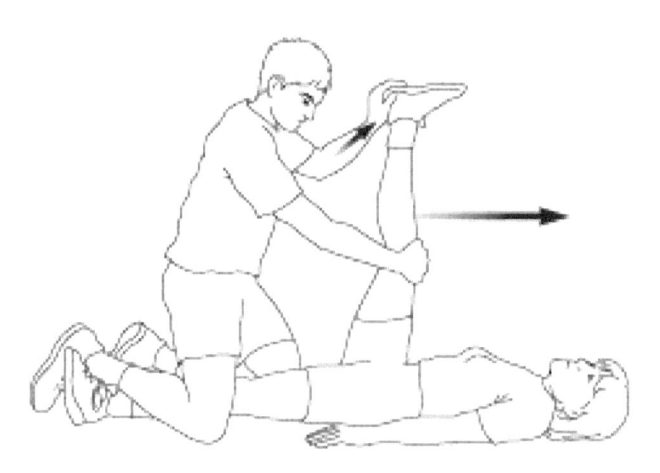

Figure 6.1 Sequence of Action PNF Stretching—Step 1.
Source: *Concepts of Health-Related Fitness*. Author: Thomas M. Adams II. Reprinted with permission.

Figure 6.2 Sequence of Action PNF Stretching—Step 2 and 3.
Source: *Concepts of Health-Related Fitness*. Author: Thomas M. Adams II. Reprinted with permission.

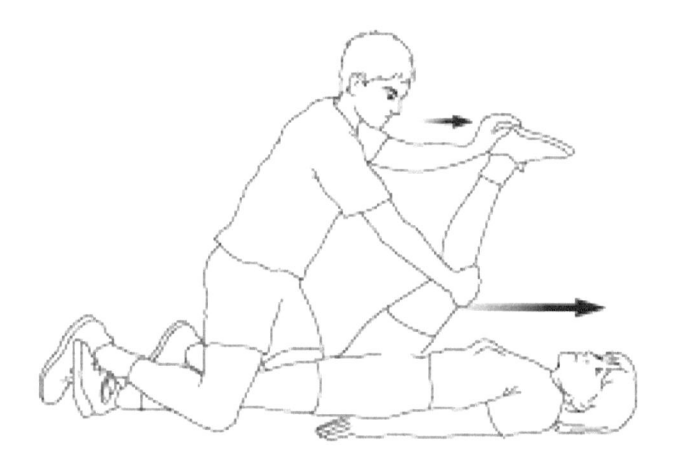

Figure 6.3 Sequence of Action PNF Stretching—Steps 4–6.
Source: *Concepts of Health-Related Fitness*. Author: Thomas M. Adams II. Reprinted with permission.

effective technique and does not initiate the stretch reflex response. **Figures 6.4** to **6.24** are examples of static stretching exercises.

Dynamic stretching involves the movement patterns and the range of motion attained when performing sport-specific whole body movements. Dynamic stretching consists of large muscle group activities such as brisk walking, slow jogging, light calisthenics, or other similar large group dynamic activity. Dynamic stretching increases whole body and muscle temperature.

PNF stretching may be more effective at increasing flexibility because it produces greater muscle relaxation compared to static stretching. PNF integrates passive stretching with isometric and concentric muscle actions. Some PNF stretching exercises require a partner to perform as illustrated above. The PNF technique begins with a static stretch for at least ten seconds to the point of mild discomfort for by the muscles being stretched (the hamstrings in **Figure 6.1**). Consistent, even pressure is slowly applied by a partner to the subject's heel or ankle stretching the hamstring muscle (the hamstrings in **Figure 6.1**). Next, a partner instructs the subject to hold and resist movement such that an isometric contraction occurs in the muscle group opposite to that passively stretched (quadriceps in **Figure 6.2**), and is held for at least 10 seconds. This second stretch will elicit greater range of motion (ROM) than the first stretch. Next, the partner applies resistance such that the subject performs a concentric contraction of the muscle group opposite to that passively stretched through a full range of motion. The subject then relaxes and another passive stretch is performed and held for thirty seconds of greater ROM compared to the first passive stretch. The third step involves concentric contraction (of the quadriceps) causing the hip to flex and descend further into a new greater ROM (**figure 6.3**).

PNF also requires knowledge of proper technique to safely implement a PNF flexibility program.

Flexibility Guidelines

- Warm-up for at least five to ten minutes before stretching with brisk walking, slow jogging, light calisthenics, or other similar large group dynamic activity. Warm muscles are more elastic than cold muscles and therefore less prone to injury. Never stretch a cold muscle.

- Stretch to the point of mild discomfort. Do not stretch to the point of pain. Hold the stretch for ten to thirty seconds. Stretching exercises are recommended 2 to 3 times per week, including four repetitions per muscle group.

- Choose specific exercises for each joint in the body. Flexibility is joint-specific, therefore, exercises for each joint in the body should be included in your program.

- When stretching, exhale into the stretch and breathe comfortably while holding the stretch. Avoid holding your breath when stretching.

- Performing flexibility exercises after an aerobic workout is beneficial because muscles are already warm.

- Do not perform contraindicated exercises (those not recommended due to potential harm they may cause).

The exercises found in **Lab 6.1** assess flexibility and can assist in developing a safe and effective flexibility program.

Stretching Exercises

The following stretching exercises can be used to improve your flexibility.

Upper Body

Neck

Figure 6.4 Anterior (Front) Neck Stretch.
Source: *Concepts of Health-Related Fitness*. Author: Thomas M. Adams II. Reprinted with permission.

Figure 6.5 Posterior (Rear) Neck Stretch.
Source: *Concepts of Health-Related Fitness*. Author: Thomas M. Adams II. Reprinted with permission.

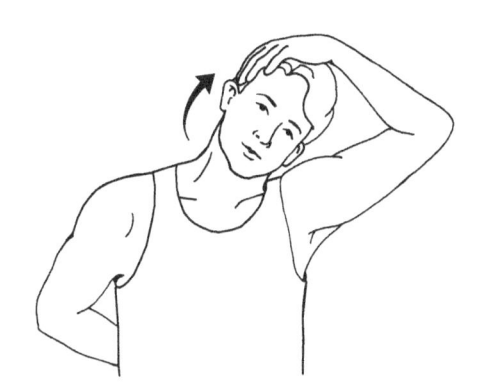

Figure 6.6 Lateral (Side) Neck Stretch.
© VHI, Inc.

108 Lifetime Fitness & Wellness

Arm

Figure 6.7 Anterior Arm (Biceps).
Source: *Concepts of Health-Related Fitness*. Author: Thomas M. Adams II. Reprinted with permission.

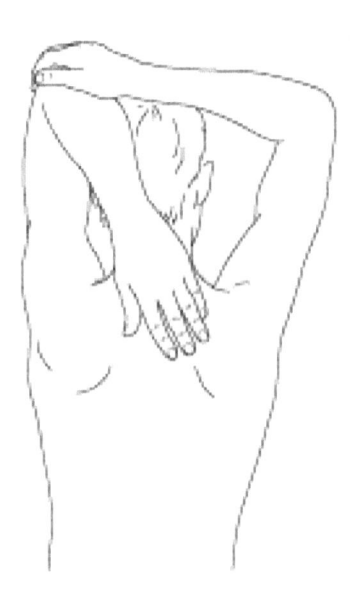

Figure 6.8 Posterior Arm (Triceps).
Source: *Concepts of Health-Related Fitness*. Author: Thomas M. Adams II. Reprinted with permission.

Shoulder

Figure 6.9 Anterior Shoulder Stretch.
Source: *Concepts of Health-Related Fitness*. Author: Thomas M. Adams II. Reprinted with permission.

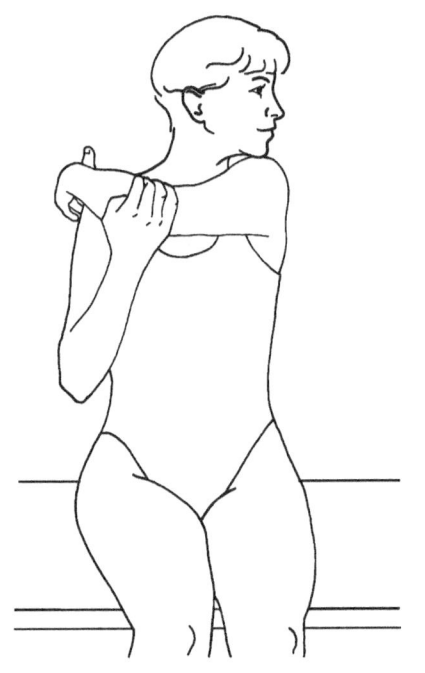

Figure 6.10 Posterior Arm (Triceps).
© VHI, Inc.

Chest

Figure 6.11 Chest Stretch.
Source: *Concepts of Health-Related Fitness*. Author: Thomas M. Adams II. Reprinted with permission.

Back

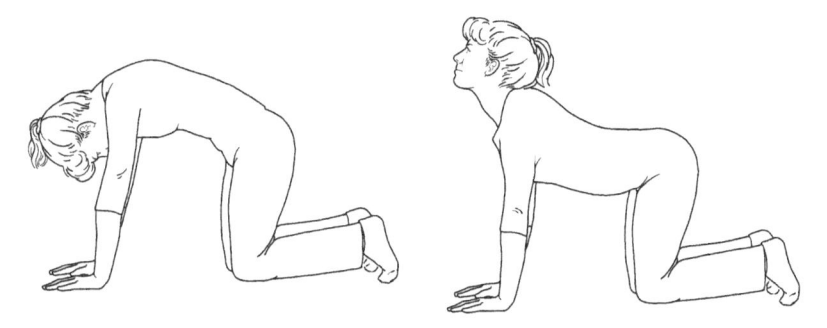

Figure 6.12 Cat Stretch.
© VHI, Inc.

Figure 6.13 Double Leg Hip Flexion.
© VHI, Inc.

Figure 6.14 Supine Single Leg Trunk Rotation.
Source: *Concepts of Health-Related Fitness*. Author: Thomas M. Adams II. Reprinted with permission.

110   Lifetime Fitness & Wellness

Figure 6.15   Supine Double Leg Hip Rotation.
Source: *Concepts of Health-Related Fitness.* Author: Thomas M. Adams II. Reprinted with permission.

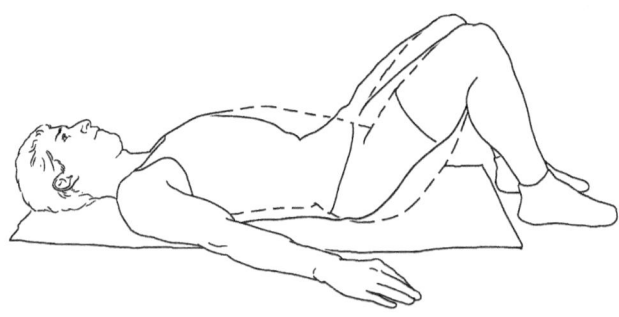

Figure 6.16   Pelvic Tilt.
© VHI, Inc.

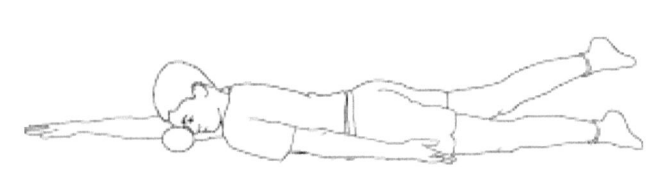

Figure 6.17   Prone (Face Down) Leg Lift.
Source: *Concepts of Health-Related Fitness.* Author: Thomas M. Adams II. Reprinted with permission.

Figure 6.18   Kneeling Arm and Leg Extension.
Source: *Concepts of Health-Related Fitness.* Author: Thomas M. Adams II. Reprinted with permission.

Abdominal Stretching Exercise

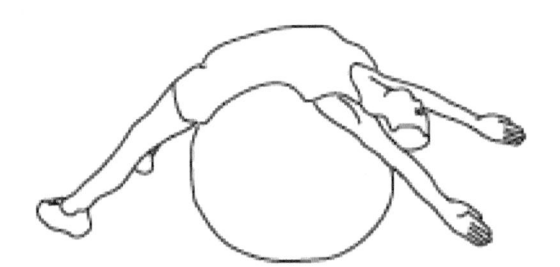

Figure 6.19   Abdominal Stretch.

Lower Body Stretching Exercises

Figure 6.20 Posterior Lower Leg (Calf) Stretch.
© VHI, Inc.

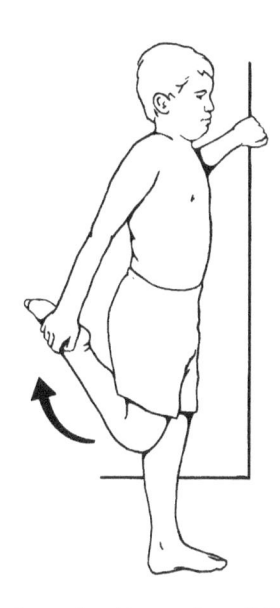

Figure 6.21 Anterior Upper Leg (Thigh) Stretch.
© VHI, Inc.

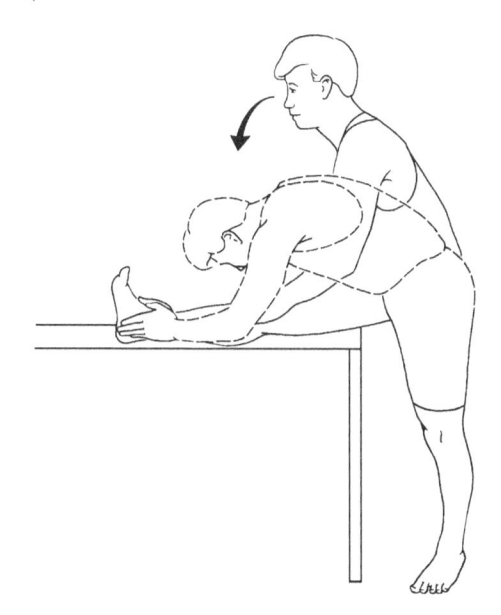

Figure 6.22 Posterior Upper Leg (Thigh) Stretch.
© VHI, Inc.

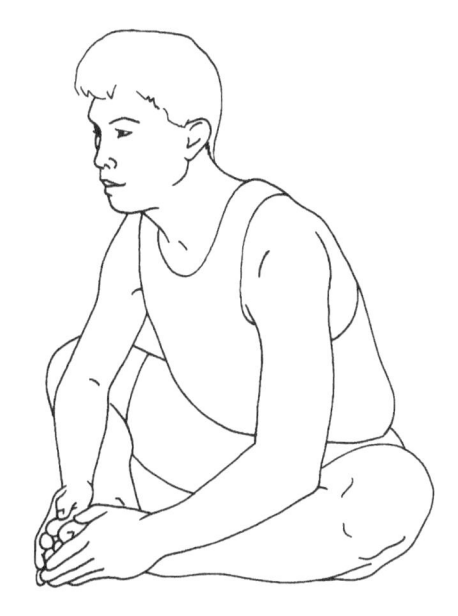

Figure 6.23 Adductor (Inner Thigh) Stretch.
© VHI, Inc.

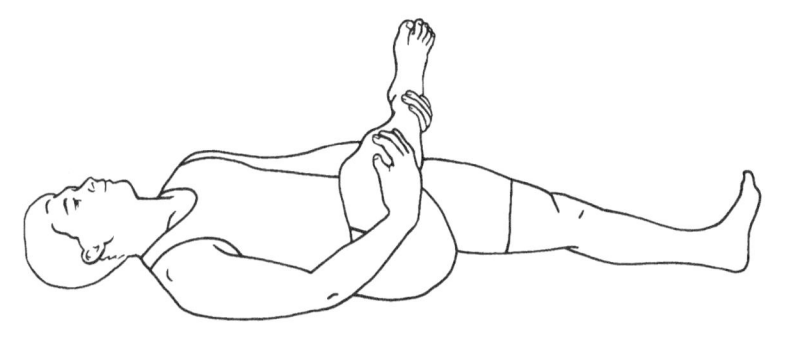

Figure 6.24 Hip Stretch.
© VHI, Inc.

Stretching Exercises to Avoid

Some stretching exercises are potentially harmful due to excessive stress placed on muscles and joints of the neck, shoulders, lower back, and knees. Exercises that are potentially harmful are termed contraindicated. **Figures 6.25–6.30** are examples of contraindicated exercises that are inappropriate for general use. However, these contraindicated exercises may not be inappropriate for individuals who participate in gymnastics, dance, or martial arts due to the high degree of flexibility required by participants in these activities.

Contraindicated Exercises

Figure 6.25 Hurdles Stretch.
Source: *Concepts of Health-Related Fitness*. Author: Thomas M. Adams II. Reprinted with permission.

Figure 6.26 Full or Deep Knee Squats.
Source: *Concepts of Health-Related Fitness*. Author: Thomas M. Adams II. Reprinted with permission.

Figure 6.27 Standing Straight Leg Toe Touch.
© VHI, Inc.

Figure 6.28 Standing Straight Leg Straddle Toe Touch.
© VHI, Inc.

Figure 6.29 Full Neck Rolls.
© VHI, Inc.

Figure 6.30 Straight Leg Sit-Ups.
Source: *Concepts of Health-Related Fitness*. Author: Thomas M. Adams II. Reprinted with permission.

Designing a Flexibility Program

1. Assess your current level of flexibility (**Lab 6.1**).
2. Apply the overload, progression and specificity training principles according to your unique needs.
3. Select stretching exercise for all joints (see **Figures 6.4** to **6.24**).
4. *Frequency:* Stretching exercises should be performed at least 3 times per week.
5. *Intensity:* Stretch to the point of mild discomfort.
6. *Duration:* Hold the final stretched position for 30 seconds. Perform two to four repetitions of each exercise.

Lab 6.1 at the end of this chapter will be used to assist in the development of your personalized flexibility program.

Back Health

Low back pain can occur as a result of the following:

- Poor flexibility caused by too tight posterior thigh and hip muscles.
- Excess body weight—excess body weight carried in the abdominal area places undue strain on the lower back region.
- Poor posture—standing with the knees fully locked or hyperextended causes swayback and places excess stress on the low back area.

- Poor muscular fitness.
- Injury caused by improper lifting or carrying technique or lifting objects that are too heavy.

Strategies to prevent low back pain include the following:

- Maintain ideal body weight.
- Strengthen weak abdominal and back muscles.
- Stretch tight posterior (rear) thigh and hip muscles to increase flexibility.
- Use proper body mechanics when standing, sitting and lying down.

    Standing for extended time periods—place one foot on a footrest or small stool to relieve strain on the lower back.

    Sitting—the back should be straight, with the knees higher than the hips.

    Lying on your side—the knees should be bent to flatten the lower back and maintain proper alignment of the spine (back bone).

    Lying on your back—bend the knees to flatten your lower back area, with the knees higher than the hips.

- Use correct lifting techniques—bend the knees (not the waist), lift using the legs, (not the back), keep the back straight. This allows you to use the stronger thigh and leg muscles to lift objects.
- Use correct technique when carrying objects—carry objects close to your body using both hands.

Summary

- Flexibility is the ability of a joint to move through its full range of motion and is important for effective and efficient participation in daily and recreational activities.
- The benefits of improved flexibility include enhanced muscle relaxation, reduced incidence of injury, improved movement capability, and improved posture.
- Joints can be classified according to the amount of movement they permit.
- Flexibility is influenced by the structure of the joint, muscle elasticity and plasticity, muscle temperature, age, gender, and activity level.
- A whole body warm-up should be performed before the execution of stretching exercises.
- Warm muscles are more flexible and, therefore less prone to injury.
- Correct posture and lifting techniques can reduce the incidence of back pain and injury.
- The three stretching techniques are ballistic, static, and proprioceptive neuromuscular facilitation.

References

Adams, T. (2002). *Concepts of health related fitness.* Dubuque, IA. Kendall/Hunt.

Baechle, T. and Earle, R. eds. *Essentials of strength training and conditioning.* Champaign, IL: Human Kinetics.

Bouchard, C., Shepard, R. J., & Stephens T. (1987). *Physical activity, fitness, and health.* Champaign, IL: Human Kinetics.

Foss, M.L. Keteyian, S.J. (1998). *Fox's physiological basis for exercise and sport.* Boston: WBC McGraw-Hill.

High, D.M., Howley, E.T. (1989). The effects of static stretching and warm-up on prevention of delayed-onset muscle soreness. *Research quarterly,* 60:357.

Kurz, T. (1994). *Stretching scientifically: A guide to flexibility training.* Island Pond, VT:Stadion Publishers.

McArdle, W.D., Katch, F.I., and Katch, V.I. *Essentials of exercise physiology.* Philadelphia: Lippincott, Williams & Wilkins.

McAtee, R.E. (1993). *Facilitated stretching.* Champaign, IL: Human Kinetic Press.

Plowman, S.A. (1993). "Physical fitness and healthy low back function," President's Council on Physical Fitness and Sports: *Physical activity and fitness research digest,* Series 1 (3)3. U.S. Surgeon General (1996). *Physical activity and health: A report of the surgeon general.* Washington: U.S. Government Printing Office.

Gilmore, J.H., & Costill, D.L. (1999). *Physiology of sport and exercise.* Champaign, IL: Human Kinetics.

Lab 6.1
Flexibility Program

Name: _____   Date: _____

Purpose: To design your personalized flexibility program. List at least one exercise for each body area for the upper and lower body.

Describe your warm-up: _____
_____

How many times each week will you perform the flexibility exercises in your program? _____

List the days of the week you will perform the flexibility exercises in your program? _____
_____

Body Area	Exercise	Muscle (s) stretched	Stretch duration	Repetitions
Upper Body	********************	**********************	*******	********
Chest				
Upper back				
Lower back				
Arms				
Lower Body	********************	**********************	*******	********
Front thigh				
Back thigh				
Inner thigh				
Calf				

Chapter 7

Fitness-Related Injuries

Objectives
Introduction
Fitness-Injury Prevention—Tips for Exercising
  Safely
Fitness-Related Injuries

Treating Fitness-Related Injuries
Injuries Caused by Environmental Conditions
Summary
References
Internet Sources

Objectives

Upon completion of this chapter, you will be able to:

1. Identify guidelines for preventing fitness-related injuries.
2. Differentiate between injuries caused by overuse and those caused by accidents.
3. Describe the most common types of fitness-related injuries, and recognize the warning signs and symptoms associated with each.
4. Describe the appropriate treatment for fitness-related injuries.
5. Know when to seek medical help for fitness-related injuries.
6. Identify injuries associated with exercising in environmental conditions.

Introduction

Correct application of the FIT principle can reduce your risk of fitness related injuries due to over training. Very few fitness-related injuries are associated with moderate participation. Like anything else, however, too much activity can be harmful. As you increase the number and type of fitness activities that you are involved in, the greater the chances of acquiring fitness-related injuries. The types of movements performed during fitness activities contribute to various types of fitness-related injuries. For example, running and aerobic dancing can cause ankle and knee sprains or strains, as well as shin splints; playing tennis can cause tendinitis in the elbow (tennis elbow); jogging can cause tendonitis in the heel (Achilles tendinitis); and a stress fracture may be the result of overtraining. This chapter describes techniques for preventing fitness-related injuries as well as ways to recognize some of the most common fitness-related injuries and methods for treating those injuries.

Fitness-Injury Prevention—Tips for Exercising Safely

Whether you participate in fitness activities for fun, to get in shape, for health, or for a combination of reasons, injury prevention should be considered every step of the way. While some injuries are beyond control, you can prevent the vast majority of fitness injuries by following these guidelines:

- medical screening examination.
- proper warm up and cool down.
- use the appropriate equipment and safety devices.
- wear proper attire.
- use common sense.

Get a Medical Screening Examination

Today more and more people are leading more active lifestyles. Most individuals can safely participate without any worries. However, some people should check with their doctor before they start a fitness program—especially those just getting started or those who have not participated in a fitness program in several years. A medical screening examination will alert you to any predisposing facts which might cause injury or death while engaging in fitness activities. Predisposing conditions which may include high blood pressure, diabetes, cardiovascular problems, and obesity. The Physical Activity Readiness-Questionnaire in Chapter 2 may also assist in determining whether or not an individual should seek the advice of a medical doctor before starting a fitness program if you are between the ages of 15 to 69. If you answer "yes" to one or more of the questions on the questionnaire, it is recommended that you talk with your doctor before becoming physically active.

Properly Warm Up and Cool Down

The time frame before and after fitness activities are critical periods for preventing unnecessary injury and pain. Warming-up at least five minutes before engaging in activities such as running in place, walking, cycling, or jogging, increases blood flow to inactive muscles and gradually elevates the heart rate to its target zone. Similarly, you can gradually lower your heart rate to its resting rate by walking five minutes after exercise.

Static stretching is considered part of a warm-up and cool down process. After warming up, stretching exercises increase flexibility in tight muscles and joints, thereby reducing the risk of sprains and tears. Concentrate on stretching muscle groups utilized during selected physical activity. For example, swimmers will definitely stretch the upper body, and runners would concentrate on the legs. Static stretching after exercise is also recommended to prevent muscle soreness.

Use the Right Equipment and Safety Devices

Injuries sustained while participating in fitness activities can be reduced by using the correct equipment for the activity. For example, bikers should select the right size bicycle frame to reduce back and knee pain, wear a bicycle helmet, use padded grips, and wear padded biking shorts and gloves to reduce biking injuries such as head injuries and cyclist's palsy, which is numbness and tingling in the ring and little fingers; eye goggles should be worn while playing racquetball and squash to prevent eye injuries. Swimmers should wear earplugs while swimming to help prevent swimmer's ear. Wrist guards, elbow pads, knee pads, and helmets should be worn while in-line skating to prevent injuries to the wrist, elbow, knee, and head. Tennis players should have proper strung racquets to prevent tennis elbow. Whatever activity selected, be sure to use the appropriate equipment and make certain it is in top condition before risking your health and safety.

Wear Proper Attire

The selection of fitness and leisure activity attire is very important in the prevention of fitness-related injuries. Make sure that you select the proper footwear and appropriate clothing for your activity of choice. How can you be sure that you've chosen the right footwear for your activity? These guidelines can help:

Running Shoes. Activities that involve the feet striking the ground forcefully for an extended period of time (such as running and jogging), requires shoes with adequate cushioning for shock absorption. Shoes for these activities must also provide arch and heel support to prevent the foot from turning in and out. Padded heels to protect the Achilles tendon are also important.

Walking Shoes. When selecting a good walking shoe, choose one with flexible soles. Heel cushioning is important because this is where the foot strikes the ground, but since the foot swings through as you walk, too much cushioning in the front part of the shoe may make you trip.

"Aerobic" Shoes. Like running and jogging, aerobic dance can be a high-impact activity. Aerobic shoes should have well-cushioned soles and good overall support. They should also have firm yet flexible soles for ease of movement. If you suffer from weak ankles, a high-top variety can provide additional ankle support.

Specialty Shoes. There are numerous types of footwear designed for specific sports including bicycling, golf, football, baseball, and skiing. Each shoe has characteristics designed to improve comfort and performance for specified activities. No matter what the activity, the key to the proper shoe selection is one that fits and provides adequate support and stability.

Does the Shoe Fit? A properly fit shoe should have enough toe room when standing so that neither the big nor the little toe extends over the sole of the shoe. The heel of the shoe should feel snug without pinching. For the best support, the inner side of exercise shoes should be made of a firm material to prevent the foot from collapsing inward. An arch support that conforms to one's foot is also important for good fit, support, and comfort. Whether you run, jog, walk, or dance, shoes can make a difference (see **Figure 7.1**). The best exercise shoe is one that fits your foot. Try on several pairs of shoes by various manufacturers before making your final selection. Shoes are perhaps the most basic piece of equipment for any sport, so make sure your shoe has the right fit; then wear it.

Appropriate clothing also plays a very important role in injury prevention. The function of clothing is more important than how fashionable it is. Always wear clothes designed for the activity; a shirt on hot days to protect the skin and allow maximal body heat dissipation (light-colored), clothing on cold days that retains heat (various layers of poly-propylene and/or wool clothing), and cotton and wool socks to prevent blisters. Women should wear sport bras when exercising strenuously.

Use Common Sense

Overtraining can be a serious problem with regard to safety issues and exercise effectiveness. It can occur from consistently working out too often, too intensely, or for too long. Because overtraining can reduce performance and increase the risk of injury, employ a common-sense strategy when participating in a fitness program.

Everyone has different training goals and fitness levels, so defining overtraining is difficult. But there are common symptoms associated with overtraining. Some warning signs of overtraining include: insomnia or trouble sleeping, muscle stiffness and soreness, irritability, elevated resting heart rate and/or blood pressure, bone or joint pain, fatigue, loss of appetite, feeling of depression, decreased performance, headaches, gastrointestinal disturbances, and susceptibility to colds, flu, and injury. Overtraining is associated with the duration, frequency, and intensity of exercise as well as insufficient recovery time from exercise (optimal recovery time is 24 to 48 hours). Once signs of overtraining are identified, examine your schedule and determine the cause. If you recently boosted your training intensity, cut back and allow your body enough time to adjust.

To help prevent overtraining, make sure to eat a balanced diet for optimal performance, allow sufficient recovery between workouts, and participate in cross-training. **Cross-training**

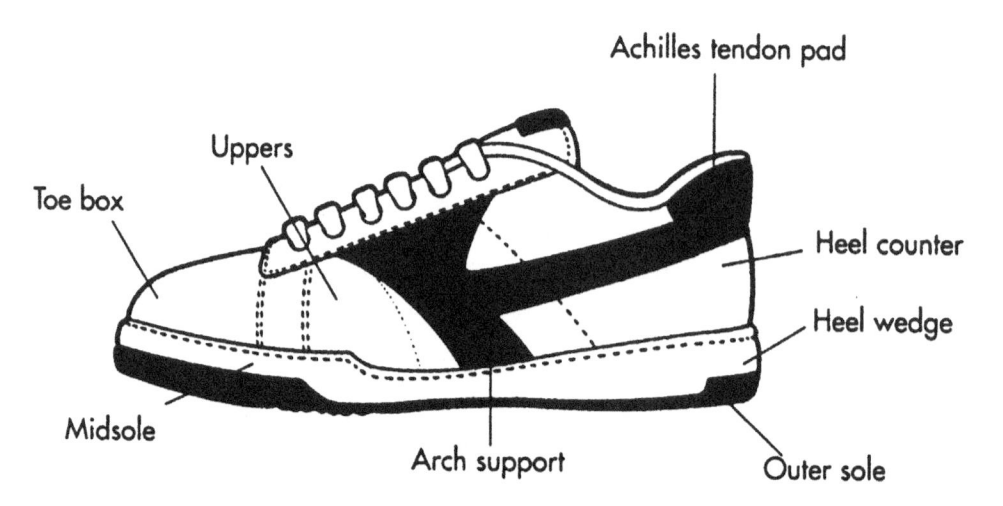

Figure 7.1 Parts of a Well-Designed Shoe.

involves performing various kinds of exercises rather than sticking to one routine. This makes you less vulnerable to injury, because the stress of working out is spread out more evenly on your muscles, joints, and bones. For example, break up your workout into various activities (15 minutes of stair stepping, 15 minutes on the treadmill and then 15 minutes on an exercise bike), alternate swimming and walking, and combine aerobic exercises with strength training in one session (alternating weight lifting with aerobics). The best way to enjoy your activity and prevent unnecessary injuries is to use common sense in applying the fitness-related injury prevention guidelines in this chapter.

Fitness-Related Injuries

Microtrauma and macrotrauma are considered the two major causes of injuries in fitness-related activities. **Microtrauma**, or overuse injuries such as stress fracture, and inflammation of the tendons (tendinitis), develop in the leg, shoulder, knee, and elbow as a result of cumulative stress during exercise over a period of time. **Macrotrauma**, or overload injuries such as muscle and/or tendon strains and ligament sprains occur as a result of an accident. The most frequent fitness-related sprain is caused by a sudden overload to the ligament in the ankle. The most common fitness-related strain is caused by a sudden or repetitive overload to the hamstring and calf.

Inflammation develops as a result of macrotrauma and microtrauma injuries to the body. Pain, swelling, redness, loss of function, and local heat are all signs and symptoms of inflammation in the injured area.

Strains

A **strain** is a stretching or tearing of a muscle and/or tendon. Together, the muscle and tendon are referred to as the **musculotendinous unit**—the functional unit of a muscle and its tendons of attachment to bone. This type of injury often occurs when muscles suddenly and powerfully contract or when a muscle stretches too far. People commonly call muscle strains pulled muscles. Hamstring injuries are among the most common strains.

A muscle becomes strained or pulled, or may even tear when it stretches unusually far or abruptly. Strains are classified as either grade I, grade II or grade III. A grade I strain is described as mild damage causing minimal loss of strength and motion. Grade I strains typically improve in approximately two to three weeks. The damage to the muscle/tendon in the grade II strain is more extensive with significant loss of strength and motion, yet the affected part is not completely ruptured. While the muscle/tendon in a grade III strain is completely ruptured with greater loss of strength and motion and severe swelling and pain. Grade III strains sometimes require surgery to repair the affected part. A muscle strain may occur when you slip on the ice, run, jump, throw, lift a heavy object, or lift in an awkward position.

For a strain, seek medical help immediately if the area quickly becomes swollen and is intensely painful, or if you suspect a ruptured muscle or broken bone. Treating a strain depends on the severity of the injury. For mild to moderate strains most doctors recommend basic self-care measures: applying ice, taking over-the-counter drugs such as ibuprofen (Advil) or acetaminophen (Tylenol) and rest. In cases of severe strains, your doctor may immobilize the area with a brace or splint, and in other cases, perform surgery to reattach the ends of the muscle or tendon.

Regular stretching and strengthening exercises specific to fitness-related activity can help reduce the risk of strains.

Sprains

A **sprain** is a stretching or tearing of ligaments. Ligaments are tough bands of fibrous tissue that connect one bone to another. They help to stabilize joints, preventing excessive movement. Sprains are frequently caused by rapid changes in direction or by a collision. Common locations for sprains are ankles and knees.

A sprain occurs when you overextend or tear a ligament while severely stressing a joint. Sprains may be classified as grade I, grade II and grade III. The ligament in a grade I sprain is stretched or slightly torn with mild swelling, tenderness, stiffness and minimal pain. The damage in a grade II sprain is greater. The ligament tear is incomplete with moderate swelling, and pain. The affected part is also tender to the touch. The grade III sprain is a complete tear of the ligament with severe bruising, swelling and pain. The affected part is unstable. A sprain of the knee or ankle may occur when walking or exercising on an uneven surface. A sprain also may happen when you land awkwardly, either at the end of a jump or while pivoting during a fitness activity.

Treating a sprain depends on the severity of the injury. In cases of a mild sprain, apply ice to minimize swelling and take an over-the-counter pain reliever such as ibuprofen (Advil) or acetaminophen (Tylenol). In cases of severe sprains, your doctor may immobilize the area in a brace or splint. Occasionally, surgery may be considered.

Stress Fractures

A **stress fracture** is a hairline crack that occurs in bones from repeated or prolonged use. The most common sites for stress fractures are the foot bones (metatarsals—22 percent), shin bone (tibia—34 percent), outer leg bone (fibula—24 percent), thigh bone (femur), and pelvis (6 percent).

Stress fractures are overuse injuries. The majority of leg injuries occur during activities such as running, jumping, or dancing, which are considered to be weight bearing activities. Symptoms linked with stress fractures include pain with activity, swelling, and bruising. Stress fractures are difficult to diagnose. Your doctor will examine you and may order an X-ray. However, X-rays do not always show a stress fracture and you may be given a more specialized test called a bone scan.

The most important treatment for a stress fracture is rest. Other treatments may include applying ice packs, taking anti-inflammatory medication, and wearing a cast for three to six weeks while the bone heals.

Tendinitis

Tendinitis is an inflammation or irritation of a tendon that is usually caused by injury or overuse during work or play. Tendons are thick fibrous cords that attach muscles to bone. The condition, which causes pain and tenderness outside a joint, is most common around the elbow (tennis elbow), heel (Achilles tendinitis), and the knee (patellar tendinitis). But it can occur in the hip, wrist, and shoulder.

Tennis elbow is an inflammation of the tendons and muscles that attach to the elbow. Activities such as painting and racquet sports that require gripping for extended periods of time may cause tennis elbow. Tendinitis involving the Achilles is caused by inflammation of the tendon that runs from the calf muscle to the heel. Changing the intensity and/or duration of your fitness activity drastically in a short period of time, may cause this tendon to become inflamed as a result of overuse. The patella, or knee cap is another area that may become aggravated while participating in fitness activities. When the tendon that attaches the quadriceps to the tibia becomes inflamed, the end result may be patella tendinitis. Endurance activities that require several repetitions, such as jogging and step aerobics, may contribute to this condition.

If tendinitis is severe and leads to the rupture of a tendon, surgical repair may be necessary. But in most cases, rest and medications to reduce pain and inflammation may be the only treatment you need.

Knee Pain

You're not alone, if you're suffering from knee pain. Knee pain is one of the most common reasons that individuals visit the emergency room or the doctor, and almost one in three Americans older than forty-five reports some type of knee pain. Most knee pain and injuries are associated with ligament injuries, tendon injuries (tendinitis), and meniscus injuries (cartilage). Some common causes of knee pain and injuries include:

- Degeneration from aging
- A blow to the knee
- Repeated stress or overuse
- Awkward landings from a fall or from jumping
- Rapidly growing bones
- Sudden turning, pivoting, and stopping
- Dislocated kneecap
- Rheumatoid arthritis – an autoimmune disease that causes inflammation of the joints, tissues around the joints and in other bodily organs
- Hyperextended knee
- Osgood-Schlatter disease – can cause a painful lump below the kneecap adolescents experiencing growth spurts
- Osteoarthritis – a degenerative disease that causes inflammation in one or more joints in the body.
- Chondromalacia of the patella – a condition in which the cartilage under the patella (knee cap) deteriorates and softens
- Bursitis

A number of factors can increase your risk of having knee problems, including:

- Age: Osgood-Schlatter disease and patellar tendinitis in young people, and gout or osteoarthritis in older adults
- Gender: Osgood-Schlatter disease more common in boys than girls
- Previous injury
- Excess weight
- High-risk sports and activities
- Overuse: repetitive activity

- Lack of muscle flexibility or strength
- Lack of neuromuscular control
- Mechanical problems: flat feet, one leg shorter than the other, and misaligned knees

The following recommendations can help alleviate joint deterioration and prevent injuries that cause knee pain.

- Listen to your body – most injuries occur when you're tired
- Keep off extra pounds – maintain a healthy weight
- Exhibit good sport or activity techniques
- Increase strength and flexibility
- Develop sound exercise routines
- Select the appropriate shoes and attire
- Protect your knees—wear proper support gear

The signs and symptoms of knee problems can vary widely. Some of the more common are pain, mild to moderate swelling, inability to bear weight, stiffness, a feeling that the knee might buckle or give way, and inflammation. The key to treating knee pain is to reduce inflammation by using RICE Therapy, nonsteroidal anti-inflammatory medication, and in some cases crutches and braces. When self-care measures aren't enough to control pain and swelling, and promote healing, your physician may recommend other options, including: physical therapy, surgical alternatives options, corticosteroid injections, and topical painkillers.

Not all knee pain is serious, but some knee injuries and medical conditions can lead to increasing pain, joint damage, and even disability if left untreated. If you've had a knee injury, even a minor one, it makes you more susceptible to similar injuries in the future.

Treating Fitness-Related Injuries

The most common fitness-related injuries are "soft tissue" injuries; strains, sprains, and bruises. While the best means of dealing with these injuries is prevention, accidents do occur, and knowing what to do first if you should become injured can help prevent further damage as well as help speed recovery. However, consult with a doctor if this injury causes loss of function.

RICE Therapy

As a response to soft-tissue (musculoskeletal) injury, the injured area swells (inflammation). This swelling causes pain, heat, and redness. For most soft-tissue injuries, the first-aid treatment is RICE: *Rest, Ice, Compression,* and *Elevation.*

Rest. Rest means restricting movement. As soon as you experience pain, stop your activity. By resting an injury for the first few days, you'll help stop excess internal and external bleeding and will promote healing of damaged tissues. In some cases, splints, tape, or bandages, and even casts are used to prevent the injured area from moving (see **Figure 7.2**).

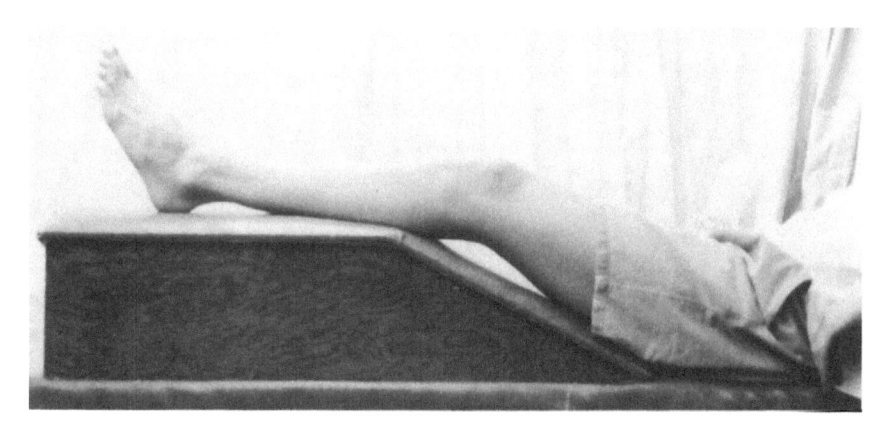

Figure 7.2 **Rest** for approximately 48 hours after the injury to prevent reinjury and to allow healing.
From *Fitness Assessment Workbook* by Jan Duquette and Duane Cain. Copyright © 2002 by Kendall/Hunt Publishing Company. Reprinted by permission.

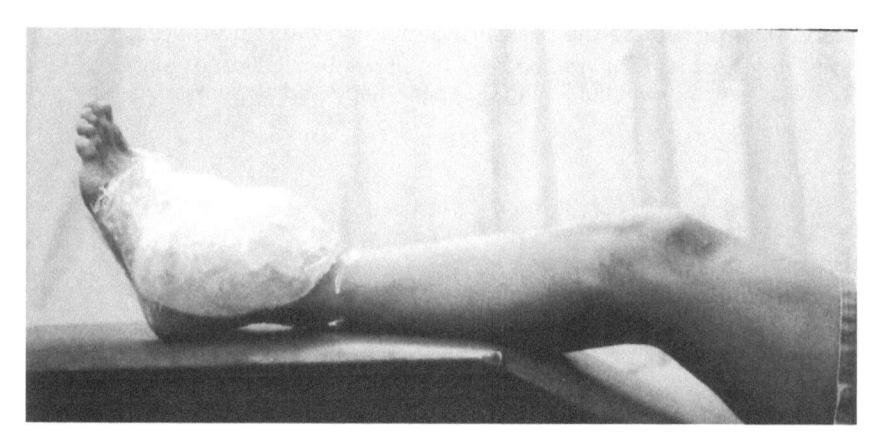

Figure 7.3 **Ice** packs will reduce bleeding from the torn blood vessels. Apply an ice pack (or cold water) to the injured area for 20 minutes every hour, over a forty-eight-hour period if possible.
From *Fitness Assessment Workbook* by Jan Duquette and Duane Cain. Copyright © 2002 by Kendall/Hunt Publishing Company. Reprinted by permission.

Ice. Applying cold compresses to soft-tissue injuries reduces bleeding (**hemorrhaging**) and swelling by constricting blood vessels. Generally, apply the ice to the injury for approximately 20 minutes on and 40 minutes off. Always wrap ice or bags of frozen vegetables or other cold compresses in a towel or cloth; applying ice directly to the injured area can cause frostbite. Coldness is transmitted faster to the injured area if a wet towel or cloth is used instead of one that is dry. Use cold compresses for the first 24 to 36 hours following an injury to reduce pain and swelling (see **Figure 7.3**).

Compression. Compression, or pressure, helps to reduce swelling and blood flow to the injured area. Compression and icing should always be performed together. You can even soak the pressure bandage in cold water before application to aid cooling. Wrap the bandage in a spiral or figure-8 pattern to ensure indirect pressure is being applied to the damaged blood vessels. While pressure bandages must be tight enough to restrict blood flow, they should not cut off blood flow altogether. If your toes or fingers feel numb, lose their color, or have a throbbing limb, loosen the compression wrap or bandage (see **Figure 7.4**).

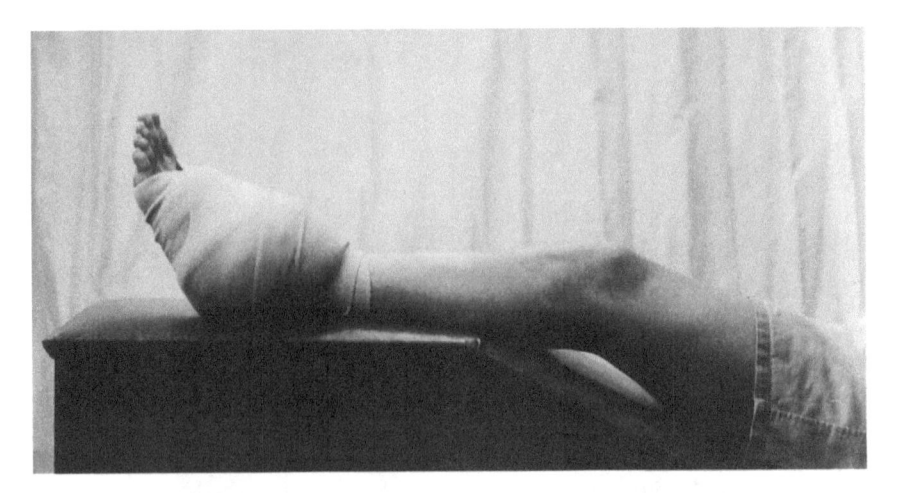

Figure 7.4 **Compression** should be used as with an ace bandage to contain the swelling. Firmly bandage the injured area, but don't bandage it so tightly that it will be uncomfortable, and **elevation** is important, so that the injured area is raised allowing blood to flow toward the heart. This will reduce the pressure of fluid on the injured area.

From *Fitness Assessment Workbook* by Jan Duquette and Duane Cain. Copyright © 2002 by Kendall/Hunt Publishing Company. Reprinted by permission.

Table 7.1 Common Fitness-Related Injuries

Injury	Signs/Symptoms	Treatment
Bruise (contusion)	Pain, swelling, discoloration	Cold application, compression, rest
Shin splints	Pain, spasm in front lower leg (shinbone/tibia)	Cold application prior to and following any physical activity, rest, heat
Muscle soreness	Tenderness, pain	Mild stretching, low-intensity exercise, warm bath
Blisters	Clear or reddish liquid forms a pocket beneath the skin	Wash area; apply ice; cover with bandage; if broken, apply antibiotic ointment
Runner's knee	Pain, swelling, redness, tenderness	Mild stretching of hamstring and quadriceps, arch supports in shoes
Swimmer's shoulder	Pain, inflammation	Ice, rest, anti-inflammatory medication
Plantar fascia	Inflammation, tenderness, pain on bottom of foot	Ice massage, stretching
Muscle cramps	Localized pain, intense contractions	Mild stretching, stay well-hydrated, apply moist heat, rest

Elevation. Elevation reduces internal bleeding and pooling of blood in the injured area, and helps blood return to the heart more easily. To be effective, the injured area should be elevated above heart level. Keep the injured area elevated whenever possible, not just during icing. Elevation also helps eliminate pain by reducing the throbbing sensation caused by blood circulating to the injured site.

Continue the RICE therapy for at least 48 hours after the injury has occurred. **Table 7.1** offers strategies for the care of common fitness-related injuries.

When to Seek Medical Care

While many minor fitness injuries can be treated safely at home, never hesitate to call a doctor if a more serious injury is suspected or if any of the following occurs for more than three days: you are unable to move the affected area, severe swelling occurs; there is pain in a specific area on or around a bony area; experience radiating pain or numbness; develop an infection, pus, red streaks, swollen lymph nodes, or fever; experience neurological symptoms; or an injured joint or a minor injury doesn't heal in three weeks.

If in doubt, seek professional medical help.

Injuries Caused by Environmental Conditions

Exercising in hot and cold weather may put you at risk for environmentally related injuries such as hyperthermia and hypothermia.

Hyperthermia

Hyperthermia is excessively high body temperature caused by excessive heat production or impaired heat loss capacity. If the relative humidity is too high, body heat cannot be lost through evaporation because the atmosphere is already saturated with water vapor reducing the cooling effect. The following are descriptions of first-aid measures for the three hyperthermia or heat-induced injuries:

Heat Cramps. Symptoms include cramps, spasms, and muscle twitching usually in the legs, arms, and abdomen. These cramps seem to be connected to excess exposure to heat, dehydration, and poor conditioning, rather than to lack of salt or other mineral imbalances. To relieve heat cramps, stop exercising, get out of the heat into a cool environment, massage the painful area, stretch slowly, and drink plenty of fluids (water, fruit drinks, or electrolyte drinks).

Heat Exhaustion. Symptoms include fainting, nausea, vomiting, dizziness, rapid heartbeat, profuse sweating, cold and clammy skin, weakness, and headache, a moderately increased temperature (101–102° F) which is not truly a fever, but caused by the heat. Heat exhaustion is the result of prolonged sweating without adequate fluid replacement. If you experience any of these symptoms, stop and locate a cool environment. If conscious, drink cool water, loosen or remove clothing, and rub your body with a cool/wet towel or ice packs. Elevate your legs 8–12 inches, while in a supine position. Seek medical help if you have not recovered in 30 minutes.

Heat Stroke. Symptoms include hot dry skin, disorientation, rapid heartbeat, rapid and shallow breathing, elevated or lowered blood pressure (caused by the breakdown of the body's cooling mechanism), sweating stops, vomiting, diarrhea, and unconsciousness. When the body temperature reaches 104–105° F, the individual may feel a cold sensation in the trunk of the body, goose bumps, nausea, throbbing in the temples, and numbness in the extremities. If the temperature exceeds 106° F the individual may experience brain damage, permanent disability, and death may be imminent. Heat stroke requires immediate emergency medical attention. While waiting for help, get into a cool environment; you should be placed in a semi-seated position, sprayed with cool water, and rubbed with cool towels. If possible place cold packs on the neck, head, armpits, or groin-areas with abundant blood supply. It is possible to prevent heat-related injuries. The important thing is to stay well-hydrated to make sure that your body can get rid of extra heat, and to be sensible about exertion in hot, humid weather.

Hypothermia or Cold Injuries

Hypothermia is a decrease in body temperature to below 95° F, usually as a result of being in extreme cold for a long time. It typically occurs when body heat is lost faster than it can be produced. Hypothermia can happen anywhere outdoors as well as indoors. Temperatures as mild as 50° F when combined with rainy or windy conditions can cause hypothermia if a person is not well prepared for the weather.

Signs that a person may have mild hypothermia include slurred speech; confused thinking; drowsiness; stiff muscles that may cause stumbling and difficulty performing tasks such as zipping up clothing; a pale, puffy face with blotchy skin; and skin that is cool to the touch, especially on the stomach and back, or in areas that are normally warm like the armpits and groin. As hypothermia becomes more severe the heartbeat may become irregular and weak, breathing becomes shallow, and muscles become rigid. In it's most severe form, unconsciousness or death can occur.

When the symptoms of hypothermia appear, immediate medical attention is required. Take the person's temperature. A temperature of 95° F or lower signals a medical problem. If the person's temperature is less than 92° F, they will stop shivering and will need prompt medical attention. When body temperature drops to between 80 and 90° F, victims are in serious condition. With a temperature below 80° F, chances for survival decrease.

Since hypothermia can be life-threatening, it is important to take steps to prevent it from developing when outdoors. Here are some common-sense prevention tips:

- Dress warmly—down and natural fabrics like cotton and wool are the best insulators.
- Wear a hat—hats drastically reduces heat loss.
- Keep dry—wet clothing is twenty times colder than dry clothing.
- Stay with at least one buddy when doing outdoor activities in remote places.
- Wear several layers of clothing to prevent excessive heat loss.

Summary

Important concepts that you have learned in this chapter include the following:

- Fitness-injury prevention involves medical screening examination, proper warm-up and cool down, using the appropriate equipment and safety devices, wearing proper attire, and using common sense.

- To avoid overtraining, participate in cross-training activities to decrease overuse of muscles, tendons, and joints.

- Conscientious exercisers always key in on intensity, duration, and frequency changes in their workout program.

- Macrotrauma injuries result from accidents and microtrauma injuries result from cumulative stress placed on body parts.

- Muscle strains, tendonitis, stress fractures, ligament sprains, and general inflammation conditions are musculoskeletal injuries.

- Pain, swelling, and loss of function are the warning signs and symptoms of common fitness-related injuries.

- If there is a loss of function as a result of a fitness-related injury, seek medical care immediately.

- The acceptable technique for first-aid treatment of most fitness-related injuries is RICE—Rest, Ice, Compression, and Elevation.

- Hyperthermia and hypothermia are injuries related to environmental conditions.

References

Corbin, C.B., Welk, G.J., Corbin, W.R., & Welk, K.A. (2008). *Concepts of fitness and wellness*, 6th ed., New York, NY: McGraw-Hill.

Dennis, K., Henson, B., & Adams T.M. (2005). *Destination: Fit, Well, and Healthy: A Roadmap for Your Journey*, Dubuque, IA: Kendall/Hunt Publishing Company.

Hoeger, W.K., & Hoeger, S.A. (2006). *Principles and labs for fitness and wellness*, 8th ed., Belmont, CA: Wadsworth Publishing Company.

Thomas, S., Reading, R., and Shepard, R.J. (1992). Revision of the physical activity readiness questionnaire (PAR-Q). *Canadian journal of sport science*, 17:338–345.

Internet Sources

www.bodytrends.com/articles/injury/bewareovertrainav.html

www.yourhealth.com/ahl/1756.html

www.mayoclinic.com/health/knee-pain/D500555

www.acsm.org

www.nsca-lift.org

Chapter 8

Body Composition and Weight Control

Objectives
Introduction
Obesity and Overweight
Body Fat Distribution
Body Composition Assessment Techniques
Eating Disorders
Strategies for Successful Weight Control
Summary

References
Internet Sources
Lab 8.1: Calculating Body Mass Index
Lab 8.2: Body Composition Program

Objectives

Upon completion of this chapter, you will be able to:

1. Describe the components of body composition.
2. Distinguish between obesity and overweight.
3. Describe body fat distribution patterns.
4. Discuss strategies for successful weight control.
5. Describe various body composition assessment techniques.
6. Distinguish between essential fat and storage fat.
7. Describe factors that influence daily energy expenditure.
8. Discuss eating disorders.

Introduction

The human body consists of two entities relative to body composition: lean body mass and fat mass. **Body composition** refers to the relative amount of **lean body mass** or fat-free mass to fat mass. **Lean body mass** includes all tissues that are not fat, such as bone, internal organs (kidney, liver, lungs, heart, etc.), connective tissues, and muscle. **Fat mass** refers specifically to fat tissue. Physical activity level, dietary practices and genetics determine your body composition. Physical activity participation and dietary practices are the primary influences of the amount of lean body mass and fat mass you possess. Body fat can be classified as **essential fat** or **storage fat**. The body cannot function normally without adequate amounts of essential fat. It serves as an insulator and padded protection of internal organs as well as an energy source for the body. Essential body fat deposits can be found in the brain, heart, central nervous system, liver, spleen, lungs, intestines, cell membranes, and bone marrow. The essential levels for women and men are 12 percent and 5 percent respectively. Females have higher levels of essential fat for reproductive and hormonal functions. Females whose body fat percentage drops below essential levels typically experience **amenorrhea** or **oligomenorrhea**. Amenorrhea is the complete cessation of the menstrual cycle. Oligomenorrhea is the delayed onset of menstruation or an irregular menstrual cycle. Female athletes such as long distance runners, dancers, and gymnasts suffer from these conditions as well as individuals with eating disorders. Storage of nonessential fat is body fat above that needed for normal physiological functioning. Most storage fat is located under the skin and serves as a depository for excess calories not used by the body and stored as fat. Excess storage of body fat leads to overweight and obesity conditions.

Obesity and Overweight

Overweight is defined as having excess body weight for one's height. **Obesity** is defined as having excess body fat **above normal for one's body type, age, and gender**. Individuals whose percent of body fat levels exceed 30% for women and 20% for men are considered obese. Excess body fat can have a significant impact on health status. The risk of disease and premature death increases substantially when body fat percentages exceed optimal levels. A high percentage of body fat increases one's risk of developing obesity, heart disease, diabetes, hypertension, cancer, elevated cholesterol levels, and other health problems. In fact, obese individuals experience diabetes and heart disease at a rate more than twice that of individuals of ideal or optimal body fat percentages. **Table 8.1** contains standards for body fat.

A variety of factors contribute to overweight and obese conditions, such as physical inactivity, the overuse of technology resulting in reduced body movement and inappropriate dietary practices that create a state of positive caloric balance for an extended time period.

Table 8.1 Standards for Body Fat Percentage

Category	Women	Men
Essential Fat	10%–12%	2%–5%
Ideal	13%–22%	6%–13%
Acceptable	23%–29%	14%–19%
Obese	30% or higher	20% or higher

Figure 8.1 Energy Balance.
Source: *Concepts of Health-Related Fitness*. Author: Thomas M. Adams II. Reprinted with permission.

Positive caloric (energy) balance (see **Figure 8.1**) refers to the consumption of more calories than expended for energy. **Negative caloric (energy) balance** refers to expending more calories than consumed. Negative caloric balance results in weight reduction, while positive caloric balance results in weight gain. Negative caloric balance is achieved by making appropriate lifestyle choices, such as consistent participation in physical activity and making proper dietary modifications. Achieving and maintaining your ideal body weight requires making long-term positive lifestyle changes. Your ideal body weight is the body weight at which you look and feel best.

Body Fat Distribution

Genetics play a role in determining your body fat distribution pattern. Body fat distribution pattern refers to the locations of fat stores on your body. For example, one individual may

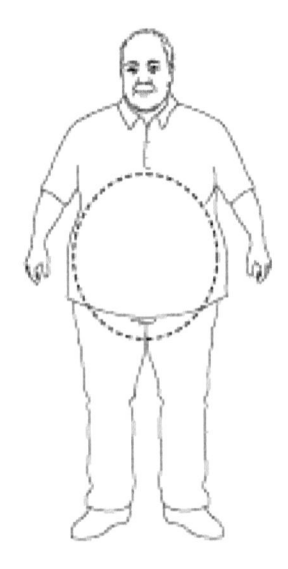

Figure 8.2 Central Obesity.
Source: *Concepts of Health-Related Fitness.* Author: Thomas M. Adams II. Reprinted with permission.

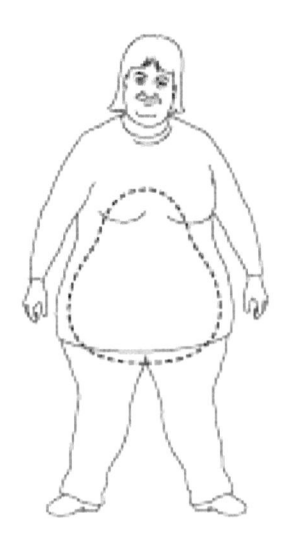

Figure 8.3 Gynoid Obesity.
Source: *Concepts of Health-Related Fitness.* Author: Thomas M. Adams II. Reprinted with permission.

tend to store more body fat in their hip and thigh regions, while another individual may tend to store more fat in their abdominal area. There are two basic body fat distribution patterns: central, also known as android and gynoid (see **Figures 8.2** and **8.3**) The android pattern is apple-shaped, characterized by deposits of excess fat in the abdominal area and typically seen in males. This pattern is also linked to a higher risk of heart disease, hypertension, and elevated cholesterol levels. Fat cells located in the abdominal area tend to be larger in size compared to fat cells in other body areas. The gynoid pattern is pear shaped, characterized by deposits of excess fat in the hips and thighs, and typically seen in females. Excessive waist circumference can be used as an indicator of health risk. The waist circumference is commonly defined as the smallest portion of the waist measured one inch above the umbilicus or navel and below the xiphoid process. The goal for weight management is a waist circumference of less than 35 inches in women and less than 40 inches in men. A waist circumference of 43 inches in women and 47 inches in men is considered very high health risk. A very low health risk is associated with a waist circumference of less than 27.5 for women and 31.5 for men.

Body Composition Assessment Techniques

A variety of diagnostic tools can be used to assess body composition, such as hydrostatic weighing, skinfold measurement, dual-energy X-ray absorptiometry, bioelectrical impedance, air displacement plethysmography, near infrared interactance, and body mass index.

Hydrostatic Weighing

Hydrostatic or underwater weighing is a technique that computes body density (the ratio of body mass to body volume) by comparing an individual's body weight while completely submerged underwater with that on land and estimating percent body fat using a mathematical equation. Hydrostatic weighing is based on Archimedes' Principle which states that a submerged object will possess a buoyant force equal to the volume of water it displaces. Buoyant force is the force that causes you to rise to the surface after jumping in a body of water. It causes an object to weigh less under water than it does on land. Hydrostatic weighing is conducted in a special underwater weighing apparatus or a swimming pool. It also requires other specialized equipment to measure lung function. This technique requires expensive equipment, highly trained technicians, and is not appropriate for individuals who are uncomfortable underwater.

Skinfold Measurement

Skinfold or anthropometric measurements are taken using calipers at specific sites on the body. Typical sites include the triceps, suprailiac, biceps, subscapular, and abdomen. The rationale for using skinfolds to estimate body fat is based on the idea that most of the body's fat stores are located directly beneath the skin (subcutaneous fat). The skinfold measurement is taken by pinching the subcutaneous fat between the thumb and index finger. The caliper is then placed on the most parallel section of the fold to measure its thickness. Mathematical equations are used to estimate total body fat from the sum of the skinfold sites measured with the caliper. The accuracy of skinfold evaluation depends on the technical skill and precise site selection by the individual making the measurements. This method is not suitable for obese persons or those whose skin tissue is very tight making it difficult to pinch a parallel skinfold between the thumb and index finger. The cost of skinfold measurement is typically much less than other methods using sophisticated equipment. The most accurate calipers employ a constant pressure of 10 g/mm$_2$ by the caliper jaws on the skinfold. The technique for measuring skinfolds is not complicated, but to become proficient you must practice measuring at different sites for all ages and both sexes.

The five steps below describe the basic procedure for measuring skinfolds.

1. Locate and mark each site according to the directions in **Figures 8.4** through **8.8**.

2. Pinch the site between the thumb and index finger, lifting the fold such that only fat tissue underneath the skin is included in the fold.

3. Take two measurements at each site unless there is a difference of more than one millimeter between the two; if there is, take a third measurement and average the closest readings.

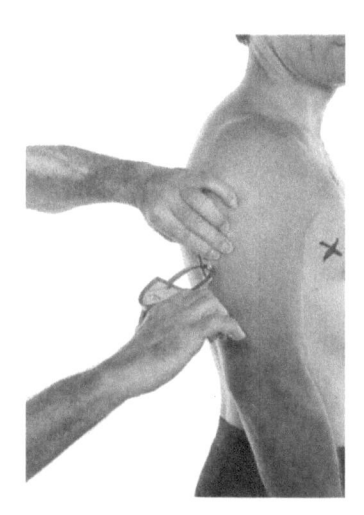

Figure 8.4 Triceps skinfold.
Take a vertical fold on the midline of the upper arm over the triceps, halfway between the tip of the shoulder and the elbow: The arm should be extended and relaxed when the measurement is taken. All skinfold measurements should be taken on the right side. From *Fitness for Wellness* by Frank D. Rosato. Copyright © 2000 by Frank D. Rosato. Reprinted with permission.

138 *Lifetime Fitness & Wellness*

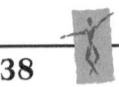

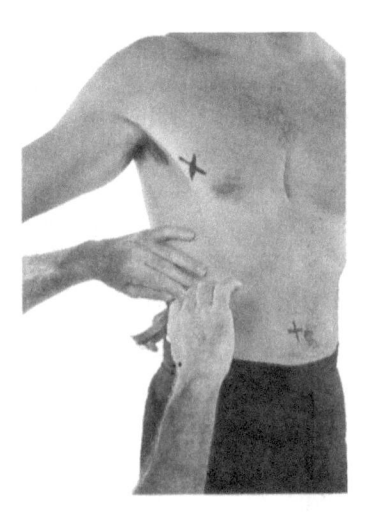

Figure 8.5 **Suprailium skinfold.**
Take a diagonal fold above the crest of the ilium directly below the armpit. From *Fitness for Wellness* by Frank D. Rosato. Copyright © 2000 by Frank D. Rosato. Reprinted with permission.

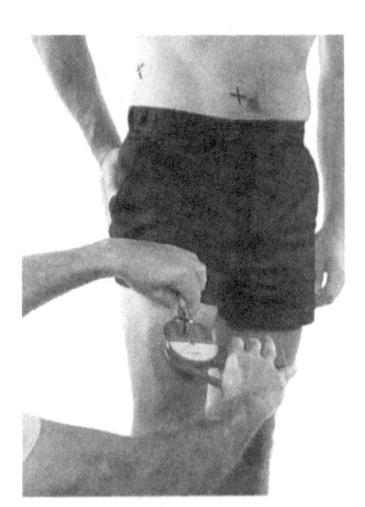

Figure 8.6 **Thigh skinfold.**
Take a vertical fold on the front of the thigh midway between the hip and the knee joint. The midpoint should be marked while the subject is seated. From *Fitness for Wellness* by Frank D. Rosato. Copyright © 2000 by Frank D. Rosato. Reprinted with permission.

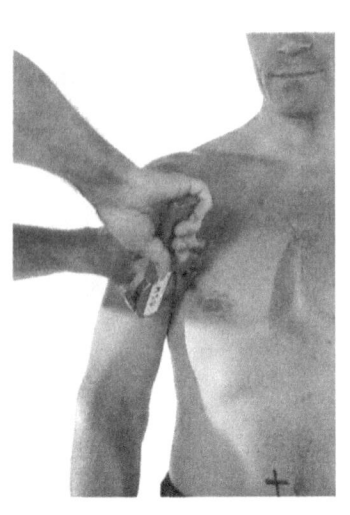

Figure 8.7 **Chest skinfold.**
Take a diagonal fold one half of the distance between the anterior axillary line and the nipple. From *Fitness for Wellness* by Frank D. Rosato. Copyright © 2000 by Frank D. Rosato. Reprinted with permission.

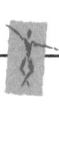

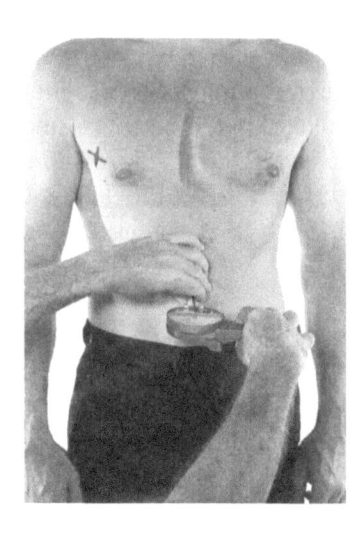

Figure 8.8 Abdominal skinfold.
Take a vertical fold about one inch above the navel. From *Fitness for Wellness* by Frank D. Rosato. Copyright © 2000 by Frank D. Rosato. Reprinted with permission.

4. Always place the caliper one quarter to one-half inch on the most parallel portion of the fold below the fingers. Be careful not to place calipers too close to the base of the fold as this will yield inaccurate readings.

5. The calipers should maintain contact with the skinfold for two to five seconds in order for the reading to stabilize.

Dual-Energy X-Ray Absorptiometry

Dual energy x-ray absorptiometry (DXA) is a high technology procedure that involves scanning the body to differentiate lean body mass, fat mass, and bone mineral content. Traditional body composition techniques are based on the two compartment model consisting of fat mass and fat free mass (i.e. hydrostatic weighing, skinfold measurement, bioelectrical impedance). DXA is based on the three compartment model of fat mass, fat free mass and total bone mineral content. DXA utilizes a total body scanner to administer low dosages of radiation to measure bone and soft tissue at the same time. The procedure takes approximately ten to twenty minutes and can illustrate precisely where fat is distributed throughout the body. It is very accurate, but employs x-ray technology and typically administered by trained operators. The equipment is very expensive and is available primarily through medical facilities.

Bioelectrical Impedance

Bioelectrical impedance is a simple, quick, noninvasive technique to analyze body composition, however the equipment is somewhat expensive. It estimates body composition by measuring the resistance of a low level, harmless, electrical current passed through the body. Bioelectrical impedance is based on the concept that different tissues conduct electrical current at different speeds. Lean tissue provides the least resistance to current flow, making it a good conductor because it contains large amounts of water. Conversely, fat tissue contains little water and produces more resistance to current flow, and is a poor electrical conductor.

Bioelectrical impedance analysis is a good predictor of body composition providing sources of error are controlled. The primary sources of error relate to the hydration status of the subject. For example, dehydration caused by body water loss due to exercise or fluid restriction will yield a lower percent body fat estimate, while hyperhydration yields a higher percent body fat estimate. Other sources of error include food intake, skin temperature, and type of equipment used. Bioelectrical impedance can be administered in less than five minutes but is not as accurate as hydrostatic weighing, DXA or air displacement. Bioelectrical impedance cannot be used by individuals with medical implants such as pacemakers and defibrillators.

Adherence to the following guidelines can reduce error:

- Comfortable room temperature
- Should not exercise within twelve hours of the test
- Should not eat or drink within four hours of the test
- Subjects should not consume alcohol within 48 hours of the test
- Diuretic medications should not be taken within seven days of the test if possible.
- Urinate within thirty minutes of taking test

Air Displacement Plethysmography

Air displacement plethysmography determines body composition by measuring body density. This technique is very accurate, quick, and easy to administer, but requires expensive equipment. Body composition is evaluated using a capsule type device known as a Bod Pod. Body volume is determined by monitoring pressure changes within the capsule when empty initially, then while a subject is seated inside the capsule. These pressure changes are extremely small and are not recognized by the subject. Elevated muscle temperature, exercise status, and hydration status can influence test accuracy. Therefore, subjects should not exercise within two hours of test administration. This technique is becoming the goal standard for body composition assessment.

Near Infrared Interactance

Near Infrared Interactance (NIR) assesses body composition by applying the principles of light absorption and reflection using a fiber optic probe with a digital analyzer. NIR is based on research that show optical densities are linearly related to total body fat. The bicep is the most commonly used single site to estimate body fat using NIR. The probe emits a low energy near infrared light beam into the biceps that is absorbed and reflected. The intensity of the re-emitted light is measured and a body fat percent computed using a prediction equation. Hydration status, skin color and the amount of pressure applied to the probe during measurement are considered potential sources of error. The concept behind NIR was developed by the US Department of Agriculture to measure the body composition of livestock and fat content of various grains. This technique has not been validated in humans and may be less accurate than skinfolds. Additional research is needed to determine the validity, accuracy, and applicability of NIR.

Body Mass Index

Body mass index (BMI) is the ratio of body weight in kilograms to height in meters squared. BMI does not evaluate the amount of body fat an individual possesses, but has been used as an indicator of obesity. A BMI of 30 or above is generally considered obese. BMI is a fair indicator of one's overweight status for individuals who do not have extensive amounts of muscle mass. High BMIs have also been linked to hypertension and elevated levels of cholesterol and triglycerides. **Lab 8.1** will help you determine your BMI.

Eating Disorders

Eating disorders are unhealthy eating patterns resulting from unrealistic perceptions about body image that have a negative impact on health. Individuals who experience these conditions require assistance from qualified health care professionals and social support to overcome their psychological problems.

Anorexia nervosa is an eating disorder characterized by a preoccupation with body weight leading to self-induced starvation. This condition usually begins with normal attempts to lose weight through dieting that is prolonged and becomes excessive. Anorexics believe themselves to be too fat despite the excessive weight loss and an emaciated appearance. The warning signs for anorexia nervosa are:

- Significant weight loss
- Cessation of menstrual cycle in females
- Frequent comments about body weight
- Refusal to eat to gain weight
- Wearing baggy clothes to disguise thin appearance
- Guilt feeling about eating
- Prefers to eat alone
- Engages in excessive, vigorous exercise
- Excessive concern about body weight and size despite previous weight loss

Bulimia nervosa is an eating disorder characterized by the consumption of large amounts of food, followed by intentional emptying of the stomach by self-induced vomiting or performing excessive exercise, ingesting laxatives or diuretics to avoid gaining weight after binge eating.

This causes damage to the lining of the stomach and esophagus over time, erodes tooth enamel, and causes electrolyte imbalances. The warning signs for bulimia nervosa are:

- Frequent gains and losses in body weight
- Irregular menstrual cycle
- Secretly binge eating, then purging
- Severe loneliness and depression
- Eating when depressed

≈ Excessive concern about body weight

≈ Visits to the bathroom after eating

≈ Compulsive dieting after binge eating episodes

Binge eating disorder is characterized by a lack of self-control, leading to the consumption of extraordinarily large amounts of food without purging behavior. Individuals with binge eating disorder experience depression and guilt as well as severe psychological distress during bingeing episodes.

Strategies for Successful Weight Control

Exercise

Regular exercise is the most effective strategy for losing body fat and achieving and maintaining ideal body weight. Exercise increases the metabolic rate and energy expenditure significantly to help achieve negative caloric balance and promote weight loss. Your metabolic rate indicates how fast your body uses energy or burn calories. The **resting metabolic rate** (RMR) represents the energy needed to sustain life under resting conditions and accounts for approximately 60 to 70 percent of one's daily energy requirement. A person's daily energy requirement is influenced by RMR, the thermic effect of food, and the thermic effect of exercise. The thermic effect of food is the energy needed to metabolize food and typically accounts for approximately 30 percent of your daily energy (caloric) requirement. The thermic effect exercise represents the energy utilized during physical activity. This may account for 30 percent or more of the daily energy (caloric) requirement.

Regular exercise maximizes fat loss and minimizes loss of fat-free mass. Body weight reduction on a weight loss program consisting of appropriate dietary changes only will result in approximately 70 to 80 percent of fat tissue loss, while a program of exercise and appropriate dietary changes will result in about 95 percent fat tissue loss. Obese adults should try reduce their current body weight by 5 to 10 percent over a six to seven month time period to significantly decrease one's risk for coronary heart disease. The American College of Sports Medicine recommends a weight loss of no more than 2.0 pounds per week. This should be accomplished by increasing energy expenditure through exercise and reducing caloric intake by approximately 500 calories per day. Cardiorespiratory endurance activities and resistance training are both crucial to increasing energy expenditure. Exercise allows your body to burn fat more efficiently. Regular exercise permits your body to mobilize fats easier and to use fat as fuel during low to moderate physical activity levels. Regular physical activity also decreases appetite to assist in achieving negative caloric balance.

Meal Planning

Advance meal planning allows you to make better food selection choices and to cognitively track your dietary habits. You should consume 5 to 7 small meals every 2 to 3 hours each day. Consuming smaller, more frequent meals each day encourages healthier food selections. Substituting reduced calorie and/or low-fat foods for high calorie/high fat foods can have a huge impact on weight loss. Replacing snacks such as potato chips, cookies and other high sugar foods with fresh fruit increases nutritional content and reduces caloric intake. Include appropriate amounts of protein and complex carbohydrates as well. Avoiding the purchase of high fat/high calorie foods is extremely helpful in achieving weight loss/weight maintenance goals. Make your snacks between meals healthy food selections.

Make a Commitment and Stick to It

Successful weight loss does not occur by accident. Consistent practice of weight loss strategies is critical. Setbacks will occur and are to be expected; however, continue to work your plan. There are no quick-fix solutions to overcoming obesity/overweight. A long term commitment is required for lifelong weight loss and weight maintenance success.

Reward Yourself

Acknowledge the success made, no matter how small or large. This builds confidence and self-esteem and enhances motivation. It is important to recognize outcome-based goals and behavioral goals. At some point the outcome-based goal of weight loss will plateau and recognition of success in attaining behavioral goals will keep you motivated and committed to your program.

Develop a Support System

Surround yourself with positive people who will assist you in reaching your goals. These individuals will help you create environments that enhance your self-esteem and motivate you to adhere to your program.

Summary

Important concepts that you have learned in this chapter include the following:

- The human body is made up of lean tissue and fat tissue.
- Obesity is a condition of excessive body fat that places a person at risk of diseases such as hypertension, diabetes, heart disease, cancer, and other health problems.
- Negative energy balance results in weight loss and positive energy balance results in weight gain.
- Daily energy expenditure is influenced by the thermic effect of food, the thermic effect of exercise, and the resting metabolic rate.
- The android body fat distribution pattern is characterized by fat stores in the abdominal area, while the gynoid pattern is characterized by fat stores in hips and thighs.
- Common body composition assessments include hydrostatic weighing, skinfold measurement, bioelectrical impedance, dual X-ray absorptionmetry, air displacement, near infrared interactance, and body mass index.
- Exercise is critical to the success of any weight-loss program.

References

National Heart, Lung, and Blood Institute. (1998). *Clinical guidelines on the identification, evaluation, and treatment of overweight and obesity in adults: The evident report.* Bethesda, MD: National Institutes of Health and Human Services, Public Health Services.

McArdle, W., Katch, F., and Katch, V. (2010). *Essentials of exercise physiology.* 4th ed., Baltimore. Lippincott, Williams & Wilkins.

Ehrman, J. (2010). *ACSM's Resource manual for guidelines for exercise testing and prescription.* 6th ed. Baltimore: Williams & Wilkins.

Rosato, F. (2000). *Fitness for wellness.* Kendall-Hunt. Dubuque, IA.

Internet Sources

http://www.new-fitness.com

http://www.shapeup.org

http://www.weightloss.about.com

http://www.nhbli.nih.gov

Lab 8.1
Calculating Body Mass Index

Name: _____   Date: _____

Purpose: To determine body mass index (BMI) as a means of examining overweight and obesity.

Equipment: Calculator

Instruction:
1. Weigh yourself to determine body weight in pounds.
2. Divide your weight in pounds by 2.2 to determine kilograms.
3. Measure your height in inches.
4. Multiply your height in inches by 2.54, and divide by 100 to convert your height to meters.
5. Multiply your height in meters by your height in meters to get your height in meters squared.
6. Divide your weight in kilograms by your height in meters squared to determine your BMI.

Worksheet for Calculating BMI

1. _____ ÷ 2.2 = _____
   Weight (lbs)   Weight (kgs)

2. _____ × 2.54 ÷ 100 = _____
   Height (in)   Height (m)

3. _____ × _____ = _____
   Height (m)   Height (m)   Height (m)^2

4. _____ ÷ _____ = _____
   Weight (kg)   Height (m)^2 Body Mass Index

   Less than 18.5   Underweight
   18.5–24.9   Normal weight
   25.0–29.9   Overweight
   30.0–39.9   Obese
   40.0 or greater   Extreme obesity

   Add Your Category: _____

Lab 8.2
Body Composition Program

Name: _____   Date: _____

Purpose: To develop a personalized body composition program

Instructions: Develop a program to enhance your body composition

Step 1: Record data from **Lab 8.1**

> Body Weight _____ pounds

> Body Mass Index _____   BMI Classification _____

Step 2: Establish long term and short term goals.

Long Term Goal

> 1.

Short Term Goals—List two short term goals that will assist you in achieving your long term goal

> 1.

> 2.

Step 3: Develop strategies to achieve goals.

> 1. List four dietary changes you can implement to improve your nutritional status and body composition.

>> a. _____

>> b. _____

>> c. _____

>> d. _____

Lab 8.2—Cont'd
Body Composition Program

Name: _____ Date: _____

2. List three specific fitness practices you can implement to improve your body composition.

    a. _____

    b. _____

    c. _____

3. List two behaviors you associate with food (i.e. watching television) that sabotage your body composition program then state how you will change each behavior.

    a. Behavior I will change: _____

    Action I will take to change my behavior: _____

    _____

    b. Behavior I will change: _____

    Action I will take to change my behavior: _____

    _____

Chapter 9

Understanding Emotional Wellness

Objectives
The Mind-Body Connection
Emotional Wellness Defined
Internal Influences Affecting Emotional Wellness
External Factors Affecting Emotional Wellness
Mental Health Continuum
Stress

Stress Management Techniques
Suicide as a Consequence
Coping Strategies
Summary
References
Internet Sources
Lab 9.1: Stress Vulnerability Questionnaire

Objectives

Upon completion of this chapter, you will be able to:
1. Define emotional wellness.
2. List the signs or characteristics of emotional wellness.
3. Understand and describe the mental health continuum.
4. Describe anxiety, burnout, fear, phobia, and dysthymia.
5. Define and describe some mental disorders.
6. Describe what causes suicide and some preventive measures for mitigating suicide.
7. Explain how the nervous and endocrine systems contribute to emotional well-being.
8. Describe internal and external influences on emotional wellness.
9. Describe stress, stressors, eustress, distress.
10. Understand and describe how to manage stress.
11. Describe the effects of stress on the body.

The Mind-Body Connection

Research has shown that our bodies respond to the manner in which we feel, think, and behave. This phenomenon is referred to as the mind-body connection. Unfortunate life events can adversely impact one's emotional health. When we do not cope effectively these events physical ailments can occur, such as headaches, undue fatigue, insomnia, chest pain, hypertension and many others. Research has also illustrated a strong correlation between exercise and higher mental functioning. Neurogenesis, the study of new cell development, has revealed some insight into why this high correlation exists. Studies show that new brain cells develop as a consequence of the increase in micro blood vessels in the brain due to exercise. Other studies have reported the formation of new neurons (nerve cells) in areas of the brain involved with cognition. Therefore, it is essential that every person understand his/her own physiological and psychological composition, set goals, and strive to attain established goals with a high degree of self-esteem. Individuals who set goals tend to think more highly of themselves and have higher levels of expectation and self-esteem. The term self-esteem refers to the overall evaluation of oneself, whether one likes or dislikes who one is, doubts or believes in oneself, and values or belittles one's worth. How you value yourself is crucial to your psychological well-being. High self-esteem, a feeling of self-worth, is closely associated with the decisions you make in the selection of peers, partners, and group affiliations such as fraternities, sororities, and clubs. Techniques to build one's self-esteem include: selecting tasks that can be easily accomplished, practicing completing tasks, and then attempting tasks that are more challenging. Other techniques include concentration on the positive aspects of one's life, associating with peers who think and act positively, and building on small successes one experiences.

Mental health and physical health are intricately connected and are important to overall health status. Mental health is defined as the successful performance of mental function, resulting in productive activities, fulfilling relationships with other people, and the ability to change and cope with adversity. Physical health is a state of well-being that permits the execution of daily tasks and activities.

Characteristics of Emotionally Well Individuals

Emotional wellness is the ability to conduct daily tasks and activities in the midst of accompanying stress, and be attentive to one's own feeling, thoughts and behaviors. Emotionally well individuals are those who exhibit adequate levels of psychological stability, positive personality traits, and have high levels of self-esteem. They view themselves as worthy individuals. The self-concept of these individuals is also positive. Emotionally individuals view themselves as "better than okay" and are able to achieve the goals that they set for themselves.

Another characteristic of emotionally well individuals is that they display an internal locus of control. Their actions are governed according to their own valve system and how they feel within themselves, and not by the authority figures or influence of other people. Emotionally well individuals are able to give others attention when needed, yet set aside some quiet time for themselves. Emotionally well individuals "know" themselves; they set realistic goals that meet their needs, are able to be flexible to modify goals when necessary, and feel they are ultimately capable of attaining their goals. Emotionally well individuals exhibit mindfulness in that they completely aware of positive and negative happenings in their surroundings. Yet they possess a profound appreciation for the world in which they live. They have an optimistic approach to life despite occasional frustrations and setbacks.

Internal Influences Affecting Emotional Wellness

Internal influences associated with a person's psychological wellness include genetic, chemical (or hormonal), electrical (or neurological), and nutritional.

Genetic Influences

Modern techniques in gene cloning, splicing, and sequencing have netted dividends that reveal explicit genetic codes associated with specific health patterns. Discoveries have shown that specific genes are responsible for conditions such as Alzheimer's disease and diabetes. Psychological disorders such as depression, anxiety disorders, and other health conditions are under investigation by biotechnology companies and scientific research entities. While controversy rages over personal and civil rights associated with gene discovery, it is simply a matter of time before many of these discoveries will be realized in the public domain. Increased discovery of individual genetic composition has and will continue to provide gene maps for the identification and targeting of psychological conditions and factors that influence fitness and wellness.

Chemical Influences

Chemicals (hormones) also impact your emotional wellness. Hormones are chemicals that transfer information and instructions between cells. Hormones are slow-acting agents and have a long-term effect on a body's systems and functions. Hormones are generated by the various organs in your body and are designed to regulate the body's functions. Hormones regulate mood swings, fear, fight or flight, and several protective emotions. They serve to balance the body's functions when other systems break down and buffers are needed. Many chemicals are used to regulate bodily functions. Adrenocorticotropic hormone, growth hormone, cortisol, as well as a host of other internal influences affect the psychological and physiological functions of your body. These influences ultimately influence the sociological aspects of your life.

Neurological Influences

As hormones or chemicals affect the internal emotional aspects of your life, electrical or neurological stimuli also affect your internal psychological disposition. The nervous system is responsible for generating electrical impulses that stimulate cells in your body to transmit information.

The central nervous system is composed of the brain and the spinal cord. The peripheral nervous system extends to the remaining parts of the body. Nerve cells emanating from the central and peripheral nervous systems act to regulate daily body functions, such as eating, breathing, and sleeping. Damage to this system may affect your self-esteem and your moods. Moreover, damage to this system could cause personality changes and other psychological problems if corrections are not made.

External Factors Affecting Emotional Wellness

External factors that have an effect on emotional wellness are environmental, social, and spiritual conditions.

Environmental Factors

Your environment plays a significant role in your mental well-being. While factors that might appear as negative influences may not cause severe mental disorders, they do create stress and imbalances in the body's systems, resulting in minor mental distractions. In some cases, these conditions may evolve into major mental health conditions. Low self-esteem resulting from the inability to purchase appropriate clothing for school and lack of funds to seek routine medical assistance occurs in families who lack sufficient financial resources. It is appropriate to realize that there are that things you can and cannot control, and to make wise choices relative to things you can control.

Social Factors

Social factors, such as your peer relationships, clubs, sororities, fraternities, and interpersonal relationships, play a significant role in your well-being. College students who join a team, club, sorority or fraternity, or other university organizations tend to complete college at higher rates than those who do not. Social connections have powerful effects on emotional and physical health because they influence our physiology.

Spiritual Factors

Research findings have found that religious faith and spirituality are associated with several positive and mental health indices. Research findings also indicate that religious faith and spirituality can help individuals recover from substance abuse, influence the occurrence of acute and chronic episodes of depression, develop greater resilience to stress and anxiety, and achieve greater overall satisfaction with life.

Mental Health Continuum

It is important to recognize that emotional wellness can be viewed as a point on a mental health continuum (see **Figure 9.1**). Mental illness is not the polar opposite of mental health, but is also a point on the continuum. Where we are on this continuum can change from minute to minute, or day to day. However, it is likely to remain in one generalized location unless a catastrophic event occurs or a concerted effort is undertaken to alter an individual's pattern of thinking.

Too much stress may lead to anxiety. **Anxiety** is a state of uneasiness caused by a reaction to vague or imagined dangers. Many college students have been found to suffer test anxiety, especially in the areas of math and science. These academic anxieties are often experienced in areas where the student is weak academically. Depending upon the level of anxiety, an individual may be rendered unable to respond to test questions that under other circumstances would be answered with ease. When anxiety becomes severe, serious conditions may develop such as Post Traumatic Stress Disorder, and Generalized Anxiety Disorder. **Post Traumatic Stress Disorder (PTSD)** is an anxiety disorder resulting from exposure to terror in which one is physically harmed or grave physical harm was threatened. Examples of individuals who experience PTSD include military troops who served in war, rescue workers and survivors of the 911 New York City terrorist attacks, survivors of Hurricane Katrina, the Virginia Tech shootings, physical and sexual abuse, and other crimes. PTSD can occur in individuals of any age, including children and adolescents. Many individuals with PTSD repeatedly re-experience the ordeal in the form of flashbacks, memories, nightmares, or frightening thoughts, especially when they are exposed to events or objects reminiscent of the trauma. Victims of PTSD also experience emotional numbness, sleep disturbances, depression, irritability, or outbursts of anger. Physical symptoms include headaches, gastrointestinal distress, immune system problems, dizziness, and chest pain. **Generalized Anxiety Disorder** (GAD) is an illness characterized by constant worry, headaches, tension, difficulty keeping your mind on one thing, hot flashes, and a tendency to feel nauseated. Treatment usually involves therapy and medication.

Another reaction to excess stress is burnout. **Burnout** is an increasingly intense pattern of psychological, physiological and behavioral dysfunction in response to a continuous flow of stressors or chronic stress. Burnout often occurs to individuals who have remained in their careers for many years or to those who perform the same task day after day. A lack of excitement and boredom characterize burnout.

Fear is another feeling that may lead to potential emotional problems. **Fear** is an emotional reaction to a real or threatened danger. While you may feel anxious about an upcoming exam, another individual may experience the stronger emotion of fear if an exam or course is failed and requires an explanation to parents. A low grade point average (G.P.A.) may bring on fear in others in anticipation of probation or suspension. Fear that becomes extreme may manifest into panic disorders. **Panic disorders** are characterized by sudden burst of fear for no apparent reason.

When fear is specific, it is considered a phobia. **Phobias** are inexplicable and illogical fears of a particular object or class of objects. Many phobias have been given special terms. For instance, fear of heights is acrophobia; fear of open spaces is agoraphobia. Agoraphobia occurs when an individual is anxious about or avoids "places or situations from which escape might be difficult or in which help may not be available in the event of having a panic attack or panic-like symptoms." Social phobia is a fear of becoming embarrassed in front of others.

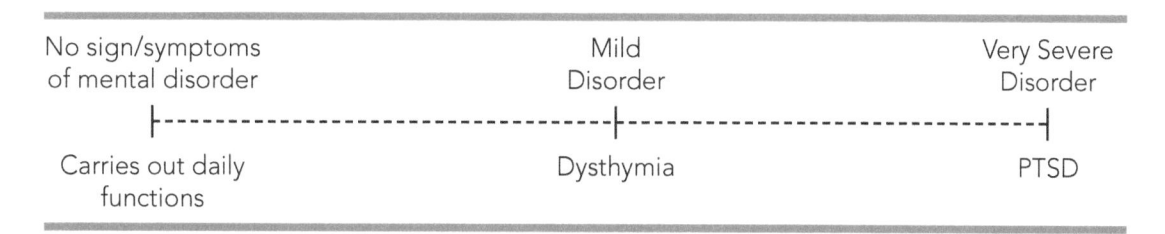

No sign/symptoms of mental disorder	Mild Disorder	Very Severe Disorder
Carries out daily functions	Dysthymia	PTSD

Figure 9.1 Mental health continuum.

This fear may interfere with a person's daily activity. The person tends to avoid speeches and other public gatherings. Phobias require professional care.

Mental depression, often referred to as depression, is another condition that debilitates the normal functioning of an individual. **Mental depression** is a lowering of one's spirit or vitality. Symptoms of mental depression include persistent sadness or despair, hopelessness, social withdrawal, inactivity, difficulty in thinking and concentrating, and deflated self-worth. Depression becomes a mental health problem when the "signs and symptoms are of sufficient intensity or duration that they meet the criteria for any mental disorder." Many college students experience acute (occasional) depression. Three of the most common depressive disorders are major (clinical) depression, dysthymia, bipolar disorder.

Major depression is a disease characterized by a group of signs and symptoms lasting a minimum of two consecutive weeks that interfere with the ability to work, sleep, and eat, and loss of interest in activities that were once interesting. Examples of symptoms include loss of appetite with a loss of body weight, or overeating with weight gain, low self-esteem, fatigue, physical problems (aches, pain), social withdrawal, feeling of hopelessness or worthlessness, guilt, rage, sleeping problems (insomnia or oversleeping), suicide thoughts or attempts. Crippling episodes of depression can occur more than once in a lifetime.

Dysthymia is a mild form of depression that is characterized by a change in eating and sleeping habits combined with the inability to concentrate, and sadness that extends at least two years or more. Many experience dysthymia, but may not recognize it, when events occur that significantly affect or alter our lifestyles. It involves chronic symptoms that do not have crippling effects, but do prevent one from functioning at an optimal level or feeling well. The events may be worldwide, national, local, or personal. Personal events that may lead to dysthymia include, but are not limited to, an unexpected death of a friend or loved one, marriage, infidelity, divorce, or relocating where you don't know anyone. Although the length of time characterizing dysthymia is at least two years, it is individual, and depends upon our unique physiological, psychological, sociological, and spiritual composition.

Bipolar disorder has been commonly referred to as manic depression. Bipolar disorder is characterized by extreme mood swings that cause an individual to experience euphoric (manic) episodes as well as severe depression. These mood swings may be rapid, but are most often gradual. Bipolar disorders include a group of mood disorders that are often chronic and recurring. When in a depressive episode the person may experience any or all of the signs and symptoms of depression. When in a manic episode a person may experience increased energy, racing thoughts, talk very fast, feel excessively high, be restless, require little sleep, exhibit intrusive or aggressive behavior, have poor judgment, increased sexual drive, and possess an unrealistic belief in one's abilities and power. This condition can be successfully treated by use of psychotherapy and medications prescribed by a psychiatrist.

Stress

Some individuals who handle daily tasks and activities while displaying little or no stress, while others find daily tasks and activities more challenging. These individuals experience higher levels of stress. It is interesting to note that responses to stress are specific to each individual, and depend upon each individual's physiological and psychological composition. **Stress** is a psychological/physiological condition caused by chemical, physical, and/or emotional factors which results in the alteration of mind and body functions. Excess stress is a common result of ill health. Any factor that places greater than normal pressure on your daily life is a stressor. **Table 9.1** lists several examples of common stressors. Stress

Table 9.1 Common Sources of Stressors

Environmental	Interpersonal
Noise	Poor time management skills
Heat/cold extremes	The way we interact with others and they with us
Odors, smoke, smog, pollution	Daily activity patterns
Drugs	Social acceptance
Exposure to pathogens	Lack of control
Overcrowding	Low self-esteem
Poor living conditions	Low self-efficacy
Lack of safe, working and living conditions	Improper diet, exercise and sleep patterns
Other people, places we go	Poor communication skills
Specific events	Inability to relax

Social	Biological/Heredity
Lack of control	Temperament
Unemployment	Injuries related to aging and illness
Isolation from others	Our own health conditions
Discrimination	

Cultural	Other Stressors
Racism	Financial matters
Sexism	Use of mind-altering drugs
Ageism	Expectations of friends and others
	Dysfunctional family and social ties
	Dating

Donatelle, R. et al., (1999); Corbin, C.B. et al., (2006); Dennis, K. et al., (2005).

may be considered positive or negative. **Eustress** is stress that inspires or stimulates us in a positive manner and is considered good stress. We might be stimulated to study harder to improve grades so that we may earn a scholarship. **Distress** is stress that inhibits or depresses in a negative fashion and is considered bad stress. This type of stress can prevent some individuals from performing well or being productive. It may also result in physical or mental illness.

The Cause of Stress

The **General Adaptation Syndrome** (GAS) developed by Hans Selye is the most well-known theory regarding the causes of stress. According to Selye the body seeks to maintain a homeostatic state or consistent internal physiological balance. Selye believed the GAS responses involved the nervous and hormonal (endocrine) systems. The GAS consists of three stages which describe how the body responds physiologically to stressors.

1. Alarm Stage
   The Alarm stage describes the body's immediate reaction to stressors as they are initially recognized. During this stage hormones such as adrenaline and cortisol are produced. The body exhibits the fight-or-flight response which functions to prepare the body for physical activity. Acute stress responses such as increased heart rate, respiration rate, and blood pressure occur to prepare the body for physical activity.

2. Resistance Stage
   If stress persists the body attempts to adapt to stress by trying to return to a homeostatic state as a means to cope. If the body is unable to effectively adapt its resources are gradually depleted.

3. Exhaustion Stage
   In this stage the body has now been chronically exposed to stress. As a result the body's immune system weakens and the individual succumbs to the negative physiological and psychological effects of stress such as hypertension, heart attack, headaches, ulcers, infections, depression, anxiety disorders, poor self-esteem, and other adverse conditions.

The Effects of Stress

Many people underestimate the effects of stress which can be acute or chronic. Acute stress exists in succinct episodes, lasting for relatively short time periods and occurs for specific reasons. Acute stress can cause pain in the back and other locations in the body, nausea, irritability, hyperventilation, perspiration, and a host of other responses. Chronic stress lasts for long time periods and may appear never-ending. Chronic stress can have a significant negative impact on immune system, cardiovascular system, and brain function. The effects of stress can impact the entire body if effective coping strategies are not implemented. **Table 9.2** contains various effects of stress.

Stress Management Techniques

Stress management techniques vary according to the level and types of stressors that a person encounters on a daily basis. However, people can take some basic steps to relieve stress. The following ways to relieve stress are recommended by David B. Posen, M.D. (1995).

1. Decrease or discontinue caffeine use. Caffeine generates a strong stress reaction in the body. Caffeine is found is chocolate, many soft drinks, coffee, and tea.

2. Exercise regularly. Exercise relieves pressure and relaxes the body by utilizing excess energy.

3. Practice relaxation and meditation techniques. These help to relieve stress by the following physiological effects: they slow the heart rate, lower pressure, and slow breathing.

4. Get the proper amount of sleep. Adults need approximately five to seven hours of sleep per night. After a night's sleep, people feel rested and the body responds to work commands better.

5. Take time out and enjoy leisure activities. Changing from rigorous study to watching an athletic contest can be relaxing and lowers your stress level. Too much stress decreases performance.

6. Set realistic expectations. Life will feel more manageable.

7. Use reframing as a technique for relieving stress. Reframing means to change the way you look at things in order to feel better about them.

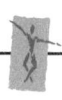

Table 9.2 The Effects of Stress

Cardiorespiratory	Nervous System
Increased heart rate	Muscle twitches and spasms
Increased respiratory rate	Insomnia
Increased blood pressure	Agitation
Hypertension	Hormonal imbalances leading to depression
Increased risk of atherosclerosis	
Hyperventilation	
Asthma	
Chest Pain	

Skin Conditions	Gastrointestinal
Rashes	Colitis
Dry skin	Diarrhea or constipation
Itching	Ulcers
Hives	Increased gastric juices, bad breath, indigestion
Acne	Stomach aches
Dermatitis	
Clammy skin	

Immunological	Psychological
Common cold	Anger
Allergies	Depression
Increased risk of infection and cancer	Frustration

Other Effects

Blurry vision
Excessive sweating
Fatigue
Vaginal discharges
Delayed menstruation
Impotence
Migraine headaches

From *Becoming Aware*, 8th Edition, by Velma Walker and Lynn Brokaw. Copyright © 2001 by Kendall Hunt Publishing Company. Reprinted by permission.

8. Belief systems cause some stress. "Men shouldn't cry" and "You can't fight city hall" are common statements that we grow up to accept. Belief systems cause stress by creating a behavior pattern.

9. Develop a ventilation/support system. Sharing problems or good news with others relieves some of the burden and can make an individual feel good about accomplishments he/she achieves.

10. Use humor as a stress reducer. Laughter relieves tension.

11. Proper nutrition. Consume a well-balanced diet to boost the body's immune system and provide increased energy levels.

12. Use strategies that improve time-management skills so that you can both work and play. Always plan ahead and don't procrastinate.

Suicide as a Consequence

Suicide is the termination of one's own life. Suicide is the most serious consequence that may occur as a result of an individual experiencing a treatable mental illness such as a major depressive disorder. Suicides occur in all ethnic populations, socioeconomic classes, and age groups. More men complete suicide compared to women, however women are more likely to attempt suicide than men. Men tend to used violent means such as guns and hanging, whereas women tend to use non-violent means (i.e. pill overdose). Many suicides are preventable and most suicidal individuals want to live, but are unable to recognize that are alternatives to their problems. Many people contemplating suicide exhibit some warning sign of their intentions to a family member or friend. The most effective way to prevent suicide is recognizing when someone is at risk, taking warning signs seriously, and responding appropriately. Talking about suicide does not cause someone to become suicidal.

Suicide Warning Signs

1. A sudden drop in academic performance in school or productivity at work.
2. A fixation with death or violence. A person exhibiting the following behaviors should be considered at immediate high risk for suicide: talking or writing about suicide, an announce that he/she has a plan to kill themselves, giving away prized possessions, neglecting personal appearance, making comments such as: I wish I were dead. You'll be better off without me. What's the point of living?
3. Depression. Depression increases a person's risk of suicide.
4. Unhealthy peer relationships. Individuals who do not have friends, suddenly reject friends, or persons involved in abuse relationships are at greater suicidal risk.
5. Securing weapons, drugs, or any item that could be used to hurt oneself.
6. Engaging in reckless or risky activities.
7. Feeling helpless, anxious, agitated, hopeless (as if no alternatives are available).
8. Experiencing dramatic mood changes.

If you think someone is suicidal:

1. Take it seriously and take action.
2. Be willing to listen, ask the person what is troubling them and be persistence if the individual is reluctant to talk. Ask them if they are considering suicide. Don't argue with the person, let them know you care, understand, that they are not alone, and that they can be helped.
3. Seek professional help. Actively encourage the person to see a physician or mental health professional immediately. Persons contemplating suicide often believe they cannot be helped, therefore you must be aggressive in your attempts to get them help.

If an Acute Crisis Exists

1. Take the person to a hospital emergency room or psychiatric care facility.

2. Do not leave the person alone until professional help is available.

3. Remove any firearms, drugs, sharp objects or other items that may be used in a suicide attempt.

4. If none of the above options are available, call 911 or the National Suicide Prevention Lifeline.

Coping Strategies

As individuals are unique in their psychological composition, so are they unique in their resiliency to illnesses, disease, or adverse conditions. While some individuals succumb more quickly or easily to illness, disease, or depression, others are able to ward off these conditions. As far as an individual's psychological functioning is concerned, self-esteem and self-concept play an enormous role. Understanding the signs and symptoms of mental/psychological disorders will significantly enhance your chances of recognizing, reporting, and obtaining medical assistance at an early stage in the progression of these conditions. Once the condition is recognized, medical attention should be sought. Mild forms of stress can be managed by some individuals through exercise, reduction or elimination of caffeine, appropriate expression of one's feelings, develop residence, relax your body and mind (via meditation, yoga, tai chi, etc.), take care of yourself, live a balanced life, and removing yourself from stressful settings when appropriate. Strategies for improving the mental health of the nation include avoiding disabling outcomes of the major mental disorders, intervening early in their course, and prevention.

Summary

Important concepts that you have learned in this chapter include:

- Emotional wellness is the ability to function normally by performing daily activities and tasks with their accompanying stressors.
- Individuals who are emotionally healthy reflect this in their behavior patterns.
- An individual's mental health status is on a continuum and may fluctuate from time to time.
- Anxiety is a state of uneasiness as result of vague or imagined dangers.
- Burnout is a dysfunction resulting from too much continuous stress.
- Fear is an emotional reaction to a real or threatened danger.
- Phobias are unexplained fears of a specific object or class of objects.
- Mental depression results in a lowering of an individual's spirit or vitality.
- Dysfunction is reflected by behavioral changes in eating and sleeping habits as well as an inability to concentrate and sadness.
- A number of mental disorders affect individuals in the United States.
- Bipolar disorder results in extreme mood swings.
- Hormones in your body impact your emotional state as well as regulate emotional responses to various situations.
- The nervous system affects the body in ways that also impact psychological and sociological behavior.
- Nutrition plays a major role in the development of and maintenance of the nervous system.
- External forces such as environment, social factors, and spiritual support affect psychological well-being.
- Environmental factors such as socioeconomic level allows for the basic needs of maintenance to be or not to be provided.
- Social relationships can provide support for an individual's wellness.
- Various aspects of religious practice, affiliation, and belief can benefit your mental health.
- An individual's psychological composition is a major factor in resiliency to illness, disease, or mental disorders.
- Prevention, early treatment, and avoiding disabling outcomes are strategies used to successfully reduce mental disorders.
- Stress is a psychological/physiological condition caused by chemical, physical, and/or emotional factors that result in an alteration of mind and body function.
- Stress that inspires or stimulates is known as eustress and stress that inhibits or depresses is known as distress.
- Stress management techniques aid in reducing stress.

References

American Psychiatric Association (1994). *Diagnostic and statistical manual of mental disorders,* 4th ed. Washington, DC: American Psychiatric Association.

Beautrais. A.L. (1998). Psychiatric contacts among youths aged 13 through 24 years who have made serious suicide attempts. *Journal of the America Academy of Child and Adolescent Psychiatry.* May.

Department of Health and Human Services (2000). Healthy People 2000 Final Review, Priority 6: Mental Health and Mental Disorders, Washington, DC: Public Health Service.

Department of Health and Human Services (2000). Healthy People 2010, 2nd ed. With understanding and improving health and objectives for improving health. 2 vols. Washington, DC: US. Government Printing Office.

Department of Health and Human Services (1990). Health People 2000: National health promotion and disease prevention objectives. Washington DC: Public Health Service.

Department of Health and Human Services (1999). Mental Health: A report of the Surgeon General. Rockville, Maryland: Department of Health and Human Services, Substance Abuse and Mental Health Services Administration, Center for Mental Health Services, National Institutes of Mental Health.

Department of Health and Human Services (2000). Tracking healthy people 2010. Washington, DC: U.S. Government Printing Office.

Ellison, C.G. (1991). Religions Involvement and Subjective Well-Being. *Journal of Health and Social Behavior,* 32, 80–99.

Koenig, H.G., Smiley, M., & Gonzales, J.A.P. (1988). *Religion, Health, and Aging.* New York: Greenwood Press.

Levin, J.S. (1994). Religion and Health: Is There an Association, Is It Valid, and Is It Casual? *Social Science and Medicine,* 38, 1475–1485.

Lieberman, A.F., Weston, D.R., & Pawl, J.H. (1991). Preventive Intervention and Outcome with Anxiously Attached Dyads. *Child Development,* 62, pp 199–209.

Miller, D.B. & Macintosh, R. (1999). Promoting resilience in urban African-American adolescents: Racial socialization and identity as protective factors. *Social Work Research,* 23, 159–161.

Munoz, R.F., Ying, Y.W., Bernal, G., Perez-Stable, E.J., Sorensen, J.L., Hargreaves, W.A., Miranda, J., Miller, L.S. (1995). Prevention of depression with primary care patients: A randomized controlled trial. *American Journal of Community Psychology,* 23, 199–222.

Neurovista, American Academy of Neurology and AAN Education & Research Foundation.

Nervous System (2001). Microsoft Encarta Online Encyclopedia.

Internet Sources

http://findarticles.com

http://www.csuchio.edu/psy/BioPsych/dopamine.html

http://www.mentalhealth.org/cmhs/surgeongeneral

http://www.surgeongeneral.gov

http://www.nimh.nih.gov/anxiety/realilliness.cmf

http://www.aaa.com/neurovista/octnov2000/article387.html

http://encarta.msn.com

http://www.afsp.org/index.cfm

http://www.sprc.org

http://www.fda.gov

http://www.healthline.com

http://www.healthatoz.com

http://www.Holistic-online.com

http://www.medicinenet.com

http://www.health.discovery.com

Lab 9.1
Health And Fitness Activity
The General Well-Being Scale

Name: _____ Date: _____

One measure of psychological status that has been used with good success in national surveys is the General Well-Being Scale (GWB). The GWB was designed by the National Center for Health Statistics, and consists of 18 questions covering such matters as energy level, satisfaction, freedom from worry, and self-control. A high score on the GWB reflects an absence of bad feelings and an expression of positive feelings. Results from national surveys have shown that higher scores for the GWB are significantly associated with increased amounts of physical activity for all age groups and for both men and women. (See: Stephens T. Physical Activity and Mental Health in the United States and Canada: Evidence from Four Population Surveys, Prev Med 17:35–47, 1988.)

The General Well-Being Scale

Instructions: The following questions ask how you feel and how things have been going for you during the *past month*. For each question, mark an "x" for the answer that most nearly applies to you. Since there are no right or wrong answers, it's best to answer each question quickly without pausing too long on any one of them.

1. How have you been feeling in general?
   - 5 ❏ In excellent spirits.
   - 4 ❏ In very good spirits.
   - 3 ❏ In good spirits mostly
   - 2 ❏ I've been up and down in spirits a lot.
   - 1 ❏ In low spirits mostly.
   - 0 ❏ In very low spirits.

2. Have you been bothered by nervousness or your "nerves"?
   - 0 ❏ Extremely so—to the point where I could not work or take care of things.
   - 1 ❏ Very much so.
   - 2 ❏ Quite a bit.
   - 3 ❏ Some—enough to bother me.
   - 4 ❏ A little.
   - 5 ❏ Not at all.

3. Have you been in firm control of your behavior, thoughts, emotions, or feelings?
   - 5 ❏ Yes, definitely so.
   - 4 ❏ Yes, for the most part.
   - 3 ❏ Generally so.
   - 2 ❏ Not too well.
   - 1 ❏ No, and I am somewhat disturbed.
   - 0 ❏ No, and I am very disturbed.

Lab 9.1—Cont'd
Health And Fitness Activity

Name: _____ Date: _____

4. Have you felt so sad, discouraged, or hopeless, or had so many problems that you wondered if anything was worthwhile?
   - 0 ❑ Extremely so—to the point I have just about given up.
   - 1 ❑ Very much so.
   - 2 ❑ Quite a bit.
   - 3 ❑ Some—enough to bother me.
   - 4 ❑ A little bit.
   - 5 ❑ Not at all.

5. Have you been under or felt you were under any strain, stress, or pressure?
   - 0 ❑ Yes—almost more than I could bear.
   - 1 ❑ Yes—quite a bit of pressure.
   - 2 ❑ Yes—some, more than usual.
   - 3 ❑ Yes—some, but about usual.
   - 4 ❑ Yes—a little.
   - 5 ❑ Not at all.

6. How happy, satisfied, or pleased have you been with your personal life?
   - 5 ❑ Extremely happy—couldn't have been more satisfied or pleased.
   - 4 ❑ Very happy.
   - 3 ❑ Fairly happy.
   - 2 ❑ Satisfied—pleased.
   - 1 ❑ Somewhat dissatisfied.
   - 0 ❑ Very dissatisfied.

7. Have you had reason to wonder if you were losing your mind, or losing control over the way you act, talk, think, feel, or of your memory?
   - 5 ❑ Not at all.
   - 4 ❑ Only a little.
   - 3 ❑ Some, but not enough to be concerned.
   - 2 ❑ Some, and I've been a little concerned.
   - 1 ❑ Some, and I am quite concerned.
   - 0 ❑ Much, and I'm very concerned.

8. Have you been anxious, worried, or upset?
   - 0 ❑ Extremely so—to the point of being sick, or almost sick.
   - 1 ❑ Very much so.
   - 2 ❑ Quite a bit.
   - 3 ❑ Some—enough to bother me.
   - 4 ❑ A little bit.
   - 5 ❑ Not at all.

Lab 9.1—Cont'd

Lab 9.1—Cont'd

Health And Fitness Activity

Name: _____   Date: _____

9. Have you been waking up fresh and rested?
   - 5 ❑ Every day.
   - 4 ❑ Most every day.
   - 3 ❑ Fairly often.
   - 2 ❑ Less than half the time.
   - 1 ❑ Rarely.
   - 0 ❑ None of the time.

10. Have you been bothered by any illness, bodily disorder, pain, or fears about your health?
    - 0 ❑ All the time.
    - 1 ❑ Most of the time.
    - 2 ❑ A good bit of the time.
    - 3 ❑ Some of the time.
    - 4 ❑ A little of the time.
    - 5 ❑ None of the time.

11. Has your daily life been full of things that are interesting to you?
    - 5 ❑ All the time.
    - 4 ❑ Most of the time.
    - 3 ❑ A good bit of the time.
    - 2 ❑ Some of the time.
    - 1 ❑ A little of the time.
    - 0 ❑ None of the time.

12. Have you felt downhearted and blue?
    - 0 ❑ All the time.
    - 1 ❑ Most of the time.
    - 2 ❑ A good bit of the time.
    - 3 ❑ Some of the time.
    - 4 ❑ A little of the time.
    - 5 ❑ None of the time.

13. Have you been feeling emotionally stable and sure of yourself?
    - 5 ❑ All the time.
    - 4 ❑ Most of the time.
    - 3 ❑ A good bit of the time.
    - 2 ❑ Some of the time.
    - 1 ❑ A little of the time.
    - 0 ❑ None of the time.

Lab 9.1—Cont'd
Health And Fitness Activity

Name: _____   Date: _____

14. Have you felt tired, worn out, used up or exhausted?
   - 0 ❑ All the time.
   - 1 ❑ Most of the time.
   - 2 ❑ A good bit of the time.v
   - 3 ❑ Some of the time.
   - 4 ❑ A little of the time.
   - 5 ❑ None of the time.

Note: For each of the tour scales below, the words at each end describe opposite feelings. Circle any number along the bar that seems closest to how you have felt generally during the past month.

15. How concerned or worried about your health have you been?

    Not concerned at all   10   8   6   4   2   0   Very concerned

16. How relaxed or tense have you been?

    Very relaxed   10   8   6   4   2   0   Very tense

17. How much energy, pep, and vitality have you felt?

    No energy at all, listless   0   2   4   6   8   10   Very energetic, dynamic

18. How depressed or cheerful have you been? Very depressed?

    Very depressed   0   2   4   6   8   10   Very cheerful

Directions: Add up all the points from the boxes you have checked for each question. Compare your total score with the norms listed below.

Your Score _____   Stress Category _____

National Norms for the General Well-Being Scale

Stress State	Total Stress Score	% Distribution U.S. Population
Positive well-being	81–110	55%
Low positive	76–80	10%
Marginal	71–75	9%
Indicates stress problem	56–70	16%
Indicates distress	41–55	7%
Serious	26–40	2%
Severe	0–25	less than 1%

Note: Figure 11.4 gives the scores for the U.S. population by age, gender, and amount of exercise. Notice that all subgroups reporting "much exercise" fell within the "positive well-being" range of 81–110.

From *Fitness and Your Health*, Seventh Edition, by David C. Nieman. Copyright © 2015 by Kendall Hunt Publishing Company. Reprinted by permission.

Chapter 10

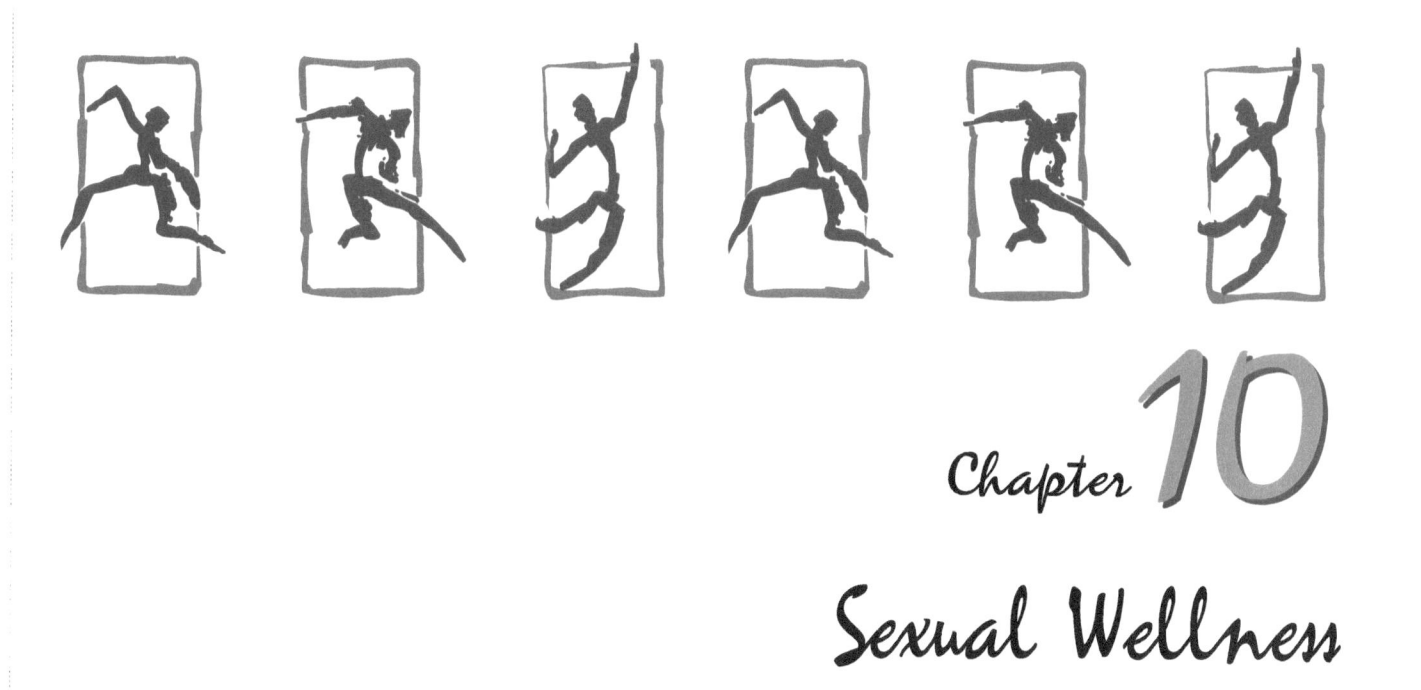

Sexual Wellness

Objectives
Introduction
Sexually Transmitted Infections
The Sexually Transmitted Infection Epidemic and Risk Factors
Sexually Transmitted Infection Risk Factors
Guidelines for Preventing Sexually Transmitted Infections

Summary
References
Internet Sources
Lab 10.1: What Is Your Risk of Contracting a Sexually Transmitted Infection?
Lab 10.2: STI Attitudes

Objectives

Upon completion of this chapter, you will be able to:

1. Describe the role of self-esteem in sexual choices.
2. Understand how to prevent sexually transmitted infections.
3. Know the risk factors for contracting a sexually transmitted infection.
4. Identify the pathogens, symptoms, and treatment for various sexually transmitted infections.
5. Understand the importance of HIV infection testing and the various types of tests.
6. Explain what sexually transmitted infections are and what causes them.
7. Identify risk factors for sexually transmitted infections.

Introduction

College students are faced with a variety of decisions vastly different from decisions made by individuals in other settings. By nature of the heterogeneous groups of young adults that are pulled together for the common purpose of obtaining an education, options and choices are magnified. One's level of self-worth and personal values are critical factors in the area of sexuality. How you select friends, casual dates, and lovers will have lasting effects upon your life. It is important to realize that your value system and self-esteem play a vital role in who you select as friends, casual acquaintances, and lovers. Therefore, it is important to analyze these factors (values/self-esteem) in order to understand how your life will be impacted. This chapter will present the symptoms, diagnosis and treatment for the most common STIs including those caused by bacteria and viruses. This chapter will also discuss STI prevention and risk factors associated with STIs.

Sexually Transmitted Infections

More than 65 million people are currently living with an incurable sexually transmitted infection (STI). An additional 15 million people become infected with one or more STIs each year, about half of whom contract lifelong infections. Despite the magnitude of the problem, most people in the United States remain unaware of the risks and consequences of all, but the most prominent STI—the human immunodeficiency virus or HIV. Many STIs go undiagnosed and even when diagnosed, many diseases are not reported. Thus, the "hidden" epidemics are magnified with each new infection that goes unrecognized and untreated.

Chlamydia

Chlamydia is a common sexually transmitted infection (STI) caused by the bacterium chlamydia trachomatic. Symptoms of chlamydia are typically mild or absent, therefore serious complications that cause irreversible damage, such as infertility, can occur before a person ever recognizes that he or she is infected. Chlamydia can be transmitted during vaginal, anal, or oral sex. A pregnant woman can transmit chlamydia to her newborn during vaginal childbirth causing conjunctivitis and pneumonia.

Chlamydia is known as a "silent" disease because 75% of infected women and 50% of infected men do not have symptoms. The infection is frequently not diagnosed or treated until complications develop. In women, the bacteria initially attack the cervix (opening of the uterus) and the urethra (urine canal). The few women with symptoms may have an abnormal vaginal discharge or a burning sensation when urinating. Some women continue not to exhibit signs and symptoms, even as the disease spreads from the cervix to the fallopian tubes. When the infection spreads into the upper reproductive tract permanent and irreversible damage can occur. In men symptoms include a discharge from the penis or burning sensation when urinating, and testicular swelling and pain may also occur. Men may also exhibit burning and itching around the opening of the penis.

Untreated, chlamydia can increase the risk of HIV infection in men and women. In men, untreated chlamydia typically causes urethral infection that may spread to the epididymis (tube that carries sperm to the testes), causing pain, fever, and potentially infertility. In women, chlamydia often infects the cervix. If not treated, infection can spread into uterus or fallopian tubes (egg canals) and cause an infection known as pelvic inflammatory disease (PID).

Chlamydia can be treated and cured with antibiotics such as doxycycline and azithromycin. Chlamydia is diagnosed using a laboratory urine test or samples taken from the woman's cervix or the man's penis. Prevention measures for chlamydia include using latex condoms correctly each time you have sex, limiting sexual partners, treatment for both sexual partners, and getting a screening test. If you think you are infected, avoid sexual contact, and see a health care provider immediately as well as notifying all your sexual partners immediately.

Gonorrhea

Gonorrhea is commonly known as "the clap" and caused by *Neisseria gonorrhoeae*, a bacterium that can grow and multiply easily in mucous membranes of the body. Gonorrhea bacteria can grow in the warm, moist areas of the reproductive tract, including the cervix (opening to the womb, uterus (womb), and fallopian tubes (egg canals) in women, and in the urethra (urine canal) in women and men. The bacteria can also grow in the mouth, throat, and anus.

Gonorrhea is spread through sexual contact (vagina, oral, or anal). Gonorrhea infection can spread to other unlikely parts of the body. For example, a person can get an eye infection after touching infected genitals and then the eyes. Individuals who have had gonorrhea and received treatment may get infected again if they have sexual contact with persons infected with gonorrhea.

When initially infected, the majority of men have some signs or symptoms. Symptoms and signs include a burning sensation when urinating and a yellowish white discharge from the penis. Sometimes men with gonorrhea get painful or swollen testicles. In women, the early symptoms of gonorrhea are often mild, and many women who are infected have no symptoms of infection. Even when a woman has symptoms, they can be so non-specific as to be mistaken for a bladder or vaginal infection. The initial symptoms and signs in women include a painful or burning sensation when urinating and a vaginal discharge that is yellow or occasionally bloody. In males, symptoms usually appear 2 to 5 days after infection, but it can take as long as 30 days for symptoms to begin. Regardless of symptoms, once a person is infected with gonorrhea, he or she can spread the infection to others if condoms or other protective barriers are not used during sex.

Many of the currently used antibiotics can successfully cure gonorrhea in adolescents and adults. Penicillin is a common antibiotic that is no longer used to treat gonorrhea, because many strains of the gonorrhea bacterium have become resistant to penicillin. Because many people with gonorrhea also have chlamydia, antibiotics for both infections are usually given together. Persons with gonorrhea should also be screened for other STIs.

Preventive measures include use of latex condoms correctly every time you have sex. Persons who choose to engage in sexual behaviors that can place them at risk for STIs should use latex condoms every time they have sex. Condoms do not provide complete protection from all STIs. Sores and lesions of other STIs on infected men and women may be present in areas not covered by the condom, resulting in transmission of infection to another person. Other prevention measures include practicing sexual abstinence, or limiting sexual contact to one uninfected partner. If you think you are infected, avoid sexual contact and see a health care provider immediately.

Syphilis

Syphilis is a complex sexually transmitted infection (STI) caused by the bacterium *treponema pallidum*. It has often been called "the great imitator" because so many of the signs and symptoms are indistinguishable from those of other diseases. Syphilis is transmitted from one person to another through direct contact with the syphilis sore which are primarily found on the external genitals, vagina, anus, and rectum. Sores may also develop on the lips and mouth. The bacterium is transmitted during vaginal, anal, and oral sex. Pregnant women can transmit syphilis to newborn babies during childbirth.

The time between infection with syphilis and the start of the first symptom can range from 10–90 days (average 21 days). The **primary stage** of syphilis is usually marked by the appearance of a single sore (called a chancre), but there may be multiple sores. The chancre is usually firm, round, small, and painless. It appears at the spot where syphilis entered the body. The chancre lasts 3-6 weeks, and it will heal on its own. If adequate treatment is not administered, the infection progresses to the secondary stage.

The **secondary stage** starts when one or more areas of the skin break into a rash that usually does not itch. Rashes can appear as the chancre is fading or can be delayed for weeks. The rash often appears as rough, red or reddish brown spots both on the palms of the hand and on the bottoms of the feet. The rash also may appear on other parts of the body with different characteristics, some of which resemble other diseases. Sometimes the rashes are so faint that they are not noticed. Rashes may clear up without treatment. In addition to rashes, second-stage symptoms can include fever, swollen lymph glands, sore throat, patchy hair loss, headaches, weight loss, muscle aches, and tiredness. A person can easily pass the disease to sex partners when primary or secondary stage signs or symptoms are present.

The **latent (hidden) stage** of syphilis begins when the secondary symptoms disappear. Without treatment, the infected person still has syphilis even though there are no signs or symptoms. It remains in the body, and it may begin to damage the internal organs, including the brain, nerves, eyes, heart, blood vessels, liver, bones, and joints. This internal damage may show up many years later in the **late** or **tertiary stage** of syphilis. Late stage signs and symptoms include not being able to coordinate muscle movements, paralysis, numbness, gradual blindness, and dementia. This damage may be serious enough to cause death.

While the health problems caused by syphilis in adults and newborns are serious in their own right, it is now known that the genital sores caused by syphilis in adults also make it easier to transmit and acquire HIV infection when syphilis is present. A single dose of penicillin, an antibiotic, will cure a person who has had syphilis for less than a year. Larger doses are needed to cure someone who has had it for longer than a year.

Genital Herpes

Herpes is a sexually transmitted infection (STI) caused by the herpes simplex viruses Type I (HSV-1) and Type 2 (HSV-2). Type 1 usually infects the mouth or lips causing cold sores or fever blisters. Type 2 infects the genitals or rectum causing genital herpes and also producing blisters. The blisters break, leaving tender ulcers (sores) that may take two to four weeks to heal the first time they occur. Typically, another outbreak can appear weeks or months after the first, but it almost always is less severe and shorter than the first episode. Although the infection can stay in the body indefinitely, the number of outbreaks tends to go down over a period of years.

HSV-1 and HSV-2 can be found and released from the sores that the viruses cause, but they also are released between episodes from skin that does not appear to be broken or to have a sore. A person almost always gets HSV-2 infection during sexual contact with someone who has a genital HSV-2 infection. A person can get HSV-1 by coming into contact with the saliva of an infected person.

Most people infected with HSV-2 are not aware of their infection. However, if signs and symptoms occur during the first episode, they can be quite pronounced. These include the aforementioned blisters, as well as fever, fatigue, swollen lymph nodes, headaches, muscle aches, and pain and itching at the sore sight. The blisters will form a scab and heal within approximately three weeks. Health care professional can test for herpes by obtaining a blood sample to look for antibodies or by examining a microscopic sample from the herpes sore.

Outbreaks or episodes can be triggered by stress, fever, illness, sunlight, and certain foods and beverages such as alcohol, coffee, and peanuts. There is no cure for herpes, but outbreaks can be shorten and controlled by antiviral medications. Even though herpes is not life threatening it can increase your risk of acquiring HIV and may cause lifelong pain and discomfort. A pregnant woman can transmit herpes to her newborn child. Consistent and correct use of latex or polyuretheane condoms can help protect against infection; however, condoms do not provide complete protection because the condom may not cover the herpes sore(s), and viral shedding may nevertheless occur. If you or your partner have genital herpes, it is best to abstain from sex when symptoms or signs are present, and use latex or polyuretheane condoms between outbreaks.

Human Papillomavirus (HPV) and Genital Warts

HPV infection is very common. Most sexually active people will be infected with HPV at some point during their lifetime. HPV causes cervical cancer in women and genital warts in women and men. It can also cause throat cancer. HPV will be resolved without treatment in 80 to 90% of the population who contract it. HPV can be spread via vaginal, anal, or oral sex and during other close skin-to-skin touching during sexual activity. **Genital HPV infection** is a sexually transmitted infection (STI) that is caused by human papillomavirus (HPV). Human papillomavirus, is the name of a group of viruses that includes more than one hundred different strains or types. Over forty of these can be sexually transmitted and some are considered "high-risk" types and may cause abnormal cells to form on the cervix that could develop into cervical cancer in women if not treated. Others are "low-risk," and cause genital warts. HPV 16 and 18 are considered high risk strains. They typically do not exhibit symptoms and account for approximately 70 percent of all cervical cancers. HPV 16 also accounts for approximately 50 percent of all cervical caners. HPV 6 and 11 are low risk strains that cause genital warts and have been associated with approximately 90% of genital warts.

Genital warts are singular or multiple growths or bumps that appear in the genital area, vulva, in or around the vagina or anus, on the cervix, and on the penis, scrotum, groin, or thigh, and sometimes form a cauliflower-like shape. The types of HPV that infect the genital area are spread primarily through sexual contact. The virus lives in the skin or mucus membranes and usually produces no symptoms. Other people get visible genital warts. Visible genital warts usually appear as soft, moist, pink, or red swellings. They can be raised or flat, single or multiple, small or large. Warts can appear within several weeks after sexual contact with an infected person, or they can take months to appear.

There is no general test to detect all HPVs. However an abnormal Pap-smear in a women may indicate HPV. Some health care providers do provide Pap tests to men who are have greater risk for anal cancer. There is no specific treatment for HPV. However, health problems cause by HPV are treatable. Early diagnosis of HPV related cancers leads to better prognosis. Genital warts can be treated by health care professionals or medication. A biopsy of a sample from a genital wart or a woman's cervix may be analyzed for HPV. Primarily genital warts are diagnosed by visual inspection. Acetic acid, a vinegar solution, can be used to identify flat warts. There is no cure for the virus, however it can be prevented through vaccination. The HPV vaccine can significantly reduce a women's risk of precancerous growths and cervical cancer. The Center for Disease Control (CDC) recommend two doses of the HPV vaccine. The Gardasil vaccine prevents infection by the HPV strains 6, 11, 16 and 18. Gardasil 9 prevents infection by strains 6,11,16,18 as well as HPV-31, HPV- 33, HPV-45,HPV-52, and HPV-58. Cervarix prevents HPV-16 and HPV-18. The HPV vaccine is recommended for all boys and girls eleven or twelve years of age, men and women with a comprised immune system through age twenty-six. The vaccine is recommended for girls, women, boys and men through age 26 if not fully vaccinated at a earlier age and men who have sex with men.

Trichomoniasis

Trichomoniasis is a common sexually transmitted infection (STI) that affects both women and men, although symptoms are more common in women. It is the most common, curable STI in young, sexually active women. Trichomaniasis is caused by the single-celled parasite *Trichomonasvaginalis.* The vagina is the most common site of infection in women, and the urethra is the most common site of infection in men. Trichomoniasis is spread through penis-to-vagina intercourse or vulva-to-vulva contact with an infected partner. Women can acquire the disease from infected men or women, whereas men usually contract it only from infected women.

Signs and symptoms of trichomoniasis may not appear in men. If symptoms do appear, men may experience an irritation inside the penis, mild discharge, or slight burning after urination or ejaculation. However, many women do have symptoms, including a frothy, yellow-green vaginal discharge with a strong odor. The infection may cause discomfort during intercourse and urination. Irritation and itching of the female genital area and, in rare cases, lower abdominal pain can also occur.

Trichomoniasis can usually be cured with the prescription drug metronidazole given by mouth in a single dose. The symptoms of trichomoniasis in infected men may disappear within a few weeks without treatment. However, an infected man, even a man who has never had symptoms or whose symptoms have stopped, can continue to infect a female partner until he has been treated. Metronidazole can be used by pregnant women.

Pelvic Inflammatory Disease (PID)

Pelvic inflammatory disease (PID) is a general term that refers to infection of the fallopian tubes (tubes that carry eggs from the ovary to the womb) and of other internal reproductive organs in women. It is a common and serious complication of STIs. Inside the lower abdominal cavity, PID can damage the fallopian tubes and tissues in and near the uterus and ovaries. Untreated PID can lead to serious consequences including infertility, ectopic pregnancy, abscess formation, and chronic pelvic pain.

Each year in the United States, more than 1 million women experience an episode of acute PID. More than 100,000 women become infertile each year as a result of PID, and a large proportion of the ectopic pregnancies occurring every year are due to the consequences of PID. More than 150 women die from this infection every year.

PID occurs when bacteria move upward from a women's vagina or cervix into the internal reproductive organs. Sexually active women in their childbearing years are most at risk. Many different organisms can cause PID, but most cases are associated with gonorrhea and Chlamydia—two very common bacterial STIs. It is estimated that 10 to 80 percent of women with either of these STIs will develop symptomatic PID.

Symptoms of PID vary from none to severe. Particularly when it is caused by chlamydia, PID may produce only mild symptoms or no symptoms at all, even while it is seriously damaging the internal reproductive organs. Because of the vague symptoms, PID goes unrecognized about two-thirds of the time. Women who do have symptoms of PID most commonly have lower abdominal pain. Other signs and symptoms include fever, unusual vaginal discharge that may have a foul odor, painful intercourse, painful urination, irregular menstrual bleeding, and pain in the right upper abdomen (rare).

PID can be cured with antibiotics. If women have pelvic pain and other symptoms caused by PID, it is critical that they seek care immediately. Prompt antibiotic treatment can prevent severe damage to pelvic organs. The longer women delay treatment for PID, the more likely they are to be infertile or to have an ectopic pregnancy in the future due to damage to the fallopian tubes. However, antibiotic treatment does not reverse any damage that has already occurred to the reproductive organs.

Women with STIs, especially gonorrhea and chlamydia, are at increased risk for developing PID. A prior episode of PID increases the risk also. Sexually active women under age 25 are more likely to develop PID than are women older than 25. The more sex partners a woman has, the greater the risk of developing PID, because of the potential for more exposure to infectious agents. Also, a woman whose partner has more than one sex partner is at greater risk of getting PID, because of the potential for more exposure to infected agents. Women who douche have a higher risk of developing PID compared with women who do not. Finally, women who have an intrauterine device (IUD) inserted may have a slightly increased risk of PID compared with women using other contraceptives or no contraceptive at all. The risk, however, is greatly reduced in women who are screened and treated for any infection prior to IUD insertion. Mutual monogamy is encouraged for women who choose to use an IUD to decrease the risk of getting PID. The main cause of PID is an untreated STI. Women can protect themselves from PID by taking action to prevent STIs or by getting early treatment if they do acquire an STI.

HIV and AIDS

Human immunodeficiency virus (HIV) is the virus that causes AIDS (Acquired Immunodeficiency Syndrome). HIV was initially recognized in 1981 and is now a worldwide epidemic. Approximately forty million people all over the world are living with HIV/AIDS of which half are women. The rate of HIV/AIDS among women continues to escalate at an alarming rate. More than one million Americans are HIV infected and more than 250,000 are unaware of their status.

HIV may cause changes in the immune system before a person who is infected feels sick, and most doctors refer to this period as "HIV disease" to cover the HIV spectrum, from the beginning of the infection to full-blown AIDS. HIV impairs the body's immune system by destroying certain immune cells, known as the CD4+ or T lymphocytes cells. The destruction of these cells diminishes the body's capacity to fight infections and certain cancers. The pattern count of the CD4+ cells over time is more important compared to a single count because values change from day to day. The pattern indicates how the virus is affecting the immune system. A CD4+ cell count (viral load) is taken when a HIV diagnosis is made to serve as a baseline for future comparisons and is typically monitored every three to six months relative to health status and the use of highly active antiretroviral therapy (HAART) medicines (used to slow the rate HIV replicates in the body). If the viral load increases steadily over several measurements, the infection is worsening. The viral load is measured using one of the following tests: Branched DNA test, reverse transcriptase polymerase chain reaction test or nucleic acid sequence-based amplification test. These all measure the amount of HIV genetic material is in the blood. An undetectable viral load means that the amount of HIV in the blood is too low for a test to detect. The patient is remains HIV positive and can infect others. The normal CD4+ cell count is 500–1500 cells per microliter (mcL) of blood. A count of less than 200mcL is indicative of AIDS and a high risk of opportunistic infections.

HIV/AID resides in cells and body fluids such as semen, vaginal secretions, blood/blood products, and breast milk. It can be transmitted through a minute break in the body's tissues (skin, mucous members) during unprotected sexual activity with an infected person. HIV/AIDS can also be transmitted by sharing infected drug paraphernalia (syringes and needles), during breastfeeding, and during childbirth by an infected mother. HIV/AIDS cannot be transmitted through casual contact such as closed-mouth kissing, hugging, or shaking hands. Open-mouth kissing is considered a low risk activity, however prolonged open-mouth kissing may cause breaks in the skin around the lips or in the mouth providing a transmission route for the virus.

Individuals with HIV disease progress thought a continuum of stages. Stage time varies for each person. For most individuals the stage progression of HIV disease is slow and takes several years from infection to severe immune suppression. When the HIV virus enters the body it attacks the CD4+ cells. The immune system then forms antibodies that can be detected by diagnostic tests for HIV. Antibodies to HIV appear in the blood between two weeks and six months after the original infection. Seroconversion is the period between infection with HIV and the point antibodies are detected in the blood. The virus can be spread from person to person during this period even though a test will not detect antibodies in the blood. The stages of HIV disease are:

1. **Primary Infection or Acute Infection**—is considered the first stage of HIV disease, and moves into seroconversion time when an HIV positive person's immune system responds to the infection by producing antibodies against the virus within three months.

2. **Clinical Latency Stage**—infected individual look and feel well for years, may have swollen lymph nodes, can infect others because the virus is still active, immune system is weakened, and requires continue periodic immune monitoring of CD4+ count. With proper treatment HIV infected individual may live for several decades during the clinical latency stage. Without proper treatment, viral load will rise and CD4 count will decrease and HIV symptoms will develop such as skin rashes, fatigue, night sweats, slight weight loss, mouth ulcers, and fungal skin and nail infections; as disease progresses the person may experience chronic oral or vaginal thrush (a fungal rash or spots), recurrent herpes blisters on the mouth (cold sores), or genitals, ongoing fevers, persistent diarrhea, and significant weight loss.

3. **Late-Stage HIV Disease (AIDS)**—This stage is characterized by severe immune system damage. The individual will experience opportunistic infections such as *Pneumocystis carinii* pneumonia (PCP), *Mycobacterium avium* complex (MAC) disease, cytomegalovirus (CMV), toxoplasmosis, and candidiasis.

Most new HIV/AIDS cases are caused by people unaware that they are infected with the virus. It may take weeks or months for the immune system to produce sufficient antibodies that can be detected in an HIV/AIDS test. Therefore, tests must be repeated three or more months after initial exposure to the virus. There are three main types of HIV tests: HIV antibody tests, RNA tests and a combination test. The immune system of individuals infected with HIV produces antibodies to neutralize the virus. However, these antibodies are unable to destroy the virus, but do serve as markers for the presence of the HIV virus. Most antibody analysis is performed using a blood sample in a laboratory setting. The results are usually available within one to three days. However rapid screening tests can be analyzed in a physician's office and are usually available in less than 30 minutes. The genetic material (RNA) of an HIV infected person differs significantly from that of the normal RNA. The HIV RNA tests are essential for detecting HIV infection within four weeks after exposure before antibodies in the blood develop. These tests are expensive and not typically used for screening purposes. Combination tests detects antibodies as well as a special protein found in the virus core known as *p24*.

The following are considered examples of HIV tests:

- Enzyme-Linked Immunosorbent Assay (ELISA)—this antibody test is used to detect HIV infection first. If positive for HIV the test is repeated.
- Western Blot test— this antibody test is used to confirm results of ELISA
- Dot Blot—a rapid screening antibody blood test, confirmation required if positive
- Home Testing System— this is home collection kit that test for antibodies in the oral fluid/saliva. The kit is then mailed to a laboratory to be analyzed.
- Polymerase Chain Reaction—this RNA test detects the genetic material (RNA) in cells infected with HIV, very useful for detecting recent infection (days or a few weeks after HIV exposure), to detect HIV infection when antibody tests are questionable and to screen blood or organs for HIV before donation, requires expensive equipment and a high level of technical skill to execute correctly.

Architect HIV Ag/Ab Combo assay – may allow for earlier HIV detection by searching for HIV antibodies and the p24 protein. Positive tests are confirmed using the Western Blot test.

The warning signs of HIV infection are:

- rapid weight loss
- profuse night sweats, fever and chills
- diarrhea lasting more than a week
- swollen lymph glands in the neck, underarms, or groin
- white spots or blemishes on the tongue, or in the mouth or throat
- pneumonia
- dry cough
- severe and unexplained fatigue
- skins sores

Get tested to determine if you have the HIV virus. Don't rely on the presence or absence of symptoms to indicate your health status. Many HIV infected people do not exhibit symptoms for years.

HIV is treated with a class of medications known as antiretroviral agents. Currently there are 21 antiretroviral medications approved by the United States Food and Drug Administration to treat HIV in adults. A physician can determine when and what specific antiretroviral medications you require based on your health status.

The Sexually Transmitted Infection Epidemic and Risk Factors

More than 25 STIs spread primarily through sexual activity, and the trends for each disease vary considerably, but together these infections comprise a significant public health problem. The latest estimates indicate that there are 9 million new STI cases in the United States each year. Approximately one-half of these new infections are in young people 18–24 years of age. And while some STIs, such as syphilis, have been brought to an all-time low, others, like genital herpes, gonorrhea, and chlamydia, continue to resurge and spread through the population.

Sexually Transmitted Infection Risk Factors

Sexually transmitted infections (STIs) are caused by pathogens, or disease-causing agents, such as bacteria, viruses, fungi and protozoa. These pathogens cause infections that may be spread through sexual contact with a person who is infected. Pathogen transmissions for sexually transmitted infections typically are through bodily fluids, such as semen, vaginal secretion, and blood. Common avenues of spreading STIs include oral-genital contact, vaginal intercourse, and anal intercourse. It doesn't matter whether you are homosexual, heterosexual, bisexual, male or female; you put yourself at greater risk for contacting STIs as a result of the following risk factors:

1. Having sex with multiple partners or with individuals who are having sex with multiple partners.
2. Having unprotected sex.
3. Consuming excessive alcohol or drugs which may reduce "inhibitions".
4. Using intravenous drugs through sharing infected needles.

Guidelines for Preventing Sexually Transmitted Infections

Practice abstinence or be in a monogamous sexual relationship to prevent the spread of STIs and HIV. The following are recommended guidelines for preventing sexually transmitted infections.

- ≈ Know your partner, don't have multiple or anonymous sexual partners.
- ≈ Discuss STIs with your perspective partner.

- Postpone sex until you believe you have found an uninfected person you can have a monogamous relationship with.
- Postpone sex until you are married.
- Unless you are in a monogamous relationship and you know your partner is not infected, practice safe sex by using a latex condom.
- Don't engage in sex with anyone whom you suspect has had multiple partners.
- Get tested for STIs, and seek proper treatment.
- Don't share toothbrushes, razors, or other items that may be contaminated with blood.
- Abstain from risky sexual activity, such as anal sex, and sex, with high-risk people (prostitutes, people with HIV or other STIs).
- Use a water-based lubricant with condoms, and use a new latex condom every time you have sex.
- Plan before you get into a sexual situation. Are you ready? Learn to say "no" to sex and drugs.

Summary

Important concepts you have learned in this chapter include:

- Self-esteem refers to the overall evaluation of oneself.
- Sexually transmitted infections (STIs) are caused by pathogens, or disease-causing agents, such as bacteria, viruses, fungi and protozoa.
- STIs are transmitted during vaginal, oral, anal sexual activity, or in some cases, by simply touching an infected area.
- Common bacterial STIs include chlamydia, gonorrhea, and syphilis.
- Untreated chlamydia is the leading cause of sterility and ectopic pregnancy, and may cause blindness if the eyes are infected.
- Untreated gonorrhea can cause sterility.
- Untreated syphilis is debilitating (skin lesions, mental deterioration, loss of balance, and vision, loss of sensation, shooting pains in the legs, and heart disease) and may be fatal.
- Genital herpes, HIV/AIDS, and HPV are caused by viruses.
- Genital herpes is a chronic, lifelong infection that results in periodic outbreaks of small red bumps in the genital area.
- HIV/AIDS attacks the body's immune system, and due to no known cure, is often fatal.
- HPV infection results in warts, usually around the genital area that may cause bleeding and obstruction in the urinary and/or anal openings if untreated.
- Responsible behavior is essential in order to prevent the transmission of STIs.

References

American College of Obstetricians and Gynecologists (ACOG) (2006). *Pelvic inflammatory disease.* ACOG Patient Education Pamphlet.

Center for Disease Control. (2007). Tracking the hidden epidemics: Trends in STDs in the United States. Atlanta, GA: CDC. http://www.cdc.gov/nchstp/dstd/STATS_trends2000.pdf.

Center for Disease Control. (2000b). Fluoroquinolone-resistance in *Neisseria gonorrhoeae*, Hawaii, 1999, and Decreased susceptibility to azithromycin in *N. gonoarrhoeae*, Missouri, 1911, MMWR. 2000:49 (No. 37):833–7.

"Sexually transmitted diseases." U.S. Centers for Disease Control and Prevention. 22 October 2013.

Internet Sources

http://www.cdc.gov/nchstp/ditd/Fact_Sheets/FactsBV.htm

http://www.cdc.gov/nchstp/dstd/Fact_Sheets/FactschlamydiaInfo.htm

http://www.cdc.gov/nchstp/dstd/Fact_Sheets/Facts_Genital_Herpes.htm

http://www.cdc.gov/nchstp/dstd/Fact_Sheets/FactsGonorrhea.htm

http://www.cdc.gov/nchstp/ditd/Fact_Sheets/FactsHPV.htm

http://www.cdc.gov/nchstp/dstd/Fact_Sheets/FactsPID.htm

http://www.cdc.gov/nchstp/dstd/Fact_Sheets/Facts_Syphilis.htm

http://www.cdc.gov/nchstp/dstd/Fact_Sheets/Facts_std_testin_and_treatment.htm

http://www.cdc.gov/nchstp/dstp/Fact_Sheets/FactsTrichomoniasis.htm

http://www.cdc.gov/hiv/topoics/aa/index.htm

http://www.cdc.gov/hiv/pbs/fag/fag9.htm

http://aidsinfo.hiv.gov

http://www.cdc.gov/hiv/pubs/fag/fag5.htm

http://www.hivtest.org/subindex.cfm

www.thebody.com/content/whatis/art2506.html

http:/aids.about.com/od/hivaidsletterg/elisadef.htm

http://www.jama.com

http://www.medicine.net

Lab 10.1
What Is Your Risk of Contracting a Sexually Transmitted Infection?

Name: _____ Date: _____

Purpose A variety of factors interact to determine your risk of contracting a sexually transmitted infection (STI). This inventory is intended to provide you with an estimate of your level of risk.

Procedure Circle the number in each row that best characterizes you. Enter the number on the line at the end of the row (score line). After assigning yourself a number in each row, total the number appearing in the score column. Your total score will allow you to interpret your risk of contracting an STI.

							Score
Points Age	1 0–9	3 10–14	4 15–19	5 20–29	3 30–34	2 35+	_____
Points Sexual practices	0 Never engage in sex	1 One sex partner	2 More than one sex partner, but never more than one at a time	4 Two to five sex partners	6 Five to ten sex partners	8 Ten or more sex partners	_____
Points Sexual attitudes	0 Will not engage in premarital sex	1 Premarital sex is okay if it is with future spouse	8 Any kind of premarital sex is okay	1 Extramarital sex is not for me	7 Extramarital sex is okay	8 Believe in complete sexual freedom	_____
Points Attitudes toward contraception	1 Would use condom to prevent pregnancy	1 Would use condom to prevent STIs	6 Would never use a condom	5 Would use the birth control pill	4 Would use other contraceptive measure	8 Would not use anything	_____
Points Attitudes toward STI	3 Am not sexually active so I do not worry	3 Would be able to talk about STIs with my partner	4 Would check an infection to be sure	6 Would be afraid to check out an infection	6 Can't even talk about an infection	6 STIs are no problem, easily cured	_____

Your total score _____

Interpretation
5–8   Your risk is well below average
9–13   Your risk is below average
14–17   Your risk is at or near average
18–21   Your risk is moderately high
22+   Your risk is high

Fitness & Wellness for Life, 6th ed. (1999), by William Prentice, McGraw-Hill: Boston, Mass.

Lab 10.2
STI Attitudes

Name: _____   Date: _____

Directions: Please read each statement carefully. STI means sexually transmissible infection. Record your reaction by circling the number.

Use This Key: 1 = Strongly Agree   2 = Agree   3 = Undecided   4 = Disagree   5 = Strongly Disagree

1 2 3 4 5   1. How one uses one's sexuality has nothing to do with getting an STI.
1 2 3 4 5   2. It is easy to use the prevention methods that reduce one's chances of getting an STI.
1 2 3 4 5   3. Responsible sex is one of the best ways of reducing the risk of STIs.
1 2 3 4 5   4. Getting early medical care is the main key to preventing harmful effects of STIs.
1 2 3 4 5   5. Choosing the right sex partner is important in reducing the risk of getting an STI.
1 2 3 4 5   6. A high rate of STI should be a concern for all people.
1 2 3 4 5   7. People with an STI have a duty to get their sex partners to medical care.
1 2 3 4 5   8. The best way to get a sex partner to STI treatment is to take him/her to the doctor with you.
1 2 3 4 5   9. Changing one's sex habits is necessary once the presence of an STI is known.
1 2 3 4 5   10. I would dislike having to follow the medical steps for treating an STI.
1 2 3 4 5   11. If I were sexually active, I would feel uneasy doing things before and after sex to prevent getting an STI.
1 2 3 4 5   12. If I were sexually active, it would be insulting if a sex partner suggested we use a condom to avoid STI.
1 2 3 4 5   13. I dislike talking about STIs with my peers.
1 2 3 4 5   14. I would be uncertain about going to the doctor unless I was sure I really had an STI.
1 2 3 4 5   15. I would feel that I should take my sex partner with me to a clinic if I thought I had an STI.
1 2 3 4 5   16. It would be embarrassing to discuss STI with one's partner if one were sexually active.
1 2 3 4 5   17. If I were to have sex, the chance of getting an STI makes me uneasy about having sex with more than one person.
1 2 3 4 5   18. I like the idea of sexual abstinence (not having sex) as the best way of avoiding STIs.
1 2 3 4 5   19. If I had an STI, I would cooperate with public health people to find the source of STIs.
1 2 3 4 5   20. If I had an STI, I would avoid exposing others while I was being treated.
1 2 3 4 5   21. I would have regular STI checkups if I were having sex with more than one partner.
1 2 3 4 5   22. I intend to look for STI signs before deciding to have sex with anyone.
1 2 3 4 5   23. I will limit my sex activity to just one partner because of the chances I might get an STI.
1 2 3 4 5   24. I will avoid sex contact anytime I think there is even a slight chance of getting an STI.
1 2 3 4 5   25. The chance of getting an STI would not stop me from having sex.
1 2 3 4 5   26. If I had a chance, I would support community efforts toward controlling STIs.
1 2 3 4 5   27. I would be willing to work with others to make people aware of STI problems in my town.

Calculate your total points using the following point values. For items 1, 10–14, 16, and 25: reverse the scoring of your circled response (1 becomes 5, 2 becomes 4, and so on). For Items 2–9, 15, 17–24, 26, and 27: add the points as you have them circled. The higher your score, the stronger your predisposition to engage in high-risk STI behaviors. The lower your score, the stronger your predisposition to practice low-risk STI behaviors. The range for the score is 27–135. Your Score_____

Chapter 11

Drug Use and Abuse

Objectives
Introduction
Drugs and Their Effects
Drugs Commonly Used, Misused, and Abused
Addictive Characteristics
Strategies Used to Overcome an Addiction

Summary
References
Internet Sources
Lab 11.1: A Letter to My Best Friend

Objectives

Upon completion of this chapter, you will be able to:

1. Define alcohol dependency.
2. Identify trends and problems associated with alcohol use and abuse.
3. Identify organizations that offer alcohol abuse assistance.
4. Identify the types of tobacco and adverse effects of tobacco use.
5. Identify approaches to quitting tobacco use.
6. Identify trends in drug use and abuse.
7. Differentiate between drug use, misuse and abuse.
8. Define addiction, dependence, tolerance, withdrawal, and craving.
9. Discuss drugs commonly used, misused, and abused on college campuses.
10. Describe the physiological and psychological effects of commonly used, misused, and abused drugs.
11. Describe the effects and risk factors associated with addiction.
12. Discuss strategies to overcome addiction.

Introduction

Alcohol, tobacco, and drug use, misuse, and abuse continue to be a detriment to society. They are serious impediments to wholesome, healthy lifestyles. Many factors can provide the impetus for one to engage in alcohol, tobacco, and drug use, misuse and abuse. This chapter is structured to provide information that will hopefully help you make correct decisions when faced with the pressures of life. It provides information about the effects and impact of drugs on society and drugs people commonly use, misuse and abuse.

Drugs and Their Effects

A **drug** is a substance that has a physiological and/or psychological effect when ingested or introduced into the body. These include prescription medications, over-the-counter-drugs, and illegal substances. Inappropriate drug use can lead to addiction. Any drug can be misused or abused. **Drug abuse** is the intentional, inappropriate use of a legal drug or the use of illegal drugs. Drug use and abuse can have physical and psychological side effects.

Most prescription and over-the-counter drugs, when taken correctly, produce insignificant side effects for the user. Yet, physical and psychological side effects are commonly experienced by individuals who use drugs. Physical side effects include the following:

- Allergic reactions—vary from mild rashes or hives to serious conditions such as anaphylactic shock
- Blindness
- Disorientation
- Seizures
- Blood disorders
- Heart failure, heart attack
- Kidney and liver failure
- Memory difficulties

Psychological side effects influence how the drug user thinks, feels and behaves. They include the following:

- Depression
- Agitation
- Mood alterations
- Anxiety
- Paranoia
- Forgetfulness
- Irritability
- Bipolar disorder

Drugs Commonly Used, Misused, and Abused

ALCOHOL

Major Signs/Symptoms

Ethanol is an addictive, intoxicating substance found in beer, wine, and distilled spirits. Alcohol is made from carbohydrates (fruit and grain products) through a process known as fermentation. Alcohol, a central nervous system depressant is quickly absorbed into the bloodstream from the stomach and small intestine at the first sip since it does not require digestion. The immediate effects of alcohol can occur within ten minutes. The amount of alcohol in the bloodstream (blood alcohol concentration-BAC) continues to rises as consumption increases. Alcohol is metabolized in small amounts (approximately a half ounce per hour) by enzymes in the liver. The liver can process moderate amounts of alcohol effectively. According to the Dietary Guidelines for Americans moderate consumption is defined as up to one drink per day for women and up to two per day for men. This definition does refer to the average amount consumed over several days, but to that consumed on any single day. Individual reactions to alcohol vary according to factors such as age, gender, family history, food consumption, health status, how much, how fast and how often on drinks. A BAC level of 0.08% is considered the legal limit for driving for individuals aged 21 and older in the United States. However, impairment of judgment, reaction time, motor skills, vision, and self-control can occur at levels below the legal limit. Alcohol abuse is a pattern of drinking that damages one's relationships, health, or ability to work. Alcoholism, also known as alcohol dependency, is a disease that includes **craving**, a strong need or urge to drink; **loss of control**, not being able to stop drinking once drinking has begun; **physical dependence**, withdrawal symptoms, such as anxiety, shakiness, sweating; and *tolerance,* the need to drink greater amounts of alcohol to get "high." Alcoholism can be divided into three stages: the *adaptive stage, dependence, and conclusion*. In the **adaptive stage** alcohol is used as a means to escape. Drinking is no longer a social activity but a habitual means of psychological escape from problems. The drinker develops a tolerance to alcohol. During the **dependence stage** is drinker is unable to stop after the initial drink. Friends, family members and co-workers become aware and very concerned about the user's drinking. The user usually attempts to conceal drinking from others, deny that a drinking problem exists and experience, hangovers, hand tremors, and blackouts. As the disease progresses, the drinker becomes more and more dependent on alcohol. The drinker experiences the physical, occupational, and social consequences of alcoholism. The **conclusion** stage of alcoholism is characterized by chronic loss of control. Alcohol is now needed by the drinker to function. Severe withdrawal symptoms such as hallucinations, seizures, tremors are experienced by the user when attempts are made to stop drinking. Death can occur as well.

Alcohol Terminology

Three general categories of information describe alcohol involvement. The categories include **alcohol consumption, alcohol dependence** (described above), and **alcohol-related consequences** or problems. The frequency and/or quantity of alcohol consumed refer to alcohol consumption. Frequency refers to how often an individual drinks, whether it is daily, weekly, or several times a month. The number of drinks consumed on a single occasion refers to quantity. A combination of quantity and frequency (Q/F) measures the total volume that an individual consumes over a specified time period. In the United States, standard measures are used to assess drinks. Standard drinks are 12 oz. of beer (approximately 5% alcohol), 5 oz. of wine (approximately 12% alcohol), 8 to 9 oz. of malt liquor (approximately 7% alcohol) 1.5 oz. of 80 proof distilled spirits (40% alcohol). It is vital that the drinker is aware of the alcohol content of the alcoholic beverage he/she consumes. The amount of alcohol in beer, wine and distilled liquor varies. A 12 ounce regular beer contains 5% alcoholic content while some light beers contain 4.2% alcoholic content. A standard glass of wine contains approximately 12% alcohol. One shot of distilled liquor (80 proof whiskey, gin, rum, tequila, vodka and other distilled liquors) contain approximately 40% alcohol. The amount of alcohol in distilled liquor is known as proof and refers to the amount of alcohol in liquor, for example an 100 proof alcohol contains 50% alcohol, and 80 proof alcohol contains 40% alcohol. Any given drink may contain more alcohol than the standard drink relative to the type of spirits used and the size of the drink. A major societal concern is heavy consumption more than light or moderate consumption. Heavy consumption on one occasion may be referred to as binge drinking, drinking to intoxication, or heavy drinking.

The Role of Heredity

Research shows that the risk of developing alcoholism does indeed run in families. Genes inherited by an individual partially explain the pattern of alcoholism, but lifestyle is also a factor. However, not all children of alcoholics become alcoholics themselves. Thus, knowing the risks and protecting yourself is important.

The Panel on Contexts and Consequences

A panel of researchers on the contexts and consequences of alcohol consumption among college students defined the magnitude of alcohol misuse on college campuses. The aim of the panel was to develop a report that would help colleges and universities reduce excessive alcohol use on campuses. Consequences refer to negative life occurrences that are a direct result of alcohol consumption. Consequences may be classified into one of four categories: social problems, legal problems, educational/vocational problems, or medical problems. An overview of the panel's findings revealed that alcohol misuse on college campuses is not a new problem. It is entrenched in the culture of many institutions of higher learning. Recent concerns have focused on the practice of binge drinking, typically defined as consuming five or more drinks in a row for men; and four or more drinks in a row for women. The U.S. Surgeon General and the U.S. Department of Health and Human Services (SUD-HHS) have identified binge drinking among college students as a major public health problem.

Drugs That Treat Alcohol Dependence

There is apparently no cure for alcoholism at this time. However, alcoholism can be treated through counseling and medications. Some medicines used to treat alcoholism are Valium and Librium. These medicines are used to assist the patient through the withdrawal stages of the disease. Naltrexone is used to help the patient remain sober. Naltrezone reduces craving and helps prevent relapse. Disulfiram discourages alcohol consumption by causing unpleasant effects such as vomiting, chest pain, headache, breathing difficulty, anxiety and mental confusion when alcohol is consumed even in very small amounts. These effects occur approximately ten minutes after alcohol is consumed and can last for an hour or longer. Anabuse discourages drinking by making the patient sick if alcohol is consumed while using the drug. Acamprosate is used to help alcoholics who have stopped drinking remain abstinence. Alcoholism disrupts the normal chemical balance within the brain. Acamprosate acts to stabilize this chemical balance so that the brain operates as it normally should.

Consequences of Alcohol and Abuse

Alcoholism cuts across gender, race, and nationality. Nearly 14 million people in the United States, one in every three adults, abuse alcohol or is an alcoholic. Alcohol problems are highest among adults ages 18–29 and lowest among adults ages 65 and older. Over exposure to alcohol by college students impairs their judgment and self-control, and can result in death, injury, assault, sexual abuse, and unsafe sex. Academic problems and other traumatic experiences are associated with overuse and abuse of alcohol on college campuses.

Excessive alcohol consumption even on a single occasion or over time can have serious consequences. Alcohol effects are experienced by every organ in the body. Alcohol impairs the brain's ability to function properly by impairing its' communication networks causing mood and behavior changes, loss of the ability to think clearly and motor coordination. In the heart alcohol can produce irregular heart rhythm, elevated blood pressure, stroke, and cardiomyopathy (a weakened heart with diminished contractility). Alcohol over indulgence can cause the pancreas to produce toxic substances that produce pancreatitis, a serious and potentially deadly inflammation of the pancreas. Chronic drinkers are more susceptible to diseases such as tuberculosis and pneumonia due to a weaken immune system and are a greater risk for cancers of the mouth, liver, esophagus, and throat. Chronic drinking depresses the appetite such that many users tend to eat poorly and become malnourished. However, alcohol has its greatest impact on the liver. The liver aids in the digestion of fats, the breakdown of cholesterol, the elimination of toxins from the blood and processes proteins and enzymes. Moderate alcohol intake is not typically related to liver disease. However, drinking large amounts of alcohol (three or more drinks per day) over several years consistently causes liver damage. There are three types of alcohol induced liver diseases: **steatosis, alcoholic hepatitis,** and **cirrhosis.** Steatosis also known as fatty liver disease, is the deposition of fat in the liver. Alcoholism is a common cause of steatosis in the liver. Steatosis is reversible if alcohol consumption ceases. If drinking continues, alcoholic hepatitis develops. Alcoholic hepatitis is inflammation of the liver. Symptoms of alcoholic hepatitis include abdominal edema and pain, loss of appetite, nausea, abnormal blood clotting, jaundice and hepatic encephalopathy (a neurological dysfunction causing mental confusion). Liver damage is reversible provided alcohol consumption if drinking stops permanently. However, if alcohol consumption continues, alcoholic cirrhosis can develop and is not reversible. Alcoholic cirrhosis is scarring of the liver. Symptoms of alcoholic cirrhosis include bleeding in the esophagus or other areas of the digestive tract, kidney failure, a comprised immune system, and improper functioning of spleen and pancreas. Untreated alcoholic cirrhosis is often fatal. However if drinking creases and treatment is received, it can stabilize. Treatment may include a low sodium and protein diet to abdominal edema and the build-up of toxins in the body and medication.

While alcohol abuse is detrimental to both men and women, women appear to be more vulnerable to adverse consequences of alcohol use. Women achieve higher concentrations of alcohol in the blood and become more impaired than men after drinking equivalent amounts of alcohol because women typically weigh less than men and have less body water which is dispersed by alcohol. Women also produce less alcohol dehydrogenase enzyme which reduces the amount of alcohol entering the bloodstream. Research suggests that women are more susceptible than men to alcohol-related organ damage and to trauma resulting from traffic crashes and interpersonal violence.

Binge drinking is most common among young people ages 18-25. Binge drinking increases the BAC level to 0.08% or greater corresponding to five or more drinks in men and four or more drinks on single occasion usually within a two hour time period. Binge drinking may lead to alcohol poisoning. **Alcohol poisoning** is an overdose of alcohol or consumption of large amounts. It can result in death due to breathing cessation, a person choking on his/her vomit, and/or heart failure. Signs and symptoms of alcohol poisoning include:

- Large quantities of alcohol consumed
- Skin cold, clammy, and very pale
- Breathing irregular or slows
- Person unconscious and cannot be awakened

Strategies used to prevent alcohol poisoning have to start with understanding how alcohol affects the body:

- Do not mix alcohol with other drugs, legal or illegal
- Drink no more than one drink per hour
- Know your limits and stick to them
- Eat a full meal shortly before you start drinking
- Drink non-alcohol drinks between alcohol drinks to slow the rate of consumption
- Do not let others pressure you to drink
- Leave any drinking situation that is out of control before you become involved
- Eat food when drinking alcohol to slow absorption into your system
- If drinking occupies a significant amount of your time, find new health alternative activities for fill that time
- Know what triggers your urge to drink and avoid those triggers. If certain people, places or activities encourage you to drink avoid them.
- Keep track of how much you drink using a recording method that works for you
- Know the standard sizes of drinks so you can accurately track your drinking

The consequences of excessive and underage drinking affect virtually all college campuses, college communities, and college students, whether they choose to drink or not. Non-drinking students are often assaulted by drinking students. Furthermore, many students 18–24 years of age are victims of alcohol related sexual assault or date rape. Many in this age group have reported being too intoxicated to know if they consented to having sex.

Organizations That Address Alcohol Use and Abuse

Information addressing alcohol use and abuse may be obtained from several organizations such as the National Institute on Alcohol Abuse and Alcoholism (NIAAA), and the National Council on Alcoholism (NCA). Both organizations provide information and support.

Additionally, Alcoholic Anonymous (AA) is an organization that directly aids alcohol-dependent individuals to become and remain sober. Alcoholic Anonymous has more than 19,000 affiliated agencies across the United States.

Al-Anon and Alateen are organizations that offer assistance to family members of alcohol-dependent individuals. These organizations are designed to aid family members acquire coping mechanisms so that they can positively address the accompanying problems and challenges of living with someone who is alcohol dependent.

TOBACCO

The use of tobacco products is a leading cause of cancer in humans as well as animals who are exposed to these products. Young people 18–25 years of age are reported to have one of the highest rates of smoking. Devastating health risks, including lung cancer, emphysema, and chronic bronchitis, do not seem to deter users from participating in tobacco use. Cancers of the mouth, larynx, and esophagus are additional risks.

The smoke from tobacco products contain more than 4000 chemicals and is harmful to almost every organ in the body. Although tar, nicotine and carbon monoxide are well known tobacco components, there are many others just as dangerous (see table 11.1). Cigarette smoking kills over 400,000 people annually. Smoking not only causes various cancers but also increase heart disease risk and exacerbates asthma in children and adults.

Other Components in Tobacco Products

Component	Common Use
Arsenic	Used in rat poisons
Benzene	Used to make dyes and synthetic rubber
Butane	A gas used in lighter fluid
Cadmium	Used in batteries
Cyanide	A deadly poison
Fungicides and pesticides	Used to kills fungus and insects
Formaldehyde	Used to preserve dead specimens
Napthalene	An ingredient in mothballs
Ammonia	A household cleaner

Tobacco Components

Three components of tobacco are toxic—tar, nicotine, and carbon monoxide. **Tar,** a dark, sticky substance, can be condensed from cigarette smoke. The potent carcinogens and chemicals found in tar irritate an individual's lung tissue, paralyzing and destroying the cilia that line the bronchi. A "smoker's cough" results; followed by the development of chronic bronchitis and emphysema, with long-term exposure often leading to lung cancer.

Nicotine, a colorless, oily compound, is extremely poisonous in concentrated amounts. Nicotine exposure can lead to heart and respiratory diseases. Short-term effects of exposure of nicotine include an increase in blood pressure and heart rate, and the narrowing of arteries caused by the additional flow of blood from the heart. The manner in which an individual smokes also determines the effects of nicotine. Shallow puffs cause the nicotine to act as a stimulant while long, deep drags depress the nervous system, causing the individual to relax.

Nicotine is considered highly addictive, even more so than cocaine or heroin. Exposure to as few as three packs of cigarettes can lead to nicotine addiction. Nicotine is so addictive that the Food and Drug Administration (FDA) has determined that it should be regulated.

Carbon monoxide, a highly toxic odorless and tasteless gas, reduces the amount of oxygen that can be carried by the blood. Carbon monoxide alters the inner walls of the arteries to encourage the accumulation of fat, a condition known as atherosclerosis. Additionally, the arteries narrow and harden, which may ultimately lead to a heart attack. Other side effects of regular exposure to carbon monoxide through smoking include an impairment of normal functioning of the nervous system and an increased risk of strokes.

Types of Tobacco

Smokeless tobacco encompasses snuff, and chewing tobacco. Chewing tobacco comes in the form of loose leaf, plug, or twist. Snuff is finely ground tobacco that van be dry, moist, or in sachets (tea-bag-like pouches). Some sniff and inhale snuff into the nose, but most smokeless tobacco is placed in the cheek or between the gum and cheek. The individual then sucks on the tobacco and spits out the juices. Smokeless tobacco is often referred to as spitting tobacco or spit. Young adult white males are the largest group drawn to the use of smokeless tobacco as they feel that it is a safe alternative to cigarettes.

Smokeless tobacco permits the effects of nicotine without the exposure to tar and carbon monoxide. However, harmful effects of nicotine exposure do exist with smokeless tobacco use due to the greater exposure of nicotine to the linings of the mouth. Bad breath, cardiovascular diseases, and decreased smell and taste ability are among the most reported side effects. Smokeless tobacco users often add more salt and sugar to their diets, thus becoming more prone to hypertension and obesity. Due to the nicotine being directly absorbed into the blood stream, dependency is believed to be much harder to break than smoking.

Leukoplakia, a pre-cancerous condition, is another major health concern related to smokeless usage. Signs and symptoms of leukoplakia include thick, rough, white patches on the gums, tongue, and inner cheeks. This condition may cause a variety of cancers around the mouth area, including the lips, pharynx, larynx, esophagus, and tongue. Moreover, dental and gum problems may arise as possible side effects.

Cigarette smoking is still the leading use of tobacco in the United States. An estimated 20.8% of all adults (45.3 million people) smoke cigarettes in the United States. Cigarette smoking is more common among men than women. Prevalence of cigarette smoking is highest among American Indians/Alaska Natives, followed by African Americans, Caucasians, Hispanics and Asians. It is more common among adults who live below the poverty level than among those living at or above the poverty level.

Respiratory ailments as well as chronic obstructive pulmonary diseases (COPD) are major health problems caused by cigarette smoking. The Surgeon General has stated that cigarette smoking is the largest preventable cause of illness and premature death in the United States. The following list contains risks associated with cigarette smoking and/or breathing secondhand cigarette smoke.

Risks Associated with Cigarette Smoking

- Allergies
- Cancers (mouth, throat, lung, other)
- Cirrhosis of the liver

- Stomach and duodenal ulcers
- Gum and dental disease
- Decreased HDL cholesterol
- Decreased platelet survival and clotting time
- Increased blood thickness
- Heart disease
- Atherosclerosis
- Blood clots
- Increased fatty acid accumulation
- Cardiac arrhythmias
- Diabetes
- Hypertension
- Peptic ulcers
- Sexual impotence

Cigars consist of the same carcinogenic and toxic compounds found in cigarettes. They are not considered a safe option to smoking cigarettes. Large cigars, cigarillos and little cigars are the three major types of cigars sold in the United States. Cigar smoking is more common among males than females and an estimated 13.3 million Americans, twelve years of age or older, were current cigar users according to the CDC. Cigar smoking has risen dramatically despite widespread tobacco prevention initiatives. An increase risk for developing cancers of the lung, oral cavity, larynx, and esophagus is associated with regular cigar smoking. Those individuals who inhale cigar smoke deeply are at increased risk for developing coronary heart disease and chronic obstructive pulmonary disease.

Secondhand smoke occurs when non-smokers are exposed to the cigarette smoke of smokers. It is also known as environmental tobacco smoke because most exposure occurs in homes, vehicles, public places and workplaces. It is a mixture of complex gases and particles that includes smoke from cigars, pipe tips, burning cigarettes, and exhaled mainstream smoke. It consists of at least two hundred fifty chemicals that are toxic, including more than fifty that can cause cancer. The chemical cotinine is measured in saliva, urine, or blood to determine the extent of exposure to nicotine and secondhand smoke.

Numerous deaths occur each year from lung cancer and heart disease that are linked to secondhand tobacco smoke. It has been estimated that approximately 60% of children under the age of five years live in a household with at least one smoker. Increased rates of asthma, ear infections, and respiratory infections occur in children under the age of five as a result of being exposed to secondhand smoke in the household. Secondhand smoke exposure is also linked to sudden infant death (SIDS).

Electronic Cigarettes

Electronic cigarettes (e-cigarettes) are battery operated device that converts a liquid solution containing nicotine, flavorings and other chemical into vapor instead of smoke. These devices often resemble pens, USB memory sticks, pipes, cigarettes, or cigars. Prior to 2016 were unregulated and could legally be purchased by individuals of all ages. The wide variety of flavorings and the easy accessibility of e-cigarettes (online or mall kiosks purchases) make them very popular among teens and preteens. Today e-cigarettes are subject to subject to the same governmental regulations as other tobacco products, making purchases by individuals under the age of 18 illegal both in-store and online. E-cigarettes have not been found to be a viable smoking cessation aid. However, they may perpetuate nicotine addiction and impede cessation efforts. Smokers who wish to quit should utilize cessation methods proven safe and effective by the Food and Drug Administration such as nicotine skin patches, gum, lozenges, nasal spray, Zyban or Chantix.

Ways and Means to "Kick the Tobacco Habit"

A number of approaches may be used to reduce and ultimately break the tobacco habit, such as gums, hypnoses, medications, patches, and smoking cessation classes are available. Since the addictive components of tobacco are so powerful, assistance from an outside source may be necessary (see **Tobacco Prevention and Assistance Organizations**).

Tobacco Prevention and Assistance Organizations

The following list of organizations offers information and assistance regarding tobacco and health.

American Council on Science and Health (ACSH)
http://www.asch.org

American Heart Association (AHA)
National Center
http://www.aha.org

American Lung Association (ALA)
www.lung.org/

Centers for Disease Control and Prevention
http://www.cdc.gov/tobacco

U.S. Department of Health and Human Services
www.hhs.gov

Americans for Nonsmoker's Rights (ANR)
http://www.no-smoke.org/

MARIJUANA

Marijuana is one of the most commonly used drug in the United States and It's use is widespread among adolescents and young adults. Marijuana use can elicit both physical and mental effects due to two main chemicals present in the plant: cannabidiol (CBD) and tetra-hydrocannabinol (THC). THC has a stronger intoxicating effect comparted to CBD. When smoked, THC quickly passes from the lungs into the bloodstream then to the brain and other organs throughout the body. THC connects to specific places on the nerve cells in the brain known as cannabinoid receptors (CBRs). THC alters the function of CBRs by over stimulating them. Cannabinoid receptors are most numerous in the hippocampus, cerebellum, cingulate cortex, and basal ganglia. These areas of the brain control memory, movement, learning, coordination, concentration, judgment and pleasure. The effects of CBRs are expressed due to its similarity to endogenous cannabinoids which occur naturally in the brain and body to help control the same mental and physical function altered by marijuana use. Long term over stimulation of the CBRs can lead to addiction and withdrawal symptoms when use is terminated. The potency of marijuana is increased over the past several years. Street names include trees, weed, roach, pot, gangster, reefer, chronic, skunk, ganja, Mary Jane, and grass. It is a greenish-gray mixture of the dried, shredded leaves, stems, seeds and flowers of *Cannabis sativa,* the hemp plant. Most individuals smoke marijuana in hand rolled cigarettes called joints or nails; some use pipes, or water pipes called bongs. Some people smoke blunts or marijuana cigars. Blunt users slice open cigars and replace the tobacco with marijuana, often combined with other drugs, such as crack cocaine. It is also brewed as tea and is sometimes mixed into foods.

The effects of marijuana start immediately after inhalation entering the brain, lasting from one to three hours. When consumed in foods or beverages the effects begin 30 minutes to one hour after consumption and last up to four hours. The heart rate increases significantly, irritating bronchial passages, expanding blood vessels in the eyes making them red in appearance. The negative effects of marijuana on memory, attention can last for days or weeks after the acute effects of the drug subsides. As a result individuals who smoke marijuana frequently may be functioning at reduced intellectual capacity most or all of the time. Research evidence also suggests that students who smoke marijuana heavily tend to get lower grades compared to non-smoking counterparts.

Marijuana smoke contains many toxins that promote cancer of the lungs. In recent years research has discovered a link between marijuana use and the later development of psychosis in a series of studies that followed subjects over time. Research indicates that marijuana can cause a brief psychotic reaction in some users that diminishes as the effects of the drug fade and can worsen the course of illness in schizophrenic patients. This relationship is influenced by the amount of drug used, the age of first use, and genetic predisposition. Marijuana use has also been reported to be associated with depression, anxiety, suicidal thoughts in adolescents and personality disturbances.

Synthetic cannabinoid compounds (commonly known as synthetic marijuana) consists of a wide variety of mixtures of dried plant material and other man-made chemicals that can produce life threatening side effects or death. Synthetic cannabinoid compounds are sold under names such as Spice, fake weed, Skunk, K2, and others and is considered not safe for human use, has no medical benefits and possesses a high potential for abuse. It is often marketed as a safe, natural alternative to marijuana and chemical detection by standard drug tests can be challenging. The U.S. Food and Drug Administration (FDA) has designated the five most active chemicals frequently found in Spice illegal to sell, purchase or possess (Schedule I controlled substances). However Spice manufacturers have substituted different chemicals to circumvent these restrictions. Spice is most commonly smoked (sometimes mixed with marijuana), prepared as a beverage for drinking and as incense.

Medical marijuana is cannabis used to treat health problems such as seizures in epilepsy, tics in Tourette syndrome, symptoms of multiple sclerosis, and nausea and vomiting caused by chemotherapy treatment for cancer. Research suggests that medical marijuana CBD does not cause the euphoric high feeling as THC does. Clinicians typically prescribe medical marijuana only when standard treatment is not effective. Many states in the United State of America have legalized marijuana for medical use. A written statement from one's physician is required to acquire medical marijuana and it must be obtained from an authorized seller. Some states have legalized small amounts for recreational use.

Researchers have distributed conflicting reports on the impact of marijuana on the body. However, recent data are more conclusive since the long-range effects of marijuana can now be determined. The U.S. Drug Enforcement Administration reported that:

- Marijuana is an addictive drug with significant health consequences. Many short- and long-term problems have been documented.

- Short-term effects of marijuana include memory loss, trouble with thinking and problem solving, loss of motor skills, decrease in strength, increased heart rate, anxiety, bloodshot eyes, dry mouth and throat, slowed reaction time, increased appetite, impairs coordination and balance, and impairs cognitive functions.

- Long term effects of marijuana use include risk of heart attack, weakened immune system, such that you are susceptible to infection and sickness, increased risk of cancer of the tongue, jaw, mouth, and lungs, impaired fertility in males, birth defects in babies of mothers who use marijuana during pregnancy, and addiction.

ECSTASY

Ecstasy, 3, 4 methylenedioxymethamphetamine or MDMA is a synthetic, psychoactive drug that is chemically similar to the stimulant methamphetamine and the hallucinogen mescaline. Ecstasy also called XTC, X, Versace, the hug drug, and the love pill is usually taken orally as a capsule or tablet. It is also inhaled or injected. It produces an energizing effect as well as feelings of euphoria, emotional warmth, and distortions in time perception and tactile experiences. Ecstasy can also produce confusion, depression, sleep problems, drug craving, severe anxiety, rapid heart rate, and even panic. For some people, ecstasy can be addictive. Overdoses may prove fatal, especially if it is taken with alcohol or another drug, such as heroin.

COCAINE

Cocaine also known as coke, snow, white girl, blow, "C," and happy dust is one of the most popular illicit drugs used in the United States. It is a powerfully addictive drug. Cocaine is derived from the leaves of the coca plant, found in Central and South America. After processing, cocaine is similar to flour. It is a fine, white, fluffy, odorless powder with a bitter taste. It is usually snorted, injected, or smoked to obtain a mild euphoric state. All three methods of cocaine abuse can lead to addiction and other severe health problems, including the risk of contracting HIV and infectious diseases.

Crack is a crystallized form of cocaine. It is 90% pure cocaine. It was given the name "crack" because of the crackling sound it makes when smoked in a cigarette or pipe. The physical effects of cocaine, smoking crack, and freebase include muscle twitching, increased heart rate and blood pressure and weight loss, decreased fatigue, temporary relief of depression, convulsions, irregular heart rhythm, and death due to overdose.

Some users spend hundreds of thousands of dollars on cocaine and crack each week and will do anything to support their habit. Many turn to drug selling, prostitution or other crimes. Cocaine and crack use has been a contributing factor in a number of drowning, car crashes, falls, burns, and suicides. Cocaine and crack addicts often become unable to function sexually. Even first users may experience seizures or heart attacks, which can be fatal.

METHAMPHETAMINE

Methamphetamine is the fastest growing illicit drug used in the United States. It is a member of a subgroup of amphetamines used to stimulate the central nervous system. The drug can be made in laboratories with inexpensive over-the-counter ingredients and industrial chemicals. It is an odorless off-white, bitter tasting powder or crystal that dissolves in water or alcohol and can be purchased as chunks or capsules. Methamphetamine comes in many forms and can be smoked, snorted, orally ingested, or injected. It is commonly known as speed, meth and chalk. When smoked it is referred to as ice, crystal, crank, and glass.

Short term effects of the drug include increased attention and decreased fatigue, hypothermia, euphoria and rush, decreased appetite, and increased activity. Long-term methamphetamine abuse results in many damaging effects, including addiction, hallucinations, cardiopulmonary damage, lethargy, severe depression, weight loss, stroke, dental destruction, and acute psychosis and paranoia.

HEROIN

Heroin usage in the United States is currently on the rise. It is a synthetic opiate drug that is highly addictive and is classified as a narcotic drug. It is made from morphine, a naturally occurring substance extracted from the seed pod of the Asian opium poppy plant. Heroin is made into a white powder, but on the streets it is brown or yellow. Street names include smack, H, ska, white death, tootsie roll, diesel, and junk. It can be smoked (which is called "chasing the dragon"), snorted, or injected. This drug is highly addictive and usage depresses the central nervous system and the user generally get's a euphoric feeling.

Symptoms of heroin use include drowsiness, nausea, and respiratory depression. Short-term effects of heroin include a surge of euphoria followed by alternately wakeful and drowsy states, and cloudy mental functioning. Other side effects include slow shallow breathing, loss of appetite, sleepiness, loss of sexual drive, and constipation.

CAFFEINE

Most **caffeine** comes from the seeds of the coffee, coco and cola plants. It is a tasteless stimulant found in some aspirin, over-the-counter cold and allergy medications, tea, some soft drinks, coffee, and chocolate. When caffeine is consumed in moderate amounts—which is about one cup—it decreases drowsiness, suppresses appetite, stimulates urinary production, and enhances attention by increasing alertness. When consumed in excess amounts over an extended period of time it is considered a drug, which results in dependency. Extended heavy use of caffeine has been linked to cancer, heart disease, digestive disorders, sleep disruption, nervousness, headaches and heart palpitations.

College students take NoDoz and Vivarin which contains caffeine during final exam week or when they have to stay up to complete assignments. Doctors often give caffeine to hyperactive children to calm them and to counteract drugs that cause depression.

SEXUAL ASSAULT AND DRUGS

Sexual assault is any type of sexual activity that a person does not agree to. Inappropriate touching, sexual intercourse, attempted rape, vaginal penetration, and rape are considered sexual assault. Drugs such as gamma hydroxybutyriuc acid (GHB), rohypnol, and ketamine can leave a person physically helpless, unable to refuse sex, and induce memory loss. This group of drugs are usually colorless, odorless, tasteless and has no smell. They can be added to flavored drinks without detection. All traces of these drugs leave the body within 72 hours of ingestion and are not typically found in a routine blood test or toxicology screen.

According to the law, sexual assault has occurred if you had sex but cannot remember the act or giving consent. Signs that sexual assault has taken place include soreness or bruising in the genital area, anal area, inner and/outer thighs, on the wrists or forearms, defensive bruises, used condoms in the area around you, vaginal fluids your body, clothes or other objects in the vicinity such as furniture. Other signs include feeling hung-over despite ingesting little or no alcohol medications or other drugs, comments from others about your behavior or the behavior of those around you, having hallucinations, fleeting memories or no clear memory of events during the prior eight to twenty-four hours. If you suspect that you have been sexually assaulted it is critical that you seek medical attention quickly and request a physical exam and testing for drugs. Most experts refer to date rape drugs as "drug-facilitated sexual assault" drugs. These drugs can affect you quickly and the effect time varies. It depends on how much of the drug is consumed and if the drug is mixed with alcohol or other substances.

According to the U.S. Department of Justice, sexual assault is a growing crime in America today. In most cases drugs are slipped into beverages of unsuspecting victims at social functions. Since the drugs are odorless, colorless, and tasteless the victim has no way of knowing that the drink is contaminated. After consuming the drink the victim is at the mercy of the perpetrator, led away, and in most cases assaulted. Any drug has the potential to be used to commit sexual assault. The following drugs have been used by perpetrators to commit sexual assault.

- GHB (gamma hydroxybutyriuc acid)
- Rohypnol (fluntrazepam)
- Ketamine (ketamine hydrochloride)

GHB can be in the form of an odorless or colorless liquid, pill, and white powder. It is an illicit depressant chemical that has become a major cause of drug-related comas in the United States and other countries. It may be listed on the internet as a sleep aid, an anti-depressant and weight loss product. This drug is naturally produced in the body in small amounts. During the 1960s, it was synthesized and sold in health food stores as a supplement for body builders.

The effects of GHB can cause numerous problems: relaxation, drowsiness, dizziness, nausea, problems seeing, unconsciousness (black out), seizures, short term memory loss while drugged, problems breathing, tremors, sweating, vomiting, slow heart rate, dream-like feeling, coma and death. GHB is abused for its euphoric and sedative effects. According to the Substance Abuse and Mental Health Services Administration (SAMHGA) this drug is one of the "designer" or "club" drugs.

Rohypnol (flenitrazepam) is an illegal drug often referred to as "roofies" and "roach." Rohypnol is a small, white, tasteless pill that dissolves in food or drink. While it alone can be dangerous, if combined with other drugs it can be fatal. Rohypnol can be physically addictive and is commonly known as a "Date Rape" drug. It is also considered to be a "designer" or "club" drug. Individuals are often unaware that they have been drugged and are unable to resist attacks. Rohypnol can cause the following problems: lower blood pressure, short term memory loss while drugged, sleepiness, stomach problems, muscle relaxation or loss of muscle control, drunk feeling, nausea, problem talking, confusion, dizziness, problem talking, difficulty with motor movements, confusion and problem seeing.

Ketamine is produced in liquid form or as a white powder. Ketamine is an injectable anesthetic that has been approved for both human and animal use in medical settings since 1970. Its slang or street names are Special K, K, Vitamin K, or Cat Valiums. Because it is odorless, tasteless, and colorless, it can be added to beverages and ingested unknowingly. High doses of ketamine cause amnesia, delirium, impaired motor functions, high blood pressure, depression, and potentially fatal respiratory problems. Low doses can result in impaired attention, learning ability, and memory. Other problems associated with ketamine use include: lost sense of time, feeling out of control, vomiting, numbness and aggressive behaviors.

It is important to be aware of tactics used by predators as they have no concern for your personal rights or safety. The tips listed below can offer some protection.

- Don't accept drinks from other people.
- Don't share drinks.
- Don't drink anything that tastes or smells strange.
- Open containers yourself.
- Keep your drink with you at all times, even when you go to the bathroom.
- Have a non-drinking friend with you to make sure nothing happens.
- Don't drink from punch bowls or other large, common, open containers. They may already have drugs in them.
- If you think that you have been drugged and/or sexual assaulted you should:
  1. Go to the police station or hospital right away.
  2. Get a urine test to test for drugs.
  3. Don't urinate before getting help
  4. Don't douche, bathe, or change clothes before getting help.
  5. You also can call a crisis center or a hotline to talk with a counselor.

Addictive Characteristics

Addiction is an advanced form of abuse characterized by compulsive use of a substance despite the loss of control and negative consequences experienced by the user. Individuals who are physically dependent on drugs develop a high tolerance to that drug, such that larger dosages are needed to get the desired effect.

There are four characteristics of addictive behavior: tolerance, withdrawal, dependence, and craving. **Tolerance** involves a diminished drug effect response due to repeated drug injection, such that larger and larger dosages are needed to get the desired effect. **Withdrawal** takes place when an addict decreases usage or stops taking the drug, which usually accompanies symptoms. **Dependence** results when an addict craves a drug while experiencing withdrawal. Individuals who are physically dependent on drugs develop a high tolerance to that drug, such that larger dosages are needed to get the desired effect. Psychological dependence refers to an intense craving for a drug's pleasure-producing effects. **Craving** refers to a compulsive desire to continue using a drug.

Risk Factors for Addictive Behavior

Individuals who are most likely to misuse or abuse drugs include individuals:

- with low self-esteem
- with the inability to control compulsion
- experiencing denial
- with the inability to control behavior
- who frequently use drugs that alter the brain's neurons, making the person more susceptible to addiction
- who feels pressure to perform or succeed to satisfy the expectations of others
- who lack a personal value system

Strategies Used to Overcome an Addiction

An addiction problem is difficult for most individuals to face. Denying the existance of an addiction makes it difficult to seek help or develop strategies to overcome the addiction. When realization of the addiction takes place, intervention is the next step to recovery.

Intervention

The purpose of a planned intervention is to confront the addict with the intent of eliminating his/her denial and to help the person acknowledge that he/she has a problem. An intervention is carried out by friends or family of the addict and a qualified professional.

Seek Treatment

Addicted individuals should seek treatment programs that possess the following characteristics:

- To build self-esteem
- To teach the addict to deal effectively with failure
- To develop stress management, problem solving, decision-making and coping skills
- To possess a systemic method to maintain adequate levels of motivation and reinforce continued modeling of new positive behaviors

Summary

Important concepts that you have learned in this chapter include:

- Electronic cigarettes contain nicotine and flavorings making them increasingly popular among teenagers.
- Alcohol dependency is a disease in which an individual craves alcohol, cannot control his or her cravings for alcohol, exhibits a physical dependence on alcohol, and needs to drink greater amounts of alcohol for the same "high".
- Alcohol misuse on college campuses is a major problem—especially binge drinking.
- Over-exposure to alcohol results in impaired judgment and loss of self-control.
- Tobacco use is the leading cause of cancer in humans.
- Cigarette smoking is the largest use of tobacco in the U.S.
- Nicotine is more addictive than either marijuana or heroin.
- Long-term effects of marijuana reveal that it is an addictive drug, as well as causes cancer and increases the risk of heart attacks.
- Caffeine is considered a drug when excessive amounts are consumed over a prolonged time period.
- Methamphetamine is one of the fastest growing illicit drug used in the United States.
- Strategies to overcome addiction include intervention and treatment.

References

Baker, F., Ainsworth, S.R., Dye, J.T., Crammer, C., Thun, M.J., & Hoffman, D., et al., (2000). Health risks associated with cigar smoking. *Journal of the American medical association,* 284, 734–740.

Bounds, L., Agnor, D., Darnell, G., & Gibbons, E. (2003). *Health and fitness: A guide to a healthy lifestyle.* Dubuque, IA: Kendall/Hunt Publishing Company.

Conrad, K.M., Flay, B.R., & Hill, D. (1992). Why children start smoking cigarettes: Predictors of onset. *British journal of addiction* 87(12):1711–1724.

Corbin, C.B., Welk, G.J., Corbin, W.R., & Welk, K.A. (2008). *Concepts of fitness and wellness,* 6th ed. New York, NY: McGraw-Hill Publishing Company.

Dennis, K., Henson, B., & Adams, T.M., (2005). *Destination: Fit, well, and healthy.* Dubuque, IA: Kendall/Hunt Publishing Company.

Donatelle, R., Snow, C., & Wilcox, A. (2009). *Wellness choices for health and fitness.* Belmont, CA: Wadsworth Publishing Company.

SAMHSA, Office of applied studies, Department of health and human services. http://www.samhsa.gov; htto://drugabusestatistics.samhas.gov; http://www.health.org.

Substance Abuse and Mental Health Services Administration, Office of Applied Studies, Department of Health and Human Services. (2006) *National household survey on drug abuse,* Rockville, MD: SAMHSA, Office of Applied Studies, Department of Health and Human Services. http://www.samhsa.gov/oas/clubdrug.pdf. Downloaded 2/18/09.

Su, S.S.; Larison, C., Ghadialy, R., et al., (1991). *Substance use among women in the United States.* SAMHSA Analytic Series A-3. Rockville, MD: Substance Abuse and Mental Health Services Administration.

U.S. Drug Enforcement Administration, (Download 2/18/09). Marijuana: The facts. http://www.usdoj.gov/dea/ongoing/marijuana.html.

Internet Sources

http://www.niaa.nih.gov/publications/aa46.htm

http://.www.collegedrinkingprevention.gov/facts/snapshot.aspx

http://www.collegedrinkingprevention.gov/facts/q-a.aspex

http://www.collegedrinkingprevention.gov/ReportsPanel101/HighRisk_02.aspx

http://www.samhsa.gov

http://www.drugabusestatistics.gov

http://www.health.org

http://www.samhsa.gov/oas/clubdrug.pdf

http://www.drugabuse.gov

http://www.usdoj.gov/dea/ongoing/marijuana.html

http://www.lungusa.org

http://www.alcoholics-anonymous.org

http://www.ca.org

http://www.casacolumbia.org

http://www.cdc.gov

http://www.drugstv.com/methamphetamine.htm

http://www.projectghb.org/ecstasy.htm

http://www.westfieldnj.com/mcadd/facts7.htm

http://www.teens.drugabuse.gov/facts/facts_mj2.asp

http://www.teens.livestrong.com

https://drugabuse.gov

Lab 11.1
A Letter to My Best Friend

Name: _____ Date: _____

Dear Friend,

I'm worried about you. You seem to be out of it all of the time. You are not acting like the real you. You didn't even remember to meet me in the student center game room yesterday. The large amount of weed/marijuana/chronic you've been smoking recently is affecting our friendship in a negative manner. I don't think you even realize what marijuana is doing to your body and mind.

Marijuana impairs various areas of the brain such as the: 1) _____,

2) _____ and 3) _____.

When these areas of your brain aren't functioning properly, you could have problems with

4) _____, 5) _____ and 6) _____.

Francis, did you know that marijuana has many short term effects such as: 7) _____

8) _____, 9) _____

I know you enjoy smoking marijuana, but it has long term negative effects such as 10) _____

11) _____ and 12) _____.

I hope the information I've shared with you helps you to understand that your chronic use will not solve any problem, but will in fact make things worse. I don't like the person you are now

because 13) _____

14) _____.

I want the real Francis back in my life because 15) _____

_____.

Your Best Friend,

_____

Chapter 12

Chronic Diseases

Objectives
Introduction
Cancer
Cardiovascular Diseases
Diabetes Mellitus
Osteoporosis

Summary
References
Internet Sources
Lab 12.1: Assessing Your Risk for Cancer
Lab 12.2: Assessing Your Risk for Osteoporosis
Lab 12.3: Coronary Heart Disease Risk Appraisal

Objectives

Upon completion of this chapter, you will be able to

1. Define *cancer, cardiovascular disease, osteoporosis,* and *diabetes.*
2. Define benign, malignant, metastasize, and chronic disease.
3. Understand how cancer starts and spreads throughout the body.
4. Identify and explain risk factors for cancer, cardiovascular disease, osteoporosis, and diabetes.
5. Discuss ways to reduce your risk for developing cancer, cardiovascular disease, osteoporosis, and diabetes.
6. Describe the early symptoms and appropriate treatments for cancer, cardiovascular disease, osteoporosis, and diabetes.
7. Describe the prevalence of cancer, cardiovascular disease, osteoporosis, and diabetes.

Introduction

A **chronic disease** is any disease that develops over time as the body's ability to resist potential pathogens and environmental threats begin to diminish (i.e., cancer, cardiovascular disease, osteoporosis, and cancer). Chronic diseases targeted by the CDC's National Center for Chronic Disease Prevention and Health Promotion are those illnesses that fit the broad definition of chronic diseases that are preventable and that pose a significant burden in mortality, morbidity, and cost. Research has linked our lifestyle choices to the most common chronic diseases that plague our society.

Chronic diseases disproportionately affect women and racial minority groups. Women comprise more than half of the people who die each year of cardiovascular disease. Deaths due to breast cancer are decreasing among Caucasian women but not among African-American women. The death rate from cervical cancer is twice as high for African-American women as it is for Caucasian women. The five-year survival rate for men with colon cancer is higher among Caucasians than African-Americans. The prevalence of diabetes is higher among non-Hispanic, African-Americans, Hispanics, American Indians, and Alaska Natives than among non-Hispanic Caucasian Americans of similar age. The death rate from prostate cancer is more than twice as high for African-American men as it is for Caucasian men. African Americans are more likely than Caucasians to get oral or pharyngeal cancer, half as likely to have those diseases diagnosed early, and twice as likely to die of these diseases.

Practical interventions exist for controlling and preventing many chronic diseases. Examples of practical interventions include the following:

- Implementing proven clinical smoking-cessation interventions
- Diabetes education
- Mammography screening
- Cervical cancer screening
- Participation in the arthritis self-help courses

In this chapter, the most common chronic diseases affecting people today will be addressed: cancer, cardiovascular (heart) disease, diabetes and osteoporosis. Factors affecting your risk for developing these diseases, treatments for the disease, and prevention strategies will also be discussed.

Cancer

Out of all the chronic diseases, cancer instills more fear in Americans than any other. Cancer afflicts all ethnic groups, ages, and socioeconomic groups in spite of major advances in cancer diagnosis, treatment, and long-term survival for some forms of cancer. According to the American Cancer Society (ACS), cancer is the second leading cause of death in this county, exceeded only by heart disease. Lung cancer remains the number one cause of cancer deaths in the United States. Cancer rates are highest among African Americans males, followed by Caucasians, American Indians, and Asian men. Among women, cancer rates are higher among Alaska-Native women, followed closely by Caucasian women.

In most cases cancer develops over time and is generally found in those over fifty. However, childhood leukemia and skin cancer attacks younger individuals, and is the major cause of death in children under the age of fifteen. Over the years an alarming number of young adults have been diagnosed with ovarian, breast, and testicular cancer—especially those with a genetic tendency for the disease.

What Is Cancer?

Cancer is a group of diseases characterized by the uncontrolled growth and rapid spread of abnormal cells. The abnormal cell divides to create other abnormal cells, which again divide, eventually forming **tumors**—masses of abnormal tissue that grow rapidly, which can be either **benign** (abnormal, noncancerous cells) or **malignant** (cancerous cells). Even though benign tumors are not considered life-threatening, they may become so large that they interfere with bodily functions.

Without treatment, cancer cells continue to grow, attacking and replacing healthy cells. This process is called **infiltration,** or invasion. They may also **metastasize,** or spread to other parts of the body via the bloodstream or lymphatic system. Some cancers metastasize quickly, while other metastases are too small to be seen or felt at the time of diagnosis. In either case, early detection is crucial for treatment and cure. Cancer is typically diagnosed by examining tissue samples removed from the body (biopsy) and cell samples under a microscope. Doctors examine the size and shape of cells and their nuclei as well as the arrangement of the cells. The consistent size and shape of healthy cells is essential to their ability to can out normal function. Cancer cells may have a nucleus that is larger or smaller than normal cells, vary in size and have an irregular shape thereby unable to carryout normal function.

Cancers are generally classified according to the type of organ (for example, brain, breast, stomach, liver, and colon in which they are initially observed. They are also classified according to tissue type, such as the following:

Carcinomas are the most common type of cancer. It starts in the epithelial tissue, the layers of the cells that cover the outer layers of the body's surface or line internal organs and glands. This type of cancer metastasize mostly through the lymphatic system. The lymphatic system is the network in the body that filters out impurities.

Sarcomas develop in the supporting, and connective tissues of the body: bones, muscles, joints, and blood vessels. This type of cancer metastasizes by way of the body.

Lymphomas develop and spread via the lymphatic system. This type of cancer can adversely impact the body's immune system because it can hinder the body's production and utilization of white blood cells.

Leukemia, the fourth type of cancer, is different from the other three types because it does not form a solid mass, but instead it is nonsolid and consists of many white blood cells. This cancer affects the blood-forming tissues.

Risk Factors for Cancer

Most doctors believe that cancer is influenced by not one but several factors. The following are some of the suggested causal agents of cancer risk:

Viruses. Researchers have linked several different viruses to cancer in humans. For example, Herpes II and the Human Papilloma viruses have been linked to an increase in cervical cancer in women and cancer of the penis. You may increase your chances of developing liver cancer if you have Hepatitis B, and the virus that causes HIV can lead to certain lymphomas and leukemias, and to a type of cancer called Kaposi's sarcoma.

Environmental Risks. Many **carcinogens**, or cancer-causing agents (i.e., asbestos, tobacco, auto emissions, dyes, petroleum, alcohol, and chemicals used as food preservatives or additives) used in industry today can cause cancer, placing both employees and neighborhood residents at risk unless safety measures are taken.

Heredity. Heredity may be responsible for 10 percent of all cancers, and approximately 13 to 14 million Americans may be at risk. Scientists have identified a variety of **oncogenes**—genes that appear to cause cancer growth. In familial cancers (i.e., breast, colon, brain, and kidney cancer), close relatives tend to develop the same type of cancer.

Lifestyle Factors. These are factors that each person can alter to reduce one's risk for cancer:

1. Diet—thirty-five percent of all cancer deaths are closely linked to dietary factors. High fat diets may increase your risk for developing cancer.
2. Stress—research suggests that stress lowers the ability of the immune system to form infection-fighting white blood cells.
3. Tobacco use—cigarettes, smokeless tobacco, and cigars are among the leading tobacco products used in America. Cigarette smoking is the single most devastating and preventable cause of cancer deaths in the Unites States. Cigarettes cause most cases of lung cancers and increase the risk of cancer of the mouth, pharynx, larynx, esophagus, pancreas, and bladder.

You can assess your risk for cancer in **Lab 12.1**.

Treatment for Cancer

Depending on the type of cancer, the cancer specialist, or oncologist, may recommend chemotherapy, surgery, radiation therapy, immunotherapy or a combination of these treatments. Understanding how each work, and what you can expect in terms of side effects, can help put a person's mind at ease and make the experience less frightening. Chemotherapy, radiation, surgery and immunotherapy are commonly used to treat cancer. **Chemotherapy** is the use of drugs to treat cancer. Cancerous cells can split off from the original tumor invade another sites the body. Chemotherapy can destroy cancerous cells that have metastasized throughout the body. There are three main objectives of chemotherapy. The first objective is to cure cancer such that it does not return, often referred to as **curative intent**. However, this is not always possible. The second objective of chemotherapy treatment is to control the growth and spread of cancer in order to help the person feel better and live longer. Cancer that is being controlled and managed, but not completely destroyed can return. In such cases, chemotherapy treatment is resumed. The third objective is **palliation**. Palliation chemotherapy is administered to reduce cancer symptoms to make the person feel more comfortable. Palliation is sometimes used during advanced stages of cancer. Chemotherapy can be used in combination with other therapies such as radiation and surgery. **Neoadjuvant** therapy is the use of chemotherapy *before* radiation or surgery to shrink a tumor. While **adjuvant** therapy is the use of chemotherapy *after* radiation or surgery to destroy any remaining cancer cells. Common side effects of chemotherapy include the following: nausea, vomiting, diarrhea, appetite changes, infection, fatigue, hair loss, dry skin, changes in skin color, constipation, weight changes, mood changes and easy bruising and bleeding.

Surgery is used to prevent, diagnose, and treat cancer. **Primary surgery** is performed when cancer is located in only one part of the body and it is possible to remove all the cancerous tissue. **Debulking surgery** is performed when only a portion of the tumor can be removed because removal of the entire tumor will damage surrounding tissues. **Supportive surgery** is performed to allow administration of other types of treatments such as the implantation of a portal to deliver chemotherapy medications. **Reconstructive surgery** is performed to improve a person's appearance after major surgery such as breast reconstruction after mastectomy. **Prophylactic surgery** is performed to remove tissue that may become cancerous, despite the absence of current cancer signs in order to reduce cancer risk.

Radiation therapy destroys cancerous cells by using radiation. Radiation is administered using three techniques: external beam radiation, internal radiation, systemic radiation. **External radiation** occurs by using a large machine to deliver high-energy x-ray beams directly to the tumor and some of the surrounding tissues. The number of radiation treatments given depends on the size, type and location of the cancer. As well as the health status of the individual and other types of treatments given. Radiation treatments are usually given five days a week for one to ten weeks for most individuals. **Internal radiation** therapy involves placing a radioactive source known as an implant inside the body. Radiation in the implant spreads a short distance, therefore the implant is placed directly on or in very close proximity to the tumor. **Systemic radiation** therapy involves intravenous or by mouth administration of radioactive drugs in liquid form that disperse throughout the body. Some radioactive fluid will remain in the body for a few days until the body can extract the liquid through the blood, sweat, saliva and urine. Side effects of radiation include loss of appetite, severe fatigue, and skin changes in the treated area.

Immunotherapy includes treatments that act to stimulate the immune system to attack cancer cells more effectively or to strengthen the immune system itself. The primary types of immunotherapy include monoclonal antibodies, immune checkpoint inhibitors, and cancer vaccines. **Monoclonal antibodies** are synthetic proteins used by the immune system to specifically target antigens found in cancer cells. These antibodies attach targeted antigen and enlist the assistance of other immune system components to destroy the cancer cells. **Immune checkpoint inhibitors** accelerate the immune system's ability to distinguish between normal cells and cancerous cells by creating areas on specific immune cells that when activated trigger the immune system to attack. Some **cancer vaccines** prevent cancer by enabling the immune system to attack cancer cells. For example, human papilloma virus (HPV) has been associated with cervical cancer in women. Vaccines given to combat HPV may protect against cervical cancer.

Cancer Prevention

Cancer is a disease that tends to develop over time as a result of what we eat and drink, how we live, and where we work. Not all cancers are preventable, and in some cases prevention is difficult due to a lack of health care. The following are lifestyle behaviors to consider on a quest to reduce your risk for cancer:

1. *Avoid environmental carcinogens whenever possible.* Eighty to 90 percent of all cancers are caused by environmental factors—chemicals used in industry, and smoke, dust or gases created by industry.

2. *Don't smoke.* Cigarette smoke is the number one carcinogen in this country, responsible for one in every three cancers.

3. *Self-examination.* Regular self-examinations can detect changes in body parts that are more susceptible to cancer and should be performed monthly. Recommended areas to perform self-exams include the breast, testicles, and moles. See **Table 12.1** for recommended cancer checkups.

Table 12.1 Screening Tests

Many cancer screening tests are in use. Some tests have been shown both to find cancer early and to lower the chance of dying from the disease. Others have been shown to find cancer early but have not been shown to reduce the risk of dying from cancer; however, they may still be offered to people, especially those who are known to be at increased risk of cancer.

On This Page
- Screening Tests That Have Been Shown to Reduce Cancer Deaths
- Other Screening Tests
- More Information

Screening Tests That Have Been Shown to Reduce Cancer Deaths

≈ Colonoscopy, sigmoidoscopy, and high-sensitivity fecal occult blood tests (FOBTs)

These tests have all been shown to reduce deaths from colorectal cancer. Colonoscopy and sigmoidoscopy also help prevent colorectal cancer because they can detect abnormal colon growths (polyps) that can be removed before they develop into cancer. Expert groups generally recommend that people who are at average risk for colorectal cancer have screening at ages 50 through 75. For more information, see the Tests to Detect Colorectal Cancer and Polyps fact sheet and the PDQ® Colorectal Cancer Screening summary.

≈ Low-dose helical computed tomography

This test to screen for lung cancer has been shown to reduce lung cancer deaths among heavy smokers ages 55 to 74. For more information, see the National Lung Screening Trial page and the PDQ® Lung Cancer Screening summary.

≈ Mammography

This method to screen for breast cancer has been shown to reduce mortality from the disease among women ages 40 to 74, especially those age 50 or older. For more information, see the Mammograms fact sheet and the PDQ® Breast Cancer Screening summary.

≈ Pap test and human papillomavirus (HPV) testing

These tests reduce the incidence of cervical cancer because they allow abnormal cells to be identified and treated before they become cancer. They also reduce deaths from cervical cancer. Testing is generally recommended to begin at age 21 and to end at age 65, as long as recent results have been normal. For more information, see the Pap and HPV Testing fact sheet and the PDQ® Cervical Cancer Screening summary.

Other Screening Tests

≈ Alpha-fetoprotein blood test

This test is sometimes used, along with ultrasound of the liver, to try to detect liver cancer early in people at high risk of the disease. For more information, see the PDQ® Liver (Hepatocelluar) Cancer Screening summary.

≈ Breast MRI

This imaging test is often used for women who carry a harmful mutation in the *BRCA1* gene or the *BRCA2* gene; such women have a high risk of breast cancer, as well as increased risk for other cancers. For more information, see the *BRCA1* and *BRCA2*: Cancer Risk and Genetic Testing fact sheet and the PDQ® Breast Cancer Screening summary.

≈ CA-125 test

This blood test, which is often done together with a transvaginal ultrasound, may be used to try to detect ovarian cancer early, especially in women with an increased risk of the disease. Although this test can help in diagnosing ovarian cancer in women who have symptoms and can be used to evaluate the recurrence of cancer in women previously diagnosed with the disease, it has not been shown to be an effective ovarian cancer screening test. For more information, see the PDQ® Ovarian Cancer Screening summary.

≈ Clinical breast exams and regular breast self-exams

Routine examination of the breasts by health care providers or by women themselves has not been shown to reduce deaths from breast cancer. However, if a woman or her health care provider notices a lump or other unusual change in the breast, it is important to get it checked out. For more information, see the PDQ® Breast Cancer Screening summary.

≈ PSA test

This blood test, which is often done along with a digital rectal exam, is able to detect prostate cancer

Table 12.1 Screening Tests —cont'd

at an early stage. However, expert groups no longer recommend routine PSA testing for most men because studies have shown that it has little or no effect on prostate cancer deaths and leads to overdiagnosis and overtreatment. For more information, see the Prostate-Specific Antigen (PSA) Test fact sheet and the PDQ® Prostate Cancer Screening summary.

≈ Skin exams
Doctors often recommend that people who are at risk for skin cancer examine their skin regularly or have a health care provider do so. Such exams have not been shown to decrease the risk of dying from skin cancer, and they may lead to overtreatment. However, people should be aware of changes in their skin, such as a new mole or a change to an existing mole, and report these to their doctor promptly. For more information, see the Common Moles, Dysplastic Nevi, and Risk of Melanoma fact sheet and the PDQ® Skin Cancer Screening summary.

≈ Transvaginal ultrasound
This imaging test, which can create pictures of a woman's ovaries and uterus, is sometimes used in women who are at increased risk of ovarian cancer (because they carry a harmful *BRCA1* or *BRCA2* mutation) or of endometrial cancer (because they have a condition called Lynch syndrome). But it has not been shown to reduce deaths from either cancer. For more information, see the PDQ® Ovarian Cancer Screening summary and the PDQ® Endometrial Cancer Screening summary.

≈ Virtual colonoscopy
This test allows the colon and rectum to be examined from outside the body. However, it has not been shown to reduce deaths from colorectal cancer. For more information, see the Tests to Detect Colorectal Cancer and Polyps fact sheet and the PDQ® Colorectal Cancer Screening summary.

More Information
For complete information about screening tests by cancer type, including tests that are being developed and tests that were used in the past, see the PDQ® Cancer Information Summaries: Screening/Detection (Testing for Cancer).

Retreived from: https://www.cancer.gov/about-cancer/screening/screening-tests#screening-test

4. *Exercise on a regular basis.* Exercise aids in boosting the immune system and may enhance your body's ability in fighting off cancer.

5. *Watch your weight.* Obesity increases the risks in the development of several types of cancer.

6. *Watch what you eat.* Make sure that you eat a well-balanced diet that's low in fat and high in fruits and vegetables and whole grains. High fat foods have been linked to breast, prostate, and colon cancer.

7. *Protect yourself from the sun.* Use a sun screen with high Sun Protective Factors (SPFs) of at least 15, wear protective clothing, stay in the shade, and stay away from ultraviolet light in tanning beds.

8. *Limit alcohol intake.* Cancer of the throat, esophagus, liver, breast, and larynx are more prevalent in excessive drinkers.

9. *Know the warning signs.* The American Cancer Society suggests the following warning signs to help you recognize the presence of cancer: change in bowel or bladder habits, a sore that does not heal, unusual bleeding or discharge, thickening or lump in the breast or elsewhere, indigestion that persists or difficulty in swallowing, obvious change in a wart or mole, and nagging cough or hoarseness.

10. *Sexual cautions.* Cervical cancer has been linked to the human Papilloma virus (genital warts) and multiple sex partners. Prostate cancer in men increases with a history of sexually transmitted diseases, and multiple sex partners.

Cardiovascular Diseases

More Americans today are exercising and eating healthful diets. As a result of this trend, and in conjunction with diagnosis and treatment, the nation is seeing a decline in cardiovascular diseases. Even with the decline, heart disease is still at the top of the list of the country's most serious health problems. In fact, statistics show that cardiovascular disease is America's leading health problem, and the leading cause of death. The American Heart Association reports that cardiovascular diseases (CVD) have been the number one killer for both men and women among all racial and ethnic groups in the United States for several decades. At least 60.8 million people in this country suffer from some form of heart disease. Almost 1 million Americans die of CVDs each year, which adds up to 42 percent of all deaths. CVDs cost the nation $274 billion each year, including health expenditures and lost productivity.

What Are Cardiovascular Diseases (CVD)?

Cardiovascular disease (CVDs) includes dysfunctional conditions of the heart, arteries, and veins that supply oxygen to vital life-sustaining areas of the body—like the brain, the heart itself, and other vital organs. If oxygen is not received tissues and organs will die. CVD comes in many forms, such as, atherosclerosis, coronary artery disease, hypertension (high blood pressure), stroke, peripheral artery disease, and heart disease (congestive heart failure). High blood pressure is the most prevalent form of cardiovascular disease affecting 73.6 million Americans, 16.8 million have coronary artery disease, and 6.5 million have suffered a stroke. However, coronary artery disease is responsible for the most deaths (500,000) per year when compared with stroke and high blood pressure.

The following are examples of several types of cardiovascular diseases which may plague the cardiovascular system:

Atherosclerosis is gradual narrowing and hardening of the arteries due to the build-up of **plaque**, which is the deposit of fat, cholesterol, calcium, and other cellular substances in the inner lining of the arterial walls.

Coronary artery disease (CAD) is a condition in which the coronary arteries that carry blood to the heart have been narrowed or blocked by atherosclerosis. These blockages can restrict or totally block oxygenated blood flow, and can cause a heart attack or myocardial infraction (when blood flow to the heart is blocked).

Hypertension, or high blood pressure, is often a hidden multifactorial problem and the most common CVD. The main pathologic process involved in hypertension is atherosclerosis. The narrowing and hardening of the arteries increase their resistance and pressure, and make the heart work harder, which can then wear down this vital muscle. Untreated hypertension may lead to further heart disease including heart attacks, congestive heart failure, and stroke.

Strokes, cerebrovascular accidents, or brain attacks are diseases of the blood vessels that supply the brain. They are caused by a clot that forms and enlarges in an artery leading to the brain (thrombus), or a clot that forms elsewhere, dislodges or fractures, and circulates to one of the cerebral arteries that are too small for its passage (embolus). Strokes can also occur in blood vessels in the brain that become blocked due to plaque build-up. Cerebral hemorrhage, the bursting of a blood vessel in the brain, is a third cause of stroke, which can result from heart trauma or an aneurysm. An aneurysm is a weak spot in an artery that forms a blood-filled pouch similar to a balloon that may burst and bleed into the brain.

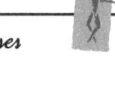

Congestive Heart Failure. Congestive heart failure occurs when the heart muscle is incapable of contracting with enough force to effectively pump blood throughout the body. The major causes are high blood pressure, heart attack, birth defects, atherosclerosis, and rheumatic fever.

Risk Factors for Cardiovascular Diseases

Researchers have identified several major controllable factors that put you at risk for CVDs, including smoking, hypertension, high blood cholesterol, obesity, diabetes, stress, and physical inactivity. Some uncontrollable risk factors for CVDs include heredity and race, age and gender. CVDs rarely develops from a single risk factor. You will have an opportunity to evaluate your risk for heart disease in **Lab 12.3**.

Smoking. Exposure to cigarette smoke acts with other factors to greatly increase your risk of CVD by damaging blood vessels.

Hypertension. High blood pressure places more "wear and tear" on the lining of arteries, predisposing them to atherosclerosis. Additionally, high blood pressure puts an extra work load on the heart, which can be particularly problematic if the coronary arteries are narrowed due to atherosclerosis. The optimal blood pressure level is 120/80. The top number represents the heart action during contraction and the bottom number represents relaxation of the heart. A reading between 120/80 and 139/89 is considered prehypertension. Prehypertension indicates that your blood pressure is outside the optimal range, but is not yet considered hypertensive. Readings of 140/90 to 159/99 and 160/100 or higher are considered stage 1 and stage 2 hypertension respectively. The higher the blood pressure the higher the risk of cardiovascular disease.

High Blood Cholesterol. The risk of CVDs rises as your LDL blood cholesterol levels increase. Lowering blood cholesterol can lower the risk of a heart attack.

Obesity. Excessive weight increases the strain on your heart, raises blood pressure, increases blood cholesterol levels, and increases your risk of diabetes.

Diabetes. Uncontrolled blood sugar (glucose) levels seriously increases the risk of heart disease, kidney disease, and stroke by damaging blood vessels.

Stress. Some scientists have noted a relationship between CVDs and unmanaged stress in a person's life, however the mechanism by which it exerts its effects is not completely understood.

Physical Inactivity. Regular exercise is important in preventing heart and blood vessel disease. Exercise also helps control other risk factors for CVDs, such as high blood cholesterol, obesity, and stress.

Heredity and Race. If your siblings, parents or grandparents have heart disease, you may be at risk, too. Your family may have a genetic predisposition that negatively affects cholesterol levels. High blood pressure can also run in families. Race can be a factor. African-Americans have a higher risk for CVD than Caucasians, Hispanics, or Asian-Americans, and their heart disease is often more severe. High blood pressure is also more common among African-Americans in America.

Age and Sex. About four out of five people who die of CVD are age 65 or older. Heart disease takes decades to develop. Arteries also naturally thicken and harden with age, compounding existing CVDs. Men are generally at greater risk than women for heart disease. However, the risk for women increases after menopause.

Treatment for Cardiovascular Diseases

If CVDs are found, they are treated in a number of ways, depending on the seriousness of the disease. For some individuals, a CVD is managed with lifestyle changes and medications. Others with severe CVDs may need angioplasty or surgery. In any case, once a CVD develops, it requires lifelong management.

Although advances have been made in treating CVDs, changing one's habits remains the single most effective way to stop the disease from progressing. The most beneficial changes you can make include:

1. *Changing your diet.* Your diet should consist of foods low in fat, especially saturated fat and cholesterol. This will help reduce cholesterol, a primary cause of atherosclerosis. Eating less fat should also help in losing weight. Eating a diet rich in fruits and vegetables, and having at least one to two servings of fish per week can also reduce your risk of heart attack and help you lose weight.

2. *Exercising.* Research has shown that even moderate amounts of physical activity(30 minutes a day) are associated with lower death rates from CVDs. Check with a doctor to find out what types of exercise are best.

3. *Not smoking.* Smoking is a major risk factor for CVDs. Quitting smoking dramatically lowers the risk of a first or second heart attack.

In addition to lifestyle changes, your doctor may recommend drug therapy to treat CVDs. Certain medications can help prevent the progression of CVDs, and other drugs can be used to help improve blood flow to the heart. At times, a combination of medications is advised. Medications commonly used to prevent or treat CVDs include:

1. *Cholesterol-lowering drugs.* Cholesterol (a fat) is a large part of the fatty deposits that can clog heart arteries. Cholesterol-lowering drugs, also called lipid-lowering drugs, help lower the level of bad cholesterol in blood while raising the level of good cholesterol. Examples of these drugs include statins, niacin, fibrates and bile acids.

2. *Aspirin.* Aspirin, as well as other blood thinners can reduce the tendency of blood to clot, which may help prevent obstruction of coronary arteries and a heart attack.

3. *Beta-blocker.* These drugs slow heart rate and decrease blood pressure, which in turn decrease the heart's demand for oxygen.

4. *Nitroglycerin.* Nitroglycerin tablets, spray, and patches are used to control chest pain (angina) by both opening the coronary arteries and reducing the heart's demand for oxygen.

5. *Calcium channel blockers.* These medications cause the muscles that surround the coronary arteries to relax and the vessels to open more, increasing blood flow to the heart. They also control high blood pressure.

6. *Angiotensin-converting enzyme* (ACE) inhibitors. These drugs allow blood to flow from the heart more easily, decreasing the heart's workload.

7. *Other drugs that lower blood pressure.* These medications help widen blood vessels, including those to the heart, decreasing the heart's workload.

Surgery may be recommended for people who have frequent or unstable angina, despite the use of medications. At times surgical procedures also may be used for people who have severe blockages or narrowed coronary arteries cause by atherosclerosis. Types of surgical procedures to treat CVD include:

1. *Coronary angioplasty.* In this procedure, a doctor inserts a catheter with a small balloon at the tip into an artery in the groin or arm. The catheter is then threaded to the area of a blocked or narrowed artery. When the catheter reaches the blockage, the balloon is inflated to widen the artery and improve blood flow;

2. *Coronary bypass surgery.* This heart surgery procedure creates a route for blood to go around a blocked stretch of a coronary artery. A blood vessel, usually taken from the leg or chest, or grafted directly onto a narrowed artery, bypasses the blocked area.

Cardiovascular Disease Prevention

How you live your life can largely affect the health of your heart and the arteries that feed it. Taking the following steps can help you prevent CVDs, especially including heart attacks:

1. *Get regular medical checkups.* Some of the main risk factors for CVDs (high blood cholesterol, high blood pressure, and diabetes) have no symptoms in the early stages. A doctor can perform tests to check for these conditions. If a problem is found, you and your doctor can manage it early to prevent complications.

2. *Control your blood pressure.* All adults should have their blood pressure checked annually. Your doctor may recommend more frequent measurements if you have high blood pressure or a history of heart disease. Optimal blood pressure with respect to cardiovascular risk is 120/80 mm Hg.

3. *Check your cholesterol.* Have your blood cholesterol levels checked regularly, through a simple blood test at a doctor's office. If blood cholesterol levels are undesirably high, your doctor can prescribe changes to your diet and medications to help lower the numbers and protect your cardiovascular health.

4. *Don't smoke.* Smoking and secondhand smoke are major risk factors for CVDs. Nicotine constricts blood vessels and forces your heart to work harder. Carbon monoxide reduces oxygen in blood and damages the lining of blood vessels. Smoking also worsens cholesterol and increases fibrinogen, a clotting protein.

5. *Exercise regularly.* Exercise helps prevent CVD by helping one to achieve and maintain a healthy weight and control diabetes, elevated cholesterol and high blood pressure.

6. *Maintain a healthy weight.* Being only 10 percent overweight increases heart disease risk. Losing just 5 to 10 pounds may lower blood pressure.

7. *Eat a heart-healthy diet.* Excess fat and cholesterol in the diet can clog arteries to the heart. A diet high in salt can raise blood pressure. Fish containing omega-3 fatty acids should be a part of a heart-healthy diet. They help improve blood cholesterol

levels and prevent blood clots. Eating plenty of fruits and vegetables is also encouraged. Fruits and vegetables contain antioxidants, vitamins and minerals that help prevent everyday wear-and-tear on coronary arteries.

8. *Manage stress.* To reduce risk of cardiovascular disease, reduce stress in your day-to-day activities. Rethink workaholic habits and find healthy ways to minimize or deal with stressful events in your life.

Diabetes Mellitus

Diabetes mellitus is considered a serious disease, but most individuals learn how to live with it and manage the condition. Individuals with diabetes are capable of doing the same things as people without the disease if they eat the appropriate foods, monitor their blood sugar level daily, exercise on a regular basis, and take medication, if prescribed. Diabetes can lead to serious complications such as blindness, kidney problems, heart disease, stroke, and amputations. Research shows that a large percentage of people with diabetes also have high blood pressure.

What Is Diabetes Mellitus?

Diabetes mellitus is a disease of the pancreas. The pancreas is responsible for producing and releasing a hormone called **insulin** that helps the body store and use carbohydrates (i.e., sugars and starches) and fat from food eaten. In other words, insulin helps the body change food into energy. **Diabetes mellitus** occurs when the pancreas does not produce any insulin, produces very little, or when the body does not respond appropriately to insulin. Without insulin, carbohydrates which are the body's major energy source, build up in the blood. There are two types of diabetes. **Type 1 diabetes** occurs when the body does not produce any insulin, most often found in children and young adults. Type 1 diabetes was formerly known as juvenile-onset diabetes. People with Type 1 diabetes must take daily insulin injections to stay alive. This type of diabetes is present in 5 to 10 percent of all diabetes cases.

Type 2 diabetes, also known as adult-onset diabetes, occurs as a result of the body's inability to make enough, or properly use insulin. Type 2 diabetes is the most common and accounts for 90 to 95 percent of diabetes. Type 2 diabetes is on the rise, as a result of a greater prevalence of obesity, an increase in sedentary lifestyles, and an increase in the number of elderly Americans. Type 2 diabetes is more prevalent in African-Americans and Hispanics than in Caucasians. It is the fourth leading cause of death from disease in African-Americans. Approximately one in ten African-Americans develop diabetes between the ages forty-five and sixty-five. More than 75 million adults age 20 or older a **prediabetic**. Prediabetes occurs when blood glucose levels are higher than normal but is not high enough to be diagnosed with type two diabetes. These individuals are a greater risk for developing type 2 diabetes, heart disease, and stroke. The cause of diabetes is a mystery, although both genetics and lifestyle factors such as obesity and lack of exercise play roles.

Type 2 diabetes is more prevalent in African-Americans and Hispanics than in Caucasians. It is the fourth leading cause of death from disease in African-Americans. Approximately one in ten African-Americans develop diabetes between the ages forty-five and sixty-five. Diabetes is the third leading cause of death in Hispanics women when compared to one in four in African-American women. American Indians have the highest rate of Type II diabetes in the world. The cause of diabetes is a mystery, although both genetics and lifestyle factors such as obesity and lack of exercise play roles.

To gain a greater understanding of the importance of insulin, it helps to know how the body converts food into energy. Your body is composed of millions of cells. To make energy, these cells need food in a simple form. When food is initially consumed, most of it is broken down into glucose (a simple sugar). Glucose provides the body with the energy it needs to carry out daily functions. The bloodstream transports glucose both from where it is taken into the body after eating (the stomach and intestines), and where it is manufactured (in the liver), to the cells where it will be used (muscles, brain, etc.) or stored (in the liver), or converted to fat (also in the liver). When the amount of glucose in the blood reaches a certain level, the pancreas releases insulin. The insulin carries the glucose into the appropriate cells. As more glucose enters the cells, the level of glucose in the bloodstream drops. Without insulin, the glucose can't be stored, which allows the level of glucose in the blood to rise. Excess glucose in the blood is known as **hyperglycemia**. While too little glucose in the blood is known as **hypoglycemia**. A person is diagnosed with diabetes if they have a blood sugar level of 126 milligrams per deciliter (mg/dl), or more, after an overnight fast.

Diabetes can be managed successfully by monitoring blood glucose levels to insure they are within a safe range. Blood glucose levels can be monitored using a home blood glucose meter or laboratory glycohemoglobin test also known as *hemoglobin A1c*. The home glucose meter measure blood glucose levels by using a small drop of blood on a glucose strip that is inserted into meter. This device allows the user to measure blood sugar anywhere. The blood glucose level should be 70-130 mg/dl after fasting and less than 180 mg/dl two hours after a meal. The hemoglobin A1c test is performed in a laboratory and determines one's average blood glucose level over the past two to three months. The ideal hemoglobin A1c level for diabetics is less than seven percent. The normal hemoglobinA1c for most laboratories is 4.5 to 5.9 percent.

The symptoms of diabetes often occur suddenly and can be severe. They include:

- extreme thirst

- increased hunger (especially after eating)

- dry mouth

- frequent urination, especially at night

- unexplained weight loss (even though you are eating and feel hungry)

- extreme fatigue (weak, tired feeling)

- numbness or tingling of the feet or toes

- unintentional weight loss

- blurred vision

- slow-healing sores or cuts

- itching of the skin (usually in the vaginal or groin area)

- frequent yeast infections; and

- frequent infections of the skin, gums, bladder

Risk Factors for Diabetes

Although the causes of diabetes are unknown, the following are the major risk factors for diabetes: age, genetics, race or ethnic background, being overweight, abnormal cholesterol levels, and hypertension. Evaluate your risk for diabetes in **Lab 12.2**.

Age. Your risk of developing diabetes increases progressively as you get older.

Genetics. If a parent or sibling in your family has diabetes, the risk of developing diabetes is increased.

Race or Ethnic Background. The risk of diabetes is greater in Hispanics, African-Americans, Native Americans, and Asians. This may be linked to lifestyles, especially diet and physical activity.

Being Overweight. If you are 20 percent or more over your optimal body weight, you increase your risk for developing diabetes.

Abnormal Cholesterol Levels. Low HDL or "good" cholesterol level under 35 mg/dl and/or a triglyceride level over 250 mg/dl increases your risk.

Hypertension. Hypertension increases your risk of diabetes. Many diabetics have cardiovascular disease. Gestational diabetes occurs during pregnancy and resolves with birth. Risk factors include being overweight, having a family history of diabetes, having prediabetes and previously giving birth to an infant weighing nine or more pounds.

Excess sugar intake. Consuming 400ml or more of sugar daily can double the risk of developing diabetes

Treatment for Diabetes

At the present time, diabetes can't be cured, but it can be treated and controlled. The goal of treatment for individuals with diabetes is to lower blood sugar levels and improve the body's use of insulin. Most individuals with Type 1 diabetes live long, healthy lives. The key is keeping blood sugar levels within target range, which can be accomplished by meal planning (diet), exercise, and insulin ingestion (medication). The diet of a person with Type 1 diabetes should be a balanced meal plan that consists of decreasing the total amount of fat to 30 percent or less of total daily calories, reducing saturated fat and cholesterol, increasing complex carbohydrates, and lowering simple sugar intake. The exercise program should consist of aerobic activity most days of the week for at least thirty minutes, within the person's target heart rate zone. Insulin should be taken as prescribed by closely following the guidelines on how and when to take it.

    The goal of treatment for Type 2 diabetes is to lower blood sugar and improve the body's use of insulin with meal planning, exercise, and weight control. The diet of a person with Type 2 diabetes should be similar to that for Type 1 diabetes. The diet should include strategies to lose fat which is linked to weight loss. Fat loss in individuals with diabetes is associated with improved body sensitivity to insulin. The exercise program should also include aerobic exercise because it increases glucose uptake by muscle cells in the absence of insulin. It is imperative to take medications prescribed by you physician properly.

Diabetes Prevention

Type I diabetes cannot be prevented; however, you can reduce your risk of developing Type 2 diabetes by making behavior modification changes in the following lifestyle choices:

1. *Engage in aerobic activities on a regular basis.* Aerobic activities increase energy expenditure which aids in weight loss and maintenance. These activities also enable the body to use and take up blood glucose without insulin.

2. *Know the warning signs of diabetes.* The earlier the disease is caught, the earlier you can start treatment and prevent or delay the progress of the disease.

3. *Maintain normal body weight.* Exercising on a regular basis and watching your dietary fat and sugar intake can aid in controlling weight.

4. *Know your blood sugar level.* The American Diabetes Association recommends blood glucose testing starting at age 45 and, if normal, repeat at three-year intervals.

5. *Maintain normal body fat, cholesterol and blood pressure levels.* A 7% reduction in body fat levels have a significant positive impact on managing blood glucose levels increase insulin sensitivity.

6. *Consume a healthy diet.* Eat a variety of foods including whole grains, vegetables, protein and fates. If is important to minimize sugar intake.

Osteoporosis

As Linda Burns waited to be seated in a restaurant, she felt a sharp pain in her right hip. The 44 year-old Alabama woman had always been healthy and active, and suddenly she could hardly stand. When she visited her doctor, she was told that several of her vertebrae had fractured. The radiologist stated that he thought that he was reviewing the bones of a 70 year-old woman.

The scenario depicts a sometimes deadly condition known as osteoporosis. Osteoporosis is a major public health threat for an estimated 44 million Americans. In the U.S. today, 10 million American women and 2 million men are estimated to have osteoporosis and an estimated 34 million more have low bone density, placing them at increased risk for osteoporosis. Five percent of African-American women, 10 percent of Hispanic women, and 20 percent of non-Hispanic women aged 50 and older are estimated to have osteoporosis. Seven percent of non-Hispanic white and Asian men, 4 percent of non-Hispanic black men, and 3 percent of Hispanic men aged fifty and older are estimated to have osteoporosis. The estimated national direct expenditures (hospitals and nursing homes) for osteoporosis and associated fractures was $17 billion in 2001, and the cost is rising.

What Is Osteoporosis?

Osteoporosis is often called the "silent disease" because bone loss occurs without symptoms. It is often characterized by developing back pain, bone loss and deterioration of the skeleton which leads to bone fragility and increased risk of fractures of the hip, spine, and wrists. One in two women and one in eight men aged 50 and over will have an osteoporosis-related fracture in their lifetime. Osteoporosis is defined as about 25 percent bone loss compared to a healthy young adult or, on a bone density test, 2.5 standard deviations below normal. Although everyone experiences some bone loss with age, few people realize that stooped

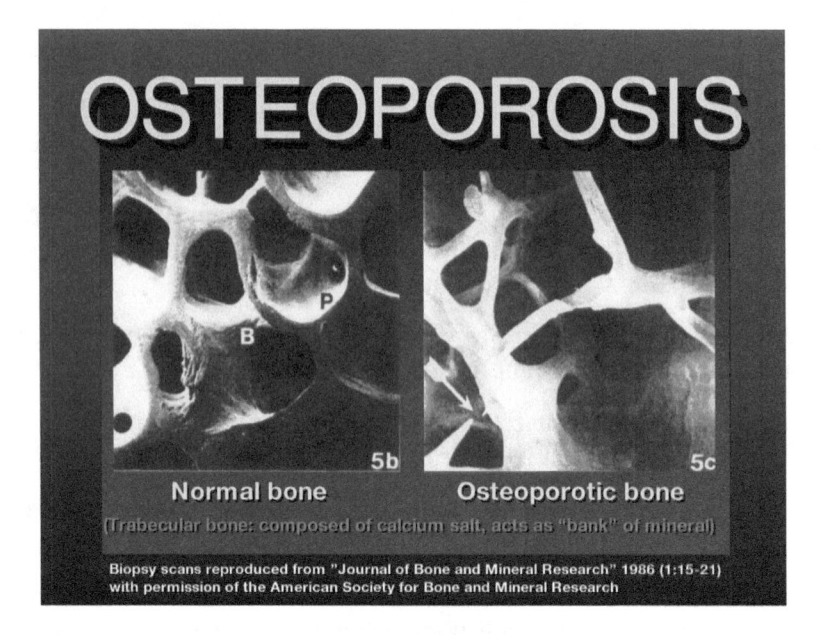

Figure 12.1
Figure from U.S. Department of Health and Human Services. The 2004 Surgeon General's Report on Bone Health and Osteoporosis: What It Means To You. U.S. Department of Health and Human Services, Office of the Surgeon General, 2004.

posture, and loss of height (greater than one to two inches) are caused by vertebral fractures due to osteoporosis.

In order to gain a greater understanding of the disease it is imperative to understand the composition of the skeleton (see **Figure 12.1**). Bone tissue has two forms: **trabecular bone** and **cortical bone.** The thick ivory-like outer portion of a bone is the cortical bone. Cortical bone provides a covering for the inner trabecular bone—a fragile network of calcium containing crystals, almost spongelike in appearance. When calcium intakes are low, hormones call first upon the trabecular bone to release calcium into the blood for use by the rest of the body. Over time, the fragile network of bones becomes less dense and fragile as calcium deposits are withdrawn.

Risk Factors for Osteoporosis

The exact cause of osteoporosis is not known. Certain people are most likely to develop the disease than others. Factors that increase the likelihood of developing osteoporosis are called "risk factors". This disease generally results from a combination of risk factors. Assess your risks for osteoporosis in **Lab 12.2.**

Alcohol and/or Caffeine Consumption. Alcohol interferes with the absorption of calcium, and caffeine stimulates the excretion of calcium through the urine.

Frame Size. People with thin or small skeletal systems are at greater risk for fractures because they have reduced bone mineral density and less fat. Fat tissue stores estrogen, which helps protect women form osteoporosis.

Low Hormonal Levels. Bone loss begins earlier in women because of women's different hormonal make-up, and the loss is accelerated at menopause (naturally or surgically), when their protective estrogen (female hormone) secretion declines. Lowered testosterone (male hormone) can significantly reduce bone mineral content which results in the development of osteoporosis.

Smoking. Cigarette smoking may decrease the estrogen level in women and lead to early menopause.

Lack of Calcium Intake. When the blood calcium level is low the body draws on stored calcium in the skeleton. In order for the skeleton to remain healthy it must have access to an adequate supply of calcium.

Heredity. You are at greater risk for osteoporosis if there is a family history of the disease.

Age. For both women and men, the longer one lives, the greater the likelihood of developing the disease.

Race. Asian and white women are more susceptible to fractures than African-American women.

Gender. Women are four times more likely to develop osteoporosis than men because estrogen production ceases at menopause and they are smaller framed.

Physical Inactivity. Exercise, especially weight-bearing activities, increase the mineral content of the bones.

Medications. Use of certain medications, such as steroids (often used to treat asthma and arthritis), and high doses of thyroid hormones, increases the risk of developing osteoporosis.

Treatment for Osteoporosis

Early diagnosis and treatment of osteoporosis is very important. Diagnosis of osteoporosis is usually done by evaluating a person's medical history, performing a physical exam, and testing bone density. Individuals who are most likely to develop the disease need to be screened for the disease before symptoms (such as broken bones) occur. Although there is no cure for osteoporosis, treatment typically includes medication, increased calcium intake, and increased intensity of weight-bearing activities. People taking medication for osteoporosis may also take calcium and vitamin D supplements. The Recommended Adequate Intake (RAI) by the Institute of Medicine (IOM) for calcium is 1300 mg/day for males and females age 14 to 18 years, 1000 mg/day for males and females ages 19 to 50 years, and 1200 mg.day for males and females 51 years and older. Weight-bearing exercises (such as walking, jogging, stair climbing, or lifting weights) stimulate new bone growth by working the muscles and bones against gravity. Keep in mind that none of these treatments reverse osteoporosis; rather, they all delay its progress.

Osteoporosis Prevention

Bone thinning is a natural part of growing older. If you start healthy habits (such as eating a nutritious diet and exercising regularly) early in life, you may be able to delay the development of osteoporosis. Young women in particular must be aware of their risk for developing osteoporosis and take steps early to slow its progress and prevent complications. Studies show that exercising during the preteen and teen years increases bone mass and greatly reduces the risk of osteoporosis as an adult (Seeman, 2000). A comprehensive program that can help prevent osteoporosis includes:

- a balanced diet rich in calcium and vitamin D;
- weight bearing exercises;
- a healthy lifestyle with no smoking and limited alcohol intake;
- cutting down on caffeine; and
- bone density testing and medication when appropriate.

Prevention is important at all ages, however, at the time of menopause these steps may not be enough without osteoporosis medication to protect from bone loss.

Summary

Important concepts that you have learned in this chapter include the following:

- Cancer is characterized by abnormal, uncontrolled cell growth in the from of either benign (noncancerous) or malignant (cancerous tumors).
- The four major types of cancer are carcinomas, sarcomas, lymphomas, and leukemia.
- The major risk factors for cancer include viruses, environmental exposure, genetics, chronic irritation, and lifestyle factors such as diet, smoking, and stress.
- Your risk for developing cancer can be reduced by avoiding stress; alcohol; tobacco; performing self-examinations; exercising regularly; controlling your weight, protecting yourself from the sun, and eating a well-balanced diet that's high in fiber and low in fat.
- The arteries that serve the heart are damaged by atherosclerosis in coronary artery disease.
- The major risk factors for cardiovascular disease include smoking, hypertension, high blood cholesterol, and physical inactivity, contributing risk factors include heredity, age, sex, diabetes, obesity, and stress.
- In order to improve cardiovascular health you must quit smoking, exercise regularly, eat a well-balanced diet, reduce body fat and reduce stress.
- Diabetes mellitus is a serious medical problem in which the pancreas produces an insufficient amount of insulin, a hormone needed by the body's cells to metabolize glucose.
- Risk factors for diabetes include age, heredity, race, and obesity.
- Insulin, diet, and exercise are the triad of control for insulin-dependent diabetes, and non–insulin-dependent diabetes can usually be controlled through a triad of diet, exercise, and weight control.
- Osteoporosis is characterized by low bone mineral content, which can lead to fractures—mostly common of the vertebra, hips, and wrists.
- Risk factors for osteoporosis include alcohol consumption, a light skeleton, low levels of estrogen or testosterone, smoking, insufficient calcium, age, physical inactivity, and reduced peak bone mass.
- You can reduce your risk of osteoporosis by increasing non-weight bearing physical activity, taking calcium, quitting smoking, reducing alcohol consumption.
- Osteoporosis treatment involves increased calcium intake, and increased levels of weight-bearing exercises.

References

Bierman, J., Virginia V. & Toohey, B. *Diabetes: The New Type 2: Your Complete Handbook to Living Healthfully with Diabetes Type 2.* New York: Tarcher, 2008

Corbin, C.B., Welk, G.J., Corbin, W.R. & Welk, K.A. (2008). *Concepts of fitness and wellness.* New York, NY: McGraw-Hill Publishing Company.

Hales, D. (2008). *An invitation to fitness and wellness.* Belmont, CA: Wadsworth Publishing Company.

Hoeger, W.W.K. & Hoeger, S.A. (2006). *Principles and labs for fitness and wellness.* 8th ed. U.S.: Thomson and Wadsworth.

Osteoporosis prevention, diagnosis, and therapy. NIH Consensus Development Conference Statement, vol. 17, no. 1 (2000) March 27–29.

Internet Sources

www.aolsvc.health.webmd.aol.com/condition_center_content/ost/article1829.50823

www.aoslvc.health.webmd.aol.com/condition_center_content/dia/article/1667.50911

www.aomc.org/HOD2/genaral/heart-UNDERSTA.html

www.cancer.org

www.cdc.gov/nccdphp/about.htm

www.diabetes.org/main/application/commercewf/origin

www.healingwithnutrition.com/cdisease/cardiovascular.html

www.healthy.net/asp/templates/article

www.hrslyhy.net/asp/templates/article.asp?Page

www.mayocline.com/findinformation/diseaseandconditions

www.nor.org/osteoporosis/stats.htm.

www.viahealth.org/disease/cardiac/stats.tem

www.americanheart.org/presenter.jhtml?identifer=4478

Lab 12.1
Assessing Your Risk for Cancer

Name: _____   Date: _____

Instructions: Circle the answer that best characterizes you for each question. Total your points for each section in the space provided.

I. Skin Cancer
1. Frequent work or play in the sun.
   a. Yes (10)   b. No (1)
2. Work in mines, around coal tars, or around radioactivity.
   a. Yes (10)   b. No (1)
3. Fair or light skin complexion.
   a. Yes (10)   b. No (1)

Skin cancer total _____

If you answered "yes" to any question, you need to protect your skin from the sun or any other toxic material. Changes in moles, warts, or skin sores are very important and need to be seen by a physician.

II. Lung Cancer
1. Gender:
   a. Male (2)   b. Female (1)
2. Age:
   a. 39 or less (1)   b. 40–49 (2)   c. 50–59 (5)   d. 60 and over (7)
3. Smoker or Nonsmoker:
   a. Smoker (8)   b. Nonsmoker (1)
4. Type of smoking:
   a. Cigarettes or little cigars (10)
   b. Pipe and/or cigar but not cigarettes (3)
   c. Ex-cigarette smoker (2)
   d. Nonsmoker (1)
5. Number of cigarettes smoked per day:
   a. 0 (1)
   b. Less than ½ pack per day (5)
   c. ½–1 pack (9)
   d. 1–2 packs (15)
   e. More than 2 packs (20)
6. Type of cigarettes:
   a. High tar/nicotine (10)
   b. Medium tar/nicotine (9)
   c. Low tar/nicotine (7)
   d. Nonsmoker (1)
7. Duration of smoking:
   a. Never smoked (1)
   b. Ex-smoker (3)
   c. Up to 15 years (5)
   d. 15–25 years (10)
   e. More than 25 years (20)

Lab 12.1—Cont'd
Assessing Your Risk for Cancer

8. Type of industrial work:
   a. Mining (3)
   b. Asbestos (7)
   c. Uranium and radioactive products (5)

Lung Cancer Total: _____

If your lung total is:
- 24 or less — You have a low risk for lung cancer.
- 24–49 — You may be a light smoker, would have a good chance of kicking the habit.
- 50–74 — You are a moderate smoker, your chances of developing lung and upper respiratory tract cancer are increased. If you stop smoking now, these risks will decrease.
- 77 and over — You are a heavy smoker, your chances of getting lung and upper respiratory tract cancer are greatly increased. Stop smoking for your health. See your doctor if you have a nagging cough, hoarseness, persistent pain, or a sore in the mouth or throat.

III. Colon and Rectal Cancer
1. Age:
   a. 39 or less (10)   b. 40–59 (20)   c. 60 and over (50)
2. Has anyone in your immediate family ever had:
   a. Colon cancer (20)
   b. One or more polyps of the colon (10)
   c. Neither (1)
3. Have you ever had:
   a. Colon cancer (100)
   b. One or more polyps of the colon (40)
   c. Ulcerative colitis (20)
   d. Cancer of the breast or uterus (10)
   e. None (1)
4. Bleeding from the rectum (other than the obvious hemorrhoids or piles):
   a. Yes (10)
   b. No (1)

Colon and Rectal Cancer Total: _____

1. Colon cancer occurs more frequently after the age of 50.
2. Colon cancer is more common in families with a previous history of this disease.
3. Polyps and bowel disease are associated with colon cancer.
4. Rectal bleeding may be a sign of colon/rectal cancer.

If your colon total is:
- 29 or less — You are at a low risk for colon/rectal cancer.
- 30–69 — You are at moderate risk. Testing by your physician may be warranted.
- 70 and over — You are in the high-risk category. See your physician for the following tests: digital rectal exam, guaiac slide test, and proctoscopic exam.

Lab 12.1—Cont'd
Assessing Your Risk for Cancer

Name: _____   Date: _____

IV. Women Only—Breast Cancer
1. Age:
   a. 20–34 (10)   b. 35–49 (40)   c. 50 and over (90)
2. Race/ethnicity:
   a. Asian (5)
   b. African-American (20)
   c. White (25)
   d. Mexican American (10)
3. Family history:
   a. Mother, sister, aunt, or grandmother with breast cancer (30)
   b. None (10)
4. Your history:
   a. Previous lumps or cysts (25)
   b. No breast disease (10)
   c. Previous breast cancer (100)
5. Maternity:
   a. First pregnancy before age 25 (10)
   b. First pregnancy after age 25 (15)
   c. No pregnancies (20)

Breast Cancer Total: _____

If your breast cancer total is:

100 or less	You are a low risk. Practice monthly breast self-examination and have your breasts examined by a physician at least once a year.
100–199	You are at moderate risk. Practice monthly breast self examination and have your breasts examined by a physician at least once a year. Periodic mammograms should be included as your doctor may advise.
200 and over	You are at high risk. You should practice monthly breast self-examination and have your breasts examined by a physician more often than once a year. See your physician for the examinations recommended for you.

Source: Adapted from *Cancer Facts & Figures* 1993 (p. 12) by American Cancer Society, New York. Copyright by American Cancer Society, Inc.

Lab 12.2
Assessing Your Risk for Osteoporosis

Name: _____ Date: _____

For each of the following questions, circle either Yes or No.
1. Do you smoke cigarettes?
   a. Yes   b. No
2. Do you have more than one drink of wine, beer, or other alcoholic beverages daily?
   a. Yes   b. No
3. Do you get little or no weight-bearing exercise such as walking, jogging, dancing, or lifting weights per week?
   a. Yes   b. No
4. Do you have a thin body build?
   a. Yes   b. No
5. Do you have a diet low in foods containing calcium, phosphorus, and Vitamin D?
   a. Yes   b. No
6. Did you go through menopause or have your ovaries removed by surgery before age 50?
   a. Yes   b. No
7. Do you take medications such as corticosteroids, or have medical conditions, such as hyperthyroidism or rheumatoid arthritis?
   a. Yes   b. No
8. Do you have ancestors of European or Asian ancestry?
   a. Yes   b. No
9. Do you overuse antacids that contain aluminum?
   a. Yes   b. No
10. Have you ever had an eating disorder (bulimia or anorexia nervosa)?
    a. Yes   b. No
11. Do you have a family history of osteoporosis?
    a. Yes   b. No
12. Are you allergic to milk products or are you lactose intolerant?
    a. Yes   b. No
13. Are you a female athlete?
    a. Yes   b. No

What's Your Risk?
If you had several yes answers, you are at a greater risk of developing osteoporosis. Talk with your doctor today about recommendations to prevent osteoporosis.

Lab 12.3
Coronary Heart Disease Risk Appraisal

Name: _____   Date: _____

Purpose: This lab will estimate your coronary heart disease risk.

Precautions: None

Equipment: Risko Coronary Heart Disease Risk Appraisal Survey

Procedure: Each subject should complete the survey as accurately as possible. For each variable, identify the descriptor that most fits you. The value in parentheses represents your score for that variable. Variable explanations are as follows:

- **Age:** Your chronological age in years.
- **Heredity:** Parents, or immediate family (i.e., brothers and sisters) who have a history of heart attack or stroke.
- **Weight:** Your body weight measured in pounds compared to standard recommended weights for individuals of your age and gender.
- **Tobacco Smoking:** Your current smoking status. If you smoke and inhale deeply and/or smoke a cigarette completely, **add** one point to the provided score. **Do not** correct by subtracting a point if you smoke partial cigarettes or do not inhale.
- **Exercise:** Your current exercising status. If you exercise consistently and frequently with moderate intensity, **subtract** one point from your score.
- **Cholesterol or Fat % in Diet:** Recent, determined serum cholesterol level. If cholesterol levels are not available, estimate as accurately as possible the amount of saturated (solid) fat that you eat.
- **Blood Pressure:** Recent, determined resting blood pressure.
- **Gender:** Your gender.

Scoring: Table 4.5 should be used to determine relative coronary heart disease risk.

Table 4.5 Relative Risk Categories: Risko

Score	Relative Risk Category
6–11	Risk well below average
12–17	Risk below average
18–24	Average risk
25–31	Moderate risk
32–40	High risk
41–62	Very high risk

Source: Adams, T., *Concepts of Health-Related Fitness*. Kendall Hunt Publishing Company, 2002, p. 92. Modified from: McArdle, W., Katch, F., and Katch, V. (1996), *Exercise Physiology: Energy, Nutrition, and Human Performance*. Philadelphia, PA: Williams & Wilkins.

Lab 12.3—Cont'd
Coronary Heart Disease Risk Appraisal

Risko: Coronary Heart Disease Risk Appraisal Survey

Age	(1) 10 to 20 years	(2) 21 to 30 years	(3) 31 to 40 years	(4) 41 to 50 years	(6) 51 to 60 years	(8) 61 and over
Heredity	(1) No known history of heart disease	(2) 1 relative with heart disease over 60	(3) 2 relatives with heart disease over 60	(4) 1 relative with heart disease under age 60	(6) 2 relatives with heart disease under age 60	(7) 3 relatives with heart disease under age 60
Weight	(0) More than 5 lbs. below standard weight	(1) -5 to +5 lbs. standard weight	(2) 6–20 lbs. overweight	(3) 21–35 lbs. overweight	(5) 36–50 lbs. overweight	(6) 51–65 lbs. overweight
Tobacco Smoking	(0) Nonsmoker	(1) Cigar and/or pipe; live or work with someone who smokes	(2) 10 cigarettes or less per day	(4) 11–20 cigarettes per day	(6) 21–30 cigarettes per day	(10) 40 or more cigarettes per day
Exercise	(1) Intensive occupational and recreational exertion	(2) Moderate occupational and recreational exertion	(3) Sedentary work and intense recreational exertion	(5) Sedentary occupational and moderate recreational exertion	(6) Sedentary work and light recreational exertion	(8) Complete lack of all exercise
Cholesterol or Fat % in diet	(1) Cholesterol below 180 mg/dl; Diet contains no animal or solid fats	(2) Cholesterol 181–205 mg/dl; Diet contains 1–10% animal or solid fats	(3) Cholesterol 206–230 mg/dl; Diet contains 11–20% animal or solid fats	(4) Cholesterol 231–255 mg/dl; Diet contains 21–30% animal or solid fats	(5) Cholesterol 256–280 mg/dl; Diet contains 31–40% animal or solid fats	(7) Cholesterol 281–300 mg/dl; Diet contains 50% animal or solid fats
Blood Pressure	(1) 100–119 systolic	(2) 120–139 systolic	(3) 140–159 systolic	(4) 160–179 systolic	(5) 180–199 systolic	(7) 200 or over systolic
Gender	(1) Female under age 40	(2) Female aged 40–50	(3) Female over age 50	(4) Male	(6) Stocky Male	(7) Bald stocky male

Source: Modified from: McArdle, W., Katch, F., & Katch, V. (1996). Exercise Physiology: Energy, Nutrition, and Human Performance. Philadelphia, PA: Williams & Wilkins.

Data/Calculations:

Subject: _____ Date: _____

Age: _____ Heredity: _____ Weight: _____ Tobacco smoking: _____ Exercise: _____

Cholesterol/Fat % in diet: _____ Blood pressure: _____ Gender: _____

Cumulative Score: _____

Relative Risk Category: _____

Appendix A

Appendix A.1 Estimated Calorie Needs Per Day by Age, Gender, and Physical Activity Level (Detailed)

Estimated amounts of calories[a] needed to maintain calorie balance for various gender and age groups at three different levels of physical activity. The estimates are rounded to the nearest 200 calories. An individual's calorie needs may be higher or lower than these average estimates.

Gender/Activity Level[b] Age (years)	Male/Sedentary	Male/Moderately Active	Male/Active	Female[c]/Sedentary	Female[c]/Moderately Active	Female[c]/Active
2	1,000	1,000	1,000	1,000	1,000	1,000
3	1,200	1,400	1,400	1,000	1,200	1,400
4	1,200	1,400	1,600	1,200	1,400	1,400
5	1,200	1,400	1,600	1,200	1,400	1,600
6	1,400	1,600	1,800	1,200	1,400	1,600
7	1,400	1,600	1,800	1,200	1,600	1,800
8	1,400	1,600	2,000	1,400	1,600	1,800
9	1,600	1,800	2,000	1,400	1,600	1,800
10	1,600	1,800	2,200	1,400	1,800	2,000
11	1,800	2,000	2,200	1,600	1,800	2,000
12	1,800	2,200	2,400	1,600	2,000	2,200
13	2,000	2,200	2,600	1,600	2,000	2,200
14	2,000	2,400	2,800	1,800	2,000	2,400
15	2,200	2,600	3,000	1,800	2,000	2,400
16	2,400	2,800	3,200	1,800	2,000	2,400
17	2,400	2,800	3,200	1,800	2,000	2,400
18	2,400	2,800	3,200	1,800	2,000	2,400
19–20	2,600	2,800	3,000	2,000	2,200	2,400
21–25	2,400	2,800	3,000	2,000	2,200	2,400
26–30	2,400	2,600	3,000	1,800	2,000	2,400
31–35	2,400	2,600	3,000	1,800	2,000	2,200
36–40	2,400	2,600	2,800	1,800	2,000	2,200
41–45	2,200	2,600	2,800	1,800	2,000	2,200
46–50	2,200	2,400	2,800	1,800	2,000	2,200
51–55	2,200	2,400	2,800	1,600	1,800	2,200
56–60	2,200	2,400	2,600	1,600	1,800	2,200
61–65	2,000	2,400	2,600	1,600	1,800	2,000
66–70	2,000	2,200	2,600	1,600	1,800	2,000
71–75	2,000	2,200	2,600	1,600	1,800	2,000
761	2,000	2,200	2,400	1,600	1,800	2,000

a. Based on Estimated Energy Requirements (EER) equations, using reference heights (average) and reference weights (healthy) for each age-gender group. For children and adolescents, reference height and weight vary. For adults, the reference man is 5 feet 10 inches tall and weighs 154 pounds. The reference woman is 5 feet 4 inches tall and weighs 126 pounds. EER equations are from the Institute of Medicine. Dietary Reference Intakes for Energy, Carbohydrate, Fiber, Fat, Fatty Acids, Cholesterol, Protein, and Amino Acids. Washington (DC): The National Academies Press; 2002.
b. Sedentary means a lifestyle that includes only the light physical activity associated with typical day-to-day life. Moderately active means a lifestyle that includes physical activity equivalent to walking about 1.5 to 3 miles per day at 3 to 4 miles per hour, in addition to the light physical activity associated with typical day-to-day life. Active means a lifestyle that includes physical activity equivalent to walking more than 3 miles per day at 3 to 4 miles per hour, in addition to the light physical activity associated with typical day-to-day life.
c. Estimates for females do not include women who are pregnant or breastfeeding.

Source: Britten P, Marcoe K, Yamini S, Davis C. Development of food intake patterns for the MyPyramid Food Guidance System. J Nutr Educ Behav 2006;38(6 Suppl):S78-S92.

Appendix A.2 USDA Food Patterns

For each food group or subgroup,[a] recommended average daily intake amounts[b] at all calorie levels. Recommended intakes from vegetable and protein foods subgroups are per week. For more information and tools for application, go to MyPyramid.gov.

Calorie Level of Pattern[c]	1,000	1,200	1,400	1,600	1,800	2,000	2,200	2,400	2,600	2,800	3,000	3,200
Fruits	1 c	1 c	1[½] c	1[½] c	1[½] c	2 c	2 c	2 c	2 c	2[½] c	2[½] c	2[½] c
Vegetables[d]	1 c	1[½] c	1[½] c	2 c	2[½] c	2[½] c	3 c	3 c	3[½] c	3[½] c	4 c	4 c
Dark-green vegetables	[½] c/wk	1 c/wk	1 c/wk	1[½] c/wk	1[½] c/wk	1[½] c/wk	2 c/wk	2 c/wk	2[½] c/wk	2[½] c/wk	2[½] c/wk	2[½] c/wk
Red and orange vegetables	2[½] c/wk	3 c/wk	3 c/wk	4 c/wk	5[½] c/wk	5[½] c/wk	6 c/wk	6 c/wk	7 c/wk	7 c/wk	7[½] c/wk	7[½] c/wk
Beans and peas (legumes)	[½] c/wk	[½] c/wk	[½] c/wk	1 c/wk	1[½] c/wk	1[½] c/wk	2 c/wk	2 c/wk	2[½] c/wk	2[½] c/wk	3 c/wk	3 c/wk
Starchy vegetables	2 c/wk	3[½] c/wk	3[½] c/wk	4 c/wk	5 c/wk	5 c/wk	6 c/wk	6 c/wk	7 c/wk	7 c/wk	8 c/wk	8 c/wk
Other vegetables	1[½] c/wk	2[½] c/wk	2[½] c/wk	3[½] c/wk	4 c/wk	4 c/wk	5 c/wk	5 c/wk	5[½] c/wk	5[½] c/wk	7 c/wk	7 c/wk
Grains[e]	3 oz-eq	4 oz-eq	5 oz-eq	5 oz-eq	6 oz-eq	6 oz-eq	7 oz-eq	8 oz-eq	9 oz-eq	10 oz-eq	10 oz-eq	10 oz-eq
Whole grains	1[½] oz-eq	2 oz-eq	2[½] oz-eq	3 oz-eq	3 oz-eq	3 oz-eq	3[½] oz-eq	4 oz-eq	4[½] oz-eq	5 oz-eq	5 oz-eq	5 oz-eq
Enriched grains	1[½] oz-eq	2 oz-eq	2[½] oz-eq	2 oz-eq	3 oz-eq	3 oz-eq	3[½] oz-eq	4 oz-eq	4[½] oz-eq	5 oz-eq	5 oz-eq	5 oz-eq
Protein foods[d]	2 oz-eq	3 oz-eq	4 oz-eq	5 oz-eq	5 oz-eq	5[½] oz-eq	6 oz-eq	6[½] oz-eq	6[½] oz-eq	7 oz-eq	7 oz-eq	7 oz-eq
Seafood	3 oz/wk	5 oz/wk	6 oz/wk	8 oz/wk	8 oz/wk	8 oz/wk	9 oz/wk	10 oz/wk	10 oz/wk	11 oz/wk	11 oz/wk	11 oz/wk
Meat, poultry, eggs	10 oz/wk	14 oz/wk	19 oz/wk	24 oz/wk	24 oz/wk	26 oz/wk	29 oz/wk	31 oz/wk	31 oz/wk	34 oz/wk	34 oz/wk	34 oz/wk
Nuts, seeds, soy products	1 oz/wk	2 oz/wk	3 oz/wk	4 oz/wk	4 oz/wk	4 oz/wk	4 oz/wk	5 oz/wk	5 oz/wk	5 oz/wk	5 oz/wk	5 oz/wk
Dairy[f]	2 c	2[½] c	2[½] c	3 c	3 c	3 c	3 c	3 c	3 c	3 c	3 c	3 c
Oils[g]	15 g	17 g	17 g	22 g	24 g	27 g	29 g	31 g	34 g	36 g	44 g	51 g
Maximum soFAS[h] limit, calories (% of calories)	137 (14%)	121 (10%)	121 (9%)	121 (8%)	161 (9%)	258 (13%)	266 (12%)	330 (14%)	362 (14%)	395 (14%)	459 (15%)	596 (19%)

Appendix A.3 Nutritional Goals for Age-Gender Groups, Based On Dietary Reference Intakes And Dietary Guidelines Recommendations

Nutrient (Units)	Source of Goal[a]	Child 1–3	Female 4–8	Male 4–8	Female 9–13	Male 9–13	Female 14–18	Male 14–18	Female 19–30	Male 19–30	Female 31–50	Male 31–50	Female 511	Male 511
Macronutrients														
Protein (g)	RDA[b]	13	19	19	34	34	46	52	46	56	46	56	46	56
(% of calories)	AMDR[c]	5–20	10–30	10–30	10–30	10–30	10–30	10–30	10–35	10–35	10–35	10–35	10–35	10–35
Carbohydrate (g)	RDA	130	130	130	130	130	130	130	130	130	130	130	130	130
(% of calories)	AMDR	45–65	45–65	45–65	45–65	45–65	45–65	45–65	45–65	45–65	45–65	45–65	45–65	45–65
Total fiber (g)	IOM[d]	14	17	20	22	25	25	31	28	34	25	31	22	28
Total fat (% of calories)	AMDR	30–40	25–35	25–35	25–35	25–35	25–35	25–35	20–35	20–35	20–35	20–35	20–35	20–35
Saturated fat (% of calories)	DG[e]	,10%	,10%	,10%	,10%	,10%	,10%	,10%	,10%	,10%	,10%	,10%	,10%	,10%
Linoleic acid (g)	AI[f]	7	10	10	10	12	11	16	12	17	12	17	11	14
(% of calories)	AMDR	5–10	5–10	5–10	5–10	5–10	5–10	5–10	5–10	5–10	5–10	5–10	5–10	5–10
alpha-Linolenic acid (g)	AI	0.7	0.9	0.9	1.0	1.2	1.1	1.6	1.1	1.6	1.1	1.6	1.1	1.6
(% of calories)	AMDR	0.6–1.2	0.6–1.2	0.6–1.2	0.6–1.2	0.6–1.2	0.6–1.2	0.6–1.2	0.6–1.2	0.6–1.2	0.6–1.2	0.6–1.2	0.6–1.2	0.6–1.2
Cholesterol (mg)	DG	,300	,300	,300	,300	,300	,300	,300	,300	,300	,300	,300	,300	,300
Minerals														
Calcium (mg)	RDA	700	1,000	1,000	1,300	1,300	1,300	1,300	1,000	1,000	1,000	1,000	1,200	1,200
Iron (mg)	RDA	7	10	10	8	8	15	11	18	8	18	8	8	8
Magnesium (mg)	RDA	80	130	130	240	240	360	410	310	400	320	420	320	420
Phosphorus (mg)	RDA	460	500	500	1,250	1,250	1,250	1,250	700	700	700	700	700	700
Potassium (mg)	AI	3,000	3,800	3,800	4,500	4,500	4,700	4,700	4,700	4,700	4,700	4,700	4,700	4,700
Sodium (mg)	UL[g]	,1,500	,1,900	,1,900	,2,200	,2,200	,2,300	,2,300	,2,300	,2,300	,2,300	,2,300	,2,300	,2,300
Zinc (mg)	RDA	3	5	5	8	8	9	11	8	11	8	11	8	11
Copper (mcg)	RDA	340	440	440	700	700	890	890	900	900	900	900	900	900
Selenium (mcg)	RDA	20	30	30	40	40	55	55	55	55	55	55	55	55
Vitamins														
Vitamin A (mcg RAE)	RDA	300	400	400	600	600	700	900	700	900	700	900	700	900
Vitamin D[h] (mcg)	RDA	15	15	15	15	15	15	15	15	15	15	15	15	15
Vitamin E (mg AT)	RDA	6	7	7	11	11	15	15	15	15	15	15	15	15
Vitamin C (mg)	RDA	15	25	25	45	45	65	75	75	90	75	90	75	90
Thiamin (mg)	RDA	0.5	0.6	0.6	0.9	0.9	1.0	1.2	1.1	1.2	1.1	1.2	1.1	1.2
Riboflavin (mg)	RDA	0.5	0.6	0.6	0.9	0.9	1.0	1.3	1.1	1.3	1.1	1.3	1.1	1.3
Niacin (mg)	RDA	6	8	8	12	12	14	16	14	16	14	16	14	16
Folate (mcg)	RDA	150	200	200	300	300	400	400	400	400	400	400	400	400
Vitamin B_6 (mg)	RDA	0.5	0.6	0.6	1.0	1.0	1.2	1.3	1.3	1.3	1.3	1.3	1.5	1.7
Vitamin B_{12} (mcg)	RDA	0.9	1.2	1.2	1.8	1.8	2.4	2.4	2.4	2.4	2.4	2.4	2.4	2.4
Choline (mg)	AI	200	250	250	375	375	400	550	425	550	425	550	425	550
Vitamin K (mcg)	AI	30	55	55	60	60	75	75	90	120	90	120	90	120

Notes for Appendix A.3

a. Dietary Guidelines recommendations are used when no quantitative Dietary Reference Intake value is available; apply to ages 2 years and older.
b. Recommended Dietary Allowance, IOM.
c. Acceptable Macronutrient Distribution Range, IOM.
d. 14 grams per 1,000 calories, IOM.
e. Dietary Guidelines recommendation.
f. Adequate Intake, IOM.
g. Upper Limit, IOM.
h. 1 mcg of vitamin D is equivalent to 40 IU.
AT 5 alpha-tocopherol; DFE 5 dietary folate equivalents; RAE 5 retinol activity equivalents.

Sources: Britten P, Marcoe K, Yamini S, Davis C. Development of food intake patterns for the MyPyramid Food Guidance System. J Nutr Educ Behav 2006; 38(6 Suppl):S78-S92.
IOM. Dietary Reference Intakes: The essential guide to nutrient requirements. Washington (DC): The National Academies Press; 2006.
IOM. Dietary Reference Intakes for Calcium and Vitamin D. Washington (DC): The National Academies Press; 2010.

Rockport 1.0 Mile Walk Test

Name: _____   Date: _____

Purpose: To assess your cardiorespiratory endurance by estimating your maximal oxygen uptake level by briskly walking one mile. This test is recommended for individuals who are unconditioned or have a low fitness level.

Instructions: Walk one mile at as a fast a possible at a brisk pace, such that the heart rate exceeds 120 beats per minute on a measured flat course. The completion time is recorded at the end of the mile. The heart rate is taken immediately at the end of the one mile walk for 15 seconds and multiplied four to determine the recovery. The heart rate may be taken during final one minute of the walk to determine the recovery heart rate. The formulas below are used to predict cardiorespiratory fitness females and males respectively. Classify your fitness level using the maximal uptake charts.

Female

VO2max (ml kg/min) = 132.853 − (0.1692 × Wt) − (0.3877 × age) − (3.2649 × time) − (0.1565 × HR)

_____ = 132.853 − (0.1692 × _____) − (0.3877 × _____) − (3.2649 × _____) − (0.1565 × _____)

Fitness Category _____

Male

VO2max (ml kg/min) = 132.853 − (0.1692 × Wt) − (0.3877 × age) − (3.2649 × time) − (0.1565 × HR)

_____ = 132.853 − (0.1692 × _____) − (0.3877 × _____) − (3.2649 × _____) − (0.1565 × _____)

Fitness Category _____

Wt = Body weight in kilograms*   Age = in years

Time = one mile time to nearest hundredth of minute   HR = recovery heart rate in beats/minute

*Conversion of body weight to kilograms: Wt in pounds × .454

_____ = _____ × .454

Appendix B

1.5 Mile Run/Walk Fitness Test

Name: _____   Date: _____

Purpose: To assess your cardiorespiratory endurance by estimating your maximal oxygen uptake level by running 1.5 miles. This test is not recommended for unconditioned individuals or this with symptom of heart disease.

Instructions: Complete the 1.5 mile distance as fast you can. Try to achieve an even running pace. It is important to pace yourself at the beginning of the fitness test so that you do not become overly fatigued early during the 1.5 mile distance. Use the VO_2max charts to classify your estimated VO_2max.

Step 1: Record your 1.5 mile completion time

1.5 mile time _____ (minutes: seconds)

Step 2: Convert the seconds to minutes by dividing by 60

Time in minutes = _____ (Time in sec) = _____ minutes
                      60

Total time in minutes = _____

Step 3: Convert your body weight (BW) in pounds to kilograms by dividing by 2.2

Body weight in kilograms (kg) = _____ (lbs) = _____ kg
                                    2.2

Step 4: Estimate your maximal oxygen uptake using the formula below.

VO_2 max = 88.02 − (0.1656 × BW) − (2.76 × time) + (3.716 × gender*)
*Gender: 1 for males 2 for females

= 88.02 − (0.1656 × _____) − (2.76 × _____) + (3.716 × _____)

= 88.02 − (_____) − (_____) + (_____)

VO_2 max (kg/ml/min) = _____   Fitness Category: _____

—Cont'd

1.5 Mile Run/Walk Fitness Test

Name: _____   Date: _____

Maximal Oxygen Uptake Charts

Females

Age	Poor	Fair	Good	Excellent
16–29	<30.9	31.0–34.9	35.0–38.9	≥39.0
20–29	<28.9	29.0–32.9	33.0–36.9	≥37.0
30–39	<26.7	27.0–31.4	31.5–35.6	≥35.7
40–49	<24.4	24.5–28.9	29.0–32.8	≥32.9
50↑	<22.7	22.8–26.9	27.0–31.4	≥31.5

Males

Age	Poor	Fair	Good	Excellent
16–29	<38.3	38.4–45.1	45.2–50.9	≥51.0
20–29	<36.4	36.5–42.4	42.5–46.4	≥46.5
30–39	<35.4	35.5–40.9	41.0–44.9	≥45.0
40–49	<33.5	33.6–38.9	39.4–43.7	≥43.8
50↑	<30.9	31.0–35.7	35.8–40.9	≥41.0

Modified from The Physical Fitness Specialist Certification Manual, The Cooper Institute for Aerobics Research, Dallas TX, revised 1997.

12 Minute Walk/Run Test

Name: _____   Date: _____

Purpose: To assess your cardiorespiratory endurance by estimating your maximal oxygen uptake level by walking and or running for 12 minutes.

Instructions: You are to run, walk or run and walk the greatest possible distance in 12 minutes on a measured flat course. The distance is recorded in meters. The equation below is used to predict fitness level. Classify your fitness level using the maximal uptake charts.

VO2max (ml kg/min) = (distance in meters − 504.9)/44.73

_____ = (_____ − 504.9)/44.73   Fitness Category _____

Muscle Endurance Assessment
(WOMEN)

Name: _____ Date: _____

Push-Ups

PURPOSE: To measure the endurance of pectorals and triceps.

EQUIPMENT: Towel or mat.

INSTRUCTION: *Keeping the body straight,* lower the body until your elbows flex 90°; return to straight arm position. A modified-position may also be performed from the knees.

SCORING: Partner counts the number of correct non-stop push-ups. Incorrect push-ups: Failure to keep body straight from heels to head throughout the movement; failure to straighten arms as body is raised.

Modified Push-Up Norms for Women

Fitness Category	|	Age in Years					
		18–25	26–35	36–45	46–55	56–65	65+
Excellent		>32	>33	>34	>28	>23	>21
Good		21–31	23–32	22–33	18–27	15–22	13–20
Fair		11–20	12–22	10–21	8–17	7–14	5–12
Poor		0–10	1–11	0–9	0–7	0–6	0–4
Very Poor			0				

Standard Push-Up Norms for Women

Fitness Category	|	Age in Years					
		18–25	26–35	36–45	46–55	56–65	65+
Excellent		25+	23+	18+	14+	10+	5+
Good		20–24	18–22	14–17	10–13	7–9	3–4
Fair		14–19	12–17	9–13	6–9	5–6	1–2
Poor		9–13	7–11	5–8	3–5	3–4	0
Very Poor		0–8	0–6	0–4	0–2	0–2	0

Saddleback College Norms (1993–1999)

PUSH-UPS _____ FITNESS CATEGORY _____

From *Fitness Assessment Workbook* by Jan Duquette and Duane Cain. Copyright © 2002 by Kendall/Hunt Publishing Company. Reprinted by permission.

Muscle Endurance Assessment
(MEN)

Name: _____   Date: _____

Push-Ups

PURPOSE: To measure the endurance of pectorals and triceps.

EQUIPMENT: Towel or mat.

INSTRUCTION: *Keeping the body straight,* lower the body until your elbows flex to 90° then return to straight arm position.

SCORING: Partner counts the number of correct non-stop push-ups. Incorrect push-ups: Failure to keep body straight from heels to head throughout the movement; failure to straighten arms as body is raised.

Fitness Category	Age in Years					
	18–25	26–35	36–45	46–55	56–65	65+
Excellent	>51	>43	>37	>31	>28	>17
Good	35–50	30–42	25–36	21–30	18–27	17–26
Fair	19–34	17–29	13–24	11–20	9–17	6–16
Poor	4–18	4–16	2–12	1–10	0–8	0–5
Very Poor	<3	<3	<1	<0		

Saddleback College Norms (1993–1999)

PUSH-UPS _____ FITNESS CATEGORY _____

From *Fitness Assessment Workbook* by Jan Duquette and Duane Cain. Copyright © 2002 by Kendall/Hunt Publishing Company. Reprinted by permission.

Muscle Endurance Assessment
(WOMEN AND MEN)

Name: _____   Date: _____

Sixty-Second Bent-Knee Curl-Ups

PURPOSE: To measure abdominal muscle endurance.

EQUIPMENT: Stop watch, towel/mat.

INSTRUCTION: Lie on your back, knees bent, and feet flat. Arms extended by the hips, with hands touching the floor. Curl forward, keeping hands in contact with the floor. (Fingers must move 3" approximately the width of a hand.) Return to starting position with shoulders touching the floor.

SCORING: Partner counts the number of correct sit-ups performed in 60-seconds. Incorrect sit-ups include; Failure to move fingers 3" or failure to return shoulders to the floor.

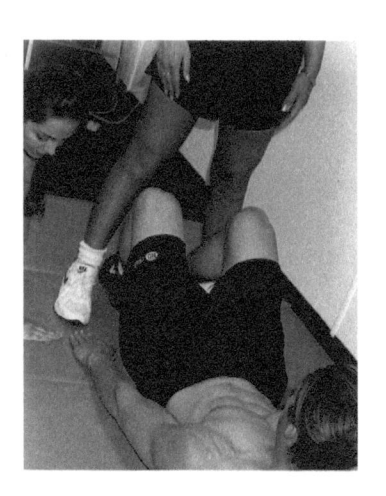

Fitness Category	Age in Years					
	<20	20–29	30–39	40–49	50–59	>60
Men						
Excellent	>51	>47	>43	>39	>35	>30
Good	48–50	44–46	40–42	35–38	30–34	24–29
Fair	39–47	37–43	33–39	28–34	22–29	18–23
Poor	36–38	33–36	30–32	24–27	19–21	15–17
Very Poor	<35	<32	<29	<23	<18	<14
Women						
Excellent	>46	>44	>35	>29	>24	>17
Good	36–45	38–43	29–34	24–28	20–23	11–16
Fair	30–35	31–37	24–28	20–23	12–19	5–10
Poor	28–29	27–30	20–23	14–18	10–11	3–4
Very Poor	<27	<26	<19	<13	<9	<2

Saddleback College Norms (1993–1999)

CURL-UPS _____ FITNESS CATEGORY _____

From *Fitness Assessment Workbook* by Jan Duquette and Duane Cain. Copyright © 2002 by Kendall/Hunt Publishing Company. Reprinted by permission.

Sit-and-Reach Flexibility Assessment

Name: _____   Date: _____

Purpose: To assess your current level of flexibility

Procedures: This test requires a flexibility testing apparatus with a reach indicator or a yardstick and a box twelve inches high. The test subject should warm-up properly before performing this assessment. The shoes are removed. The subject is seated on the floor with the back, hips, shoulders and head against a wall with the legs extended and the bottom of the feet touching the sit-and-reach box. The arms are then extended with one hand on top one the other keeping the back, hips, and head still resting against the wall. The reach indicator or yardstick is placed at the end of the subject's fingertips. The reach indicator/yardstick must be held in place for the remainder of the test. The subject now brings the back, shoulders and head away from the wall, gradually moving as far forward on the reach indicator/yardstick as possible. The final reach position is held at least two seconds for two trials. The average of the final score is used as the final score.

Trial 1: _____   Trial 2: _____   Average: _____

Classification: _____

Table 5.1 Norms for Sit and Reach Flexibility

These norms are from the YMCA's Sit and Reach Test. Units are expressed in inches.

Female Norms				
Age Group	Excellent	Good	Fair	Poor
18–25	24	21	19	18
26–35	23	20	19	17
36–45	22	19	17	16
46–55	21	18	16	14
56–65	20	17	15	14
>65	20	17	15	14

Male Norms				
Age Group	Excellent	Good	Fair	Poor
18–25	22	19	17	15
26–35	21	17	15	14
36–45	21	17	15	13
46–55	19	15	13	11
56–65	17	13	11	9
>65	17	13	10	9

Source: ACSM's Resource Manual for Guidelines for Exercise Testing and Prescription, 6th edition, Table 19-10, p. 329. Lippincott Williams & Wilkins, 2009.